Spatial Databases: A Tour

Shashi Shekhar
Sanjay Chawla

An Alan R. Apt Book

Prentice
Hall

Pearson Education Inc., *Upper Saddle River, New Jersey 07458*

Library of Congress Cataloging-in-Publication Data
  Shekhar, Shashi
    Spatial Databases: A Tour/Shashi Shekhar and Sanjay Chawla.
      p. cm.
    Includes bibliographical references and index.
    ISBN 0-13-017480-7
    1. Geographic information systems.   I. Chawla, Sanjay, II. Title.

  G70.212 .S54   2003
  910'.285–dc21   2002003694

Vice President and Editorial Director: *Marcia Horton*
Publisher: *Alan Apt*
Associate Editor: *Toni D. Holm*
Editorial Assistant: *Patrick Lindner*
Vice President and Director of Production and Manufacturing, ESM: *David W. Riccardi*
Executive Managing Editor: *Vince O'Brien*
Assistant Managing Editor: *Camille Trentacoste*
Production Editor: *Patty Donovan*
Director of Creative Services: *Paul Belfanti*
Creative Director: *Carole Anson*
Art director: *Jayne Conte*
Cover Designer: *Bruce Kenselaar*
Art Editor: *Greg Dulles*
Manufacturing Manager: *Trudy Pisciotti*
Manufacturing Buyer: *Lynda Castillo*
Marketing Assistant: *Barrie Rheinhold*

Earlier edition© 1987 by Merrill Publishing Company.

Printed in the United States of America
10   9   8   7   6   5   4   3   2   1

ISBN 0-13-017480-7

Pearson Education LTD., *London*
Pearson Education Australia PTY, Limited, *Sydney*
Pearson Education Singapore, Pte. Ltd
Pearson Education North Asia Ltd, *Hong Kong*
Pearson Education Canada, Ltd., *Toronto*
Pearson Educacion de Mexico, S.A. de C.V.
Pearson Education - Japan, *Tokyo*
Pearson Education Malaysia, Pte. Ltd
Pearson Education, *Upper Saddle River, New Jersey*

Dedicated to my two greatest teachers,
Father Prof. L. N. Sahu
and Mother Dr. (Mrs.) C. K. Gupta
and
to my wife, Ibha, and my son, Apurv Hirsh,
for wonderful support and understanding.
                                    —Shashi Shekhar

To Preeti, Ishaan, Simran and my parents.
                                    —Sanjay Chawla

Contents

List of Figures

List of Tables

Preface

Over the years it has become evident in many areas of computer applications that the functionality of database management systems has to be enlarged to include spatially referenced data. The study of spatial database management systems (SDBMS) is a step in the direction of providing models and algorithms for the efficient handling of data related to space.

Spatial databases have now been an active area of research for over two decades. Their results, example, spatial multidimensional indexing, are being used in many different areas. The principle impetus for research in SDBMs comes from the needs of existing applications such as geographical information systems (GIS) and computer-aided design (CAD), as well as potential applications such as multimedia information systems, data warehousing, and NASA's earth observation system. These spatial applications have over one million existing users.

Major players in the commercial database industry have products specifically designed to handle spatial data. These products include the spatial data engine (SDE), by Environment Systems Research Institute (ESRI); as well as spatial datablades for object-relational database servers from many vendors including Intergraph, Autodesk, Oracle, IBM and Informix. Research prototypes include Postgres, Geo2, and Paradise. The functionality provided by these systems includes a set of spatial data types such as the point, line, and polygon, and a set of spatial operations, including intersection, enclosure, and distance. An industrywide standard set of spatial data types and operations has been developed by the Open Geographic Information Systems (OGIS) consortium. The spatial types and operations can be made a part of an object-relational query language such as SQL3. The performance enhancement provided by these systems includes a multidimensional spatial index and algorithms for spatial access methods, spatial range queries, and spatial joins.

The integration of spatial data into traditional databases amounts to resolving many nontrivial issues at various levels. They range from deep ontological questions about the modeling of space, for example, whether it should be field based or object based, thus paralleling the wave-particle duality in physics to more mundane but important issues about file management. These diverse topics make research in SDBMS truly interdisciplinary.

Let us use the example of a country dataset to highlight the special needs of spatial databases. A country has at least one nonspatial datum, its name, and one spatial datum, its boundary. There is no ambiguity about storing or representing its name, but unfortunately it is not true for its boundary. Assuming that the boundary is represented as a collection of straight lines, we need to include a spatial data type *line* and the companion types *point* and *region* in the database system to facilitate spatial queries on the object *country*. These new data types need to be manipulated and composed according to some fixed rules leading to the creation of a spatial algebra. Because spatial data is inherently visual and usually voluminous, database systems have to be augmented to provide visual query processing and special spatial indexing . Other important database issues such as concurrency control, bulk loading, storage, and security have to be revisited and fine-tuned to build an effective spatial database management system.

This book evolved from the class notes of a graduate course on Scientific Databases (Csci 8705) in University of Minnesota. Researchers and students both within and outside the Computer Science Department found the course very useful and applicable to their work. Despite the good response and high level of interest in the topic, no textbook available in the market was able to meet the interdisciplinary needs of the audience. A recent book by [Scholl et al., 2001] focuses on traditional topics related to query languages and access methods while leaving out current topics such as spatial networks (e.g., road maps) and data mining for spatial patterns. A monograph by [Adam and Gangopadhyay, 1997] catalogs research papers on database issues in GIS, with little reference to the industrial state-of-the-art. Another [Worboys, 1995] also focuses on GIS and has only two chapters devoted to database issues. Many of these books neither use industry standards, e.g., OGIS, nor provide adequate instructional support, example, questions and problems at the end of each chapter to allow students to assess their understanding of the main concepts. Not surprisingly, our colleagues in academia working in databases, parallel computing, multimedia information, civil and mechanical engineering, and forestry have expressed a strong desire for a comprehensive text on spatial databases. Industry professionals involved in software development for GIS and CAD/CAM have also made several requests for information on spatial databases in a collected form.

As a first step toward developing this book, we completed a survey paper, "Spatial Databases: Accomplishments and Research Needs," for IEEE Transactions on Knowledge and Data Engineering (Jan. 1999). We noticed that the research literature in computer science was skewed with numerous publications on some topics (e.g., spatial indexes, spatial join algorithms) and relatively scarce publications on many other important topics (e.g., conceptual modeling of spatial data). We looked to GIS industry as well as GIS researchers outside computer science for ideas in these areas for the relevant chapters in the book.

Being on sabbatical for the academic year 1997–1998 facilitated initial work on the book. We completed a draft of many chapters by expanding on the course notes of CSci 8705. The first draft of the book was used in database courses at the University of Minnesota. Subsequently the book was revised using feedback from reviewers, colleagues, and students.

We believe the following features are unique aspects of this book:

- The aim of this book is to provide a comprehensive overview of spatial databases management systems. It covers current topics, example, spatial networks and spatial data mining in addition to traditional topics, example, query languages, indexing, query processing.

- A set of questions and problems is provided in each chapter to allow readers to test understanding of core concepts, to apply core concepts in new application domains, and to think beyond the material presented in the chapter. Additional instructional aids (e.g., laboratories, lecture notes) are planned on the book Web site.

- A concerted effort has been made to "look beyond GIS." Techniques from SDBMS are finding applications in many diverse areas, including multimedia information, CAD/CAM, astronomy, meteorology, molecular biology, and computational mechanics.

- In each chapter we have tried to bring out the object-relational database framework, which is a clear trend in commercial database applications. This framework allows spatial databases to reuse relational database facilities when possible, while extending relational database facilities as needed.

- We will use spatial data types and operations specified by standards (e.g., OGIS) to illustrate common spatial database queries. These standards can be incorporated into an object-relational query language such as SQL-3.

- Self-contained treatment without assuming pre-requisite knowledge of GIS or Databases.

- Complete coverage of spatial networks including modeling, querying and storage methods.

- Detailed discussion of issues related to Spatial Data Mining.

- Balance between cutting-edge research and commercial trends.

- Easy to understand examples from common knowledge application domains.

CHAPTER ORGANIZATION

The book is divided into eight chapters, each one an important subarea within spatial databases. We introduce the field of spatial databases in Chapter 1. In Chapter 2, we focus on spatial data models and introduce the field versus object dichotomy and its implications for database design. Chapter 3 discusses the necessary enhancements required to make traditional query languages compatible with spatial databases. We provide an extensive discussion of various proposals to extend SQL with spatial capabilities. Spatial databases deal with extraordinarily large amounts of data, and it is essential for DBMS to provide sophisticated storage, compression, and indexing methods to enhance the performance of query processing. Spatial data storage and indexing schemes are covered in Chapter 4. From query languages and indexing, we move on to query processing and optimization in Chapter 5. Here we discover that many standard techniques from traditional databases have to be abandoned or drastically modified in order to be applicable in a spatial context. We also introduce the filter-refine paradigm for spatial query processing. In Chapter 6, we show how spatial database technology is being applied to spatial networks. In this chapter we also cover network data models and query languages. Chapter 7 covers the emerging field of spatial data mining. In this chapter we expose the readers to the concept of spatial dependency that is prevalent in spatial data sets, and show how this can be modeled and incorporated into data mining process. Finally in Chapter 8, we discuss emerging trends in spatial databases.

ACKNOWLEDGMENTS

We have received help from many people and we are extremely grateful to them. This book would not have started without encouragement from Professor Vipin Kumar, Computer Science Department, University of Minnesota; and Dr. Jack Dangermond, President, Environmental Systems Research Institute (ESRI). This book benefitted a great deal from access to ESRI researchers and products. We are also grateful to Dr. Siva Ravada (Oracle Corporation) and Dr. Robert Uleman (Illustra Inc.) for help with understanding of their spatial datablades. We are thankful to Alan Apt and his wonderful staff at Prentice Hall for helping with the process of book-writing with constant encouragement. The presentation improved a great deal from the comments from the anonymous reviewers and we are grateful to them.

Our research related to spatial databases has been supported by many organizations including the United Nations Development Programme, the National Science Foundation, the National Aeronautics and Space Agency, the Army Research Laboratories, the U.S. Department of Agriculture, the Federal Highway Administration, the US Department of Transportation, the Minnesota Department of Transportation, the Center for Urban and Regional Affairs, and the Computing Devices International. Many of the research project resulted in surveys of research literature, as well as in development of innovative techniques for problems related to spatial databases.

Special thanks to the members of spatial database research group in the Computer Science Department at the University of Minnesota. They contributed in many different ways including literature surveys, development of examples and figures, and insights into various methods, as well in developing proper problem formulations and innovative solution methods. We are extremely grateful to Vatsavai Ranga Raju for careful review and multiple improvements to the earlier drafts. We also thank the students in different offerings of Csci 8701, and Csci 8705 for working with the earlier drafts of the books and providing helpful suggestions towards revising the material.

We benefitted from discussions with many other people over the years. They include Marvin Bauer, Yvan Bedard, Paul Bolstad, Nick Bourbakis, Thomas Burk, John Carlis, Jai Chakrapani, Vladimir Cherkassky, Douglas Chub, William Craig, Max Donath, Phil Emmerman, Max Egenhofer, Michael Goodchild, Ralf Hartmut Gueting, Oliver Gunther, John Gurney, Jia-Wei Han, Ravi Janardan, George Karypis, Hans-Peter Kriegel, Robert McMaster, Robert Pierre, Shamkant Navathe, Raymond Ng, Hanan Samet, Paul Schrater, Jaideep Srivastava, Benjamin Wah, Kyu-Young Whang, and Michael Worboys.

Foreword

Ever since Cro-Magnon hunters drew pictures of track lines and tallies thought to depict migration routes on the walls of caves near Lascaux, France, 35,000 years ago, people have been interested in graphics linked to geographic information. Today, such geographic information systems (GISs) are used in applications ranging from tracking the migration routes of caribou and polar bears, identifying the effects of oil development on animal life, aiding farmers to minimize the use of pesticide in their farms, helping corporate supply managers to predict the best places to build distribution warehouses, to relating information about rainfall and aerial photographs to wetlands drying up at certain times of the year.

A GIS, in the strictest sense, is a computer system for assembling, storing, manipulating, and displaying data with respect to their locations. However, modern GISs often assimilate data from multiple disparate sources in many different forms in order to answer queries and help analyze information. In a broad sense, a GIS not only converts and stores geographical information in digital form for analysis, but must also collects, transforms, aggregates, indexes, links, and mines related spatial databases. A modern GIS makes it possible to integrate information that is difficult to associate through any other means and combines mapped variables to build and analyze new variables.

With this broad perspective in mind, Shekhar and Chawla have done a marvelous job in presenting the fundamentals and trends in geographical information processing. The core of the book is a tour de force sequence of concepts and methods, progressively explaining models, languages and algorithms until we distinguish branches from trees and trees from forests. The authors not only explain the concepts but illustrate them well by numerous examples. They have emphasized the many nontrivial issues in integrating spatial data into traditional databases, ranging from deep ontological questions about the modeling of space to the important issues about file management. Each chapter is further supplemented by many thought-provoking exercises that aid readers in better understanding of the concepts and algorithms presented. The book ends with an excellent exposition of spatial data mining and future trends in spatial databases that helps readers appreciate emerging research issues.

This book is suitable as a textbook for an interdisciplinary course on geographic information systems, as well as a handy reference for people working in the area. Readers should find it easy to understand and apply the concepts and algorithms learned, even without any formal training in databases. Many disciplines will benefit from techniques learned in this book, leading to wider applications of the technology throughout government, business, and industry.

As the reader of the first books in this area, and I am confident that you will benefit by what you learn in this exciting and rewarding area.

Prof. Benjamin Wah
University of Illinois at Urbana-Champaign
Department of Electrical and Computer Engineering
1101 W. Springfield Avenue
Urbana, IL 61801
President, IEEE Computer Society (2001)
March 2002

Foreword

Spatial information—that is, information about objects located in a spatial frame such as the Earth's surface—has long been recognized as presenting special problems for computing. As early as 1972 the term *spatial data handling* was being used to refer to the activities of a small but dynamic community of researchers who were committed to exploiting electronic data processing in order to increase productivity in such areas as map compilation and editing; map measurement; and spatial data analysis. Spatial information is rich in high-level structures, and although each of the classical models of database management that began to emerge in the 1960s had something to offer to this application area, neither the relational model nor object-oriented modeling provide a perfect fit. The relational model handles topological relationships well, but lacks the means to represent complex hierarchical relationships that span spatial scales; while object-oriented models handle both topological and hierarchical relationships, but have difficulty dealing with phenomena that are essentially continuous in space.

Books that elucidate the complex story of spatial databases are few and far between, and thus this book is especially welcome. It covers the entire field, from representation through query to analysis, in a style that is clear, logical, and rigorous. Especially welcome is the chapter on data mining, which addresses both traditional spatial data analysis and also new techniques that have been developed in the past few years to take advantage of today's high-speed computing in processes of automated search for anomalies and patterns in very large spatial databases. It is intended for computer science students, as reflected in the sequence of topics and the style of presentation, but will also be useful for students from other disciplines looking for a more rigorous and fundamental approach than is provided by most textbooks on geographic information systems (GIS).

The importance of spatial databases is growing rapidly, partly as a result of the recognition that their applications extend well beyond the traditional domain of GIS. Location and time are powerful ways of identifying and characterizing information, because many data sets have *footprints* in space and time. This is obviously true of maps and Earth images, but is also true of many reports, books, photographs, and other types of information. Thus location is a powerful basis for search, and for finding relevant information in distributed resources such as the World Wide Web. There is growing recognition that space (and time) provides important ways of integrating information that go far beyond the traditional domains of spatial databases and GIS. The last chapter of the book discusses some of these, and gives a sense of why many believe that the importance of spatial databases is likely to continue to grow rapidly over the coming years.

Michael F. Goodchild
National Center for Geographic Information and Analysis,
    and Department of Geography,
University of California, Santa Barbara, CA 93106-4060, USA

CHAPTER 1

Introduction to Spatial Databases

1.1 OVERVIEW

We are in the midst of an information revolution. The raw material (data) which is powering this controlled upheaval is not found below the earth's surface where it has taken million of years to form but is being gathered constantly via sensors and other data-gathering devices. For example, NASA's Earth Observing System (EOS) generates one terabyte of data every day.

Satellite images are one prominent example of spatial data. To extract information from a satellite image, the data has to be processed with respect to a spatial frame of reference, possibly the earth's surface. But satellites are not the only source of spatial data, and the earth's surface is not the only frame of reference. A silicon chip can be, and often is, a frame of reference. In medical imaging the human body acts as a spatial frame of reference. In fact, even a supermarket transaction is an example of spatial data if, for example, a zip code is included. Queries, or commands, posed on spatial data are called spatial queries. For example, the query "What are the names of all bookstores with more than ten thousand titles?" is an example of a nonspatial query. On the other hand, the query, "What are the names of all bookstores within ten miles of the Minneapolis downtown?" is an example of a spatial query. This book is an exposition of efficient techniques for the storage, management, and retrieval of spatial data.

Today, data is housed in and managed via a database management system (DBMS). Databases and the software that manages them are the silent success story of the information age. They have slowly permeated all aspects of daily living, and modern society would come to a halt without them. Despite their spectacular success, the prevalent view is that a majority of the DBMSs in existence today are either incapable of managing spatial data or are not user-friendly when doing so. Now, why is that? The traditional role of a DBMS has been that of a simple but effective warehouse of business and accounting data. Information about employees, suppliers, customers, and products can be safely stored and efficiently retrieved through a DBMS. The set of likely queries is limited, and the database is organized to efficiently answer these queries. From the business world, the DBMS made a painless migration into government agencies and academic administrations.

Data residing in these mammoth databases is simple, consisting of numbers, names, addresses, product descriptions, and so on. These DBMSs are very efficient for the tasks they were designed for. For example, a query such as "List the top ten customers, in terms of sales, in the year 1998" will be very efficiently answered by a DBMS even if it has to scan through a very large customer database. Such commands are conventionally called "queries" although they are not questions. The database will not scan through all the customers; it will use an index, as you would do with this book, to narrow down the search. On the other hand, a relatively simple query such as "List all the customers who reside within fifty miles of the company headquarters" will confound the database. To process this query, the database will have to transform the company headquarters and customer addresses into a suitable reference system, possibly latitude and longitude, in which distances can be computed and compared. Then the database will have to scan through the entire customer list, compute the distance between the company and the customer, and if this distance is less than fifty miles, save the customer's name. It will not be able to use an index to narrow down the search, because traditional indices are incapable of ordering multidimensional coordinate data. A simple and legitimate business query thus can send a DBMS into a hopeless tailspin. Therefore the need for databases tailored for handling spatial data and spatial queries is immediate.

1.2   WHO CAN BENEFIT FROM SPATIAL DATA MANAGEMENT?

Professionals from all walks of life have to deal with the management and analysis of spatial data. Below we give a small but diverse list of professionals and one example of a spatial query relevant to the work of each.

Mobile phone user: Where is the nearest gas station? Is there a pet-food vendor on my way home?

Army field commander: Has there been any significant enemy troop movement since last night?

Insurance risk manager: Which houses on the Mississippi River are most likely to be affected by the next great flood?

Medical doctor: Based on this patient's Magnetic Resonance Imaging (MRI), have we treated somebody with a similar condition?

Molecular biologist: Is the topology of the amino acid biosynthesis gene in the genome found in any other sequence feature map in the database?

Astronomer: Find all blue galaxies within two arcmin of quasars.

Climatologist: How can I test and verify my new global warming model?

Pharmaceutical Researcher: Which molecules can dock with a given molecule based on geometric shapes?

Sports: Which seats in a baseball stadium provide best view of pitcher and hitter? Where should TV camera be mounted?

Corporate supply manager: Given trends about our future customer profile, which are the best places to build distribution warehouses and retail stores?

Transport specialist: How should the road network be expanded to minimize traffic congestion?

Urban sprawl specialist: Is new urban land development leading to the loss of rich agricultural land.

Ski resort owner: Which mountains on our property are ideal for a beginner's ski run?

Farmer: How can I minimize the use of pesticide on my farm?

Golf entrepreneur: Where do I build a new golf course which will maximize profit given the constraints of weather, Environmental Protection Agency pesticide regulations, the Endangered Species Act, property prices, and the neighborhood demographic profile.

Emergency service: Where is the person calling for help located? What is the best route to reach her?

1.3   GIS AND SDBMS

The Geographic Information System (GIS) is the principal technology motivating interest in Spatial Database Management Systems (SDBMSs). GIS provides a convenient mechanism for the analysis and visualization of geographic data. Geographic data is spatial data whose underlying frame of reference is the earth's surface. The GIS provides a rich set of analysis functions which allow a user to affect powerful transformations on geographic data. The rich array of techniques that geographers have packed into the GIS are the reasons behind its phenomenal growth and multidisciplinary applications. Table 1.1 lists a small sample of common GIS operations.

A GIS provides a rich set of operations over few objects and layers, whereas an SDBMS provides simpler operations on a set of objects and sets of layers. For example,

TABLE 1.1: List of Common GIS Analysis Operations [Albrecht, 1998]

Search	Thematic search, search by region, (re-)classification
Location analysis	Buffer, corridor, overlay
Terrain analysis	Slope/aspect, catchment, drainage network
Flow analysis	Connectivity, shortest path
Distribution	Change detection, proximity, nearest neighbor
Spatial analysis/Statistics	Pattern, centrality, autocorrelation, indices of similarity, topology: hole description
Measurements	Distance, perimeter, shape, adjacency, direction

a GIS can list neighboring countries of a given country (e.g., France) given the political boundaries of all countries. However it will be fairly tedious to answer set queries such as, *list the countries with the highest number of neighboring countries* or *list countries which are completely surrounded by another country.* Set-based queries can be answered in an SDBMS, as we show in Chapter 3.

SDBMSs are also designed to handle very large amounts of spatial data stored on secondary devices (e.g., magnetic disks, CD-ROM, jukeboxes, etc.), using specialized indices and query-processing techniques. Finally, SDBMSs inherit the traditional DBMS functionality of providing a concurrency-control mechanism to allow multiple users to simultaneously access shared spatial data, while preserving the consistency of that data.

A GIS can be built as the front-end of an SDBMS. Before a GIS can carry out any analysis of spatial data, it accesses that data from an SDBMS. Thus an efficient SDBMS can greatly increase the efficiency and productivity of a GIS.

1.4   THREE CLASSES OF USERS FOR SPATIAL DATABASES

The use and management of spatial data to enhance productivity has now been embraced by scientists, administrators, and business professionals alike. Equally important, the concept that spatial or geographic or geospatial data has to be treated differently, compared with other forms of data, has slowly permeated the thinking and planning of all major database vendors. As a result, specialized spatial products have appeared in the marketplace to enhance the spatial capabilities of generic DBMSs. For example, spatial attachments, with esoteric names such as *cartridge, datablade,* or more benign names such as *spatial option* have been introduced by Oracle, Informix, and IBM, respectively.

From a major database vendor perspective, there is a demand for specialized products for the management of spatial data, but this is obviously not the only form of data that businesses use. In fact, it is not the only form of specialized data. For example, besides spatial attachments, database vendors have released attachments for *temporal*, *visual*, and other multimedia forms of data.

On the other hand, GIS vendors have targeted users who are exclusively focused on the analysis of spatial data. This market by definition is relatively narrow and consists of specialists in the scientific community and/or government departments. Users of GIS typically work in an isolated environment vis-à-vis other information technology users and access specialized databases specifically designed for them. In order to manage the ever-increasing volume of spatial (and nonspatial) data and link to commercial databases, GIS vendors have introduced middleware products, such as ESRI's Spatial Data Engine. The focus in the GIS community has evolved in the last decade, as shown in Figure 1.1. GIS, which began as a software system for representing geographic information in a layered fashion, attained the status of Geographic Information (GI) science by focusing on the *algebra* of map and spatial operations. With the prominence of the personal computing, the focus has again shifted to providing geographic or spatial services over the personal computers. The prime examples are the spatially sensitive search engines and map facilities in MS Office 2000 to augment the classical spreadsheet and database tools.

With the advent of the Internet, there is another group of users who want to use spatial data but only at a very high and user friendly level. For example, one of the more popular sites on the Internet provides direction maps to visitors. Another site provides a spatially sensitive search engine. Queries such as "Find all Mexican restaurants in downtown Minneapolis" can be answered by such search engines. Another promising

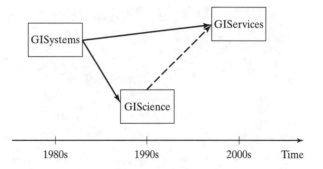

FIGURE 1.1. The evolution of the abbreviation GIS over the last two decades. In the 1980s GIS was Geographic Information System; in the 1990s, Geographic Information Science was the preferred phrase, and now the trend is toward Geographic Information Services.

use of spatial technologies is related to the location determination of mobile phones. The U.S. federal government has mandated that by October 2001, the location of all cell phones must be traceable to an accuracy of 125 meters, 67 percent of the time. Thus, although it is often remarked that the Internet revolution has "killed" the concept of geography, paradoxically, the demand for spatial technologies is continuously growing.

The recent increase in the use of personal digital assistants (PDAs), mobile phones, and two-way pagers has opened up several opportunities for new applications. Example applications are mobile workforces and location-based services. As the name suggests, the mobile workforce works from remote locations—at clients' locations, branch offices, and remote field locations. These workforces typically download a segment of data needed for a particular task, work with that segment at a remote location, and update (synchronize) their modifications with the master database at the end of the day. An important aspect of this scenario is that the client hoards data and works locally on the data in a disconnected fashion. An important trend in recent years is the availability of location-based services, that is, the services that actually change depending on the geographic location of the individual user. With the availability of global positioning systems (GPS), it is easy to precisely determine the location of any client/user and offer appropriate solutions based on the geographic location of the user. Example applications of location-based services are to locate a customer, find the nearest pizza place with a gas station on the way, display a road map for a new city with tourist locations highlighted, or location sensitive transactions and alerts. The impact and importance of the location-based services led the Open GIS Consortium (OGC) to initiate Open Location Services (OpenLS) with a vision to integrate geospatial data and geoprocessing resources into the location services and telecommunication infrastructure.

1.5 AN EXAMPLE OF AN SDBMS APPLICATION

Earlier we gave an example of a simple spatial query to illustrate the shortcomings of traditional databases. We now give a more detailed example. Figure 1.2 shows a Landsat Thematic Mapper (TM) image of Ramsey County, Minnesota. Overlaid on the image are the boundaries (thick black lines) of census blocks and the locations

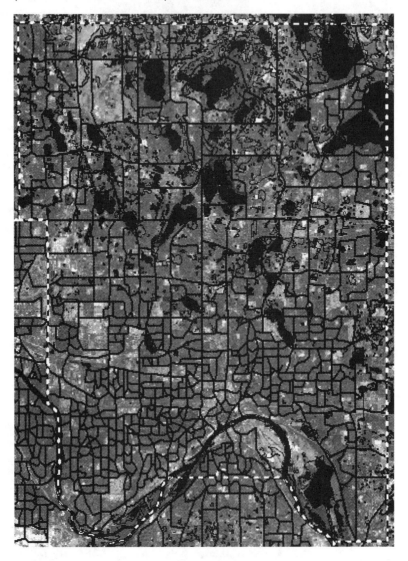

FIGURE 1.2. Landsat image of Ramsey County, Minnesota, with spatial layers of information superimposed.

of wetlands (thin black lines). From the image we can easily identify several lakes (dark patches in north) and the Mississippi river (south). This county covers about 156 square miles and covers most of the urban and suburban regions of St. Paul. This figure was created in ArcView, a popular GIS software program. A typical spatial database consists of several images and vector layers like land parcels, transportation, ecological regions, soils, etc. Here we have four layers: the basic image, a layer of census blocks, another for wetlands, and finally the layer of county boundaries (white dashed lines).

One *natural* way of storing information about the census blocks, for example, their name, geographic area, population, and boundaries, is to create the following table in the database:

```
create table census_blocks (
                            name        string ,
                            area        float,
                            population  number,
                            boundary    polyline );
```

In a (relational) database, all objects, entities, and concepts that have a distinct identity are represented as relations or tables. A relation is defined by a name and a list of distinguishing attributes that characterize the relation. All instances of the entity are stored as tuples in the table. In the preceding code fragment, we have created a table (relation) named *census_block*, which has four attributes: name, area, population, and boundary. At table creation time, the types of attributes have to be specified, and they are string, float, number, and polyline. Polyline is a datatype to represent a sequence of straight lines.

Figure 1.3 shows a hypothetical census block and how information about it can be stored in a table. Unfortunately, such a table is not natural for a traditional relational database because polyline is not a built-in datatype. One way to circumvent this problem is to create a collection of tables with overlapping attributes, as shown in Figure 1.4. Another way is to use a stored procedure. For a novice user, these implementations are quite complex. The key point is that the census block data cannot be naturally mapped onto a relational database. We need more constructs to handle spatial information in order to reduce the semantic gap between the user's view of spatial data and the database implementation. Such facilities are offered by the object-oriented software paradigm.

The object-oriented software paradigm is based on the principles of user-defined datatypes, along with inheritance and polymorphism. The popularity of such languages as C++, Java, and Visual Basic is an indicator that object-oriented concepts are firmly

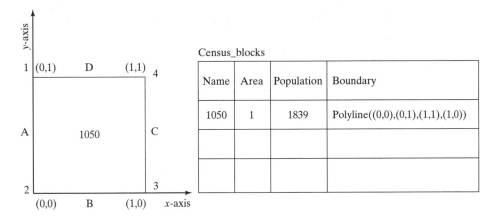

Census_blocks			
Name	Area	Population	Boundary
1050	1	1839	Polyline((0,0),(0,1),(1,1),(1,0))

FIGURE 1.3. Census blocks with boundary ID:1050.

Census_blocks

Name	Area	Population	boundary-ID
340	1	1839	1050

Polygon

boundary-ID	edge-name
1050	A
1050	B
1050	C
1050	D

Edge

edge-name	endpoint
A	1
A	2
B	2
B	3
C	3
C	4
D	4
D	1

Point

endpoint	x-coor	y-coor
1	0	1
2	0	0
3	1	0
4	1	1

FIGURE 1.4. Four tables required in a relational database with overlapping attributes to accommodate the polyline datatype.

established in the software industry. It would seem that our land parcel problem is a natural application of object-oriented design: Declare a class polyline and another class land_parcel with attribute *address*, which is a string type, and another attribute *boundary* which is of the type *polyline*. We do not even need an attribute *area* because we can define a method *area* in the polyline class which will compute the area of any land parcel on demand. So will that solve the problem? Are object-oriented databases (OODBMS) the answer? Well, not quite.

The debate between relational versus object-oriented within the database community parallels the debate between vector versus raster in GISs. The introduction of abstract data types (ADTs) clearly adds flexibility to a DBMS, but there are two constraints peculiar to databases that need to be resolved before ADTs can be fully integrated into DBMSs.

- Market adoption of OODBMS products has been limited, despite the availability of such products for several years. This reduces the financial resources and engineering efforts to performance-tune OODBMS products. As a result, many GIS users will use systems other than OODBMS to manage their spatial data in the near future.

- SQL is the lingua franca of the database world, and it is tightly coupled with the relational database model. SQL is a declarative language, that is, the user only specifies the desired result rather than the means of production. For example, in SQL the query *"Find all land parcels adjacent to MY_HOUSE."* should be able to be specified as follows:

```
SELECT   M.address
FROM     land_parcel L, M
WHERE    Adjacent(L,M) AND
         L.address = 'MYHOUSE'
```

It is the responsibility of the DBMS to implement the operations specified in the query. In particular, the function $Adjacent(L, M)$ should be callable from within SQL. The popular standard, SQL-92, supports user-defined functions and SQL-3/SQL 1999; the next revision supports ADTs and a host of data structures such as lists, sets, arrays, and bags. Relational databases that incorporate ADTs and other principles of object-oriented design are called object relational database management systems (OR-DBMS). The historical evolution of database technology is shown in Figure 1.5.

The current generation of OR-DBMSs offers a modular approach to ADTs. An ADT can be built into or deleted from the system without affecting the rest of the system. Although this "plug-in" approach opens up the DBMS for enhanced functionality, there is very little built-in support for the optimization of operations. Our focus is to specialize

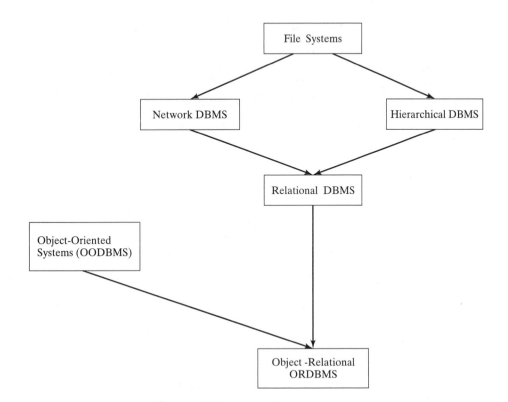

FIGURE 1.5. Evolution of databases. [Khoshafian and Baker, 1998]

an OR-DBMS to meet the requirements of spatial data. By doing so, we can extrapolate spatial domain knowledge to improve the overall efficiency of the system. We are now ready to give a definition of SDBMS for setting the scope of the book.

1. An SDBMS is a software module that can work with an underlying database management system, for example, OR-DBMS, OODBMS.

2. SDBMSs support multiple spatial data models, commensurate spatial abstract data types (ADTs), and a query language from which these ADTs are callable.

3. SDBMSs support spatial indexing, efficient algorithms for spatial operations, and domain-specific rules for query optimization.

Figure 1.6 shows a representation of an architecture to build an SDBMS on top of an OR-DBMS. This is a three-layer architecture. The top layer (from left to right) is the spatial application, such as GIS, MMIS (multimedia information system), or CAD (computer-aided design). This application layer does not interact directly with the OR-DBMS but goes through a middle layer which we have labeled spatial database (SDB). The middle layer is where most of the available spatial domain knowledge is encapsulated, and this layer is "plugged" into the OR-DBMS. No wonder commercial OR-DBMS

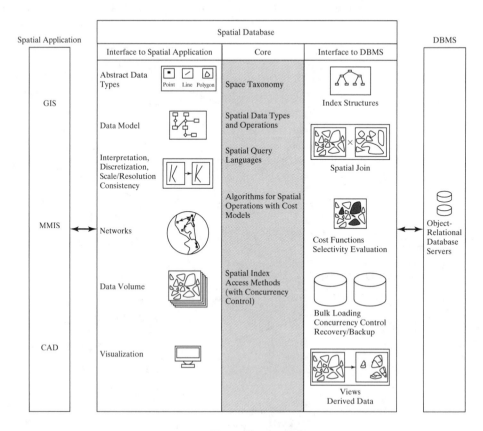

FIGURE 1.6. Three-layer architecture.

products have names such as Spatial Data Blade (Illustra), Spatial Data Cartridge (Oracle), and Spatial Data Engine (ESRI).

We close this section by recalling the core features that are essential for any DBMS to support but are implicit to a casual user:

1. *Persistence:* The ability to handle both transient and persistent data. Although transient data is lost after a program terminates, persistent data not only transcends program invocations, but also survives system and media crashes. Further, the DBMS ensures that a smooth recovery takes place after a crash. In database management systems, the state of the persistent object undergoes frequent changes, and it is sometimes desirable to have access to the previous data states.

2. *Transactions:* Transactions map a database from one consistent state to another. This mapping is atomic (i.e., it is executed completely or aborted). Typically, many transactions are executed concurrently, and the DBMS imposes a serializable order of execution. Consistency in a database is accomplished through the use of integrity constraints. All database states must satisfy these constraints to be deemed consistent. Furthermore, to maintain the security of the database, the scope of the transactions is dependent on the user's access privileges.

1.6   A STROLL THROUGH SPATIAL DATABASES

We closed the previous section by introducing a three-layer architecture to build a SDBMS on top of an OR-DBMS. We noted that most of the spatial domain knowledge is encapsulated in the middle layer. In this section, we briefly describe some of the core functionalities of the middle layer. This section can also be considered as a detailed overview of the rest of the book, or a "quick tutorial" on SDBMSs.

1.6.1   Space Taxonomy and Data Models

Space is indeed the final frontier, not only in terms of travel but also in its inability to be captured by a concise description. Consider the following refrain echoed by hapless drivers all over: "I don't remember how far Jack's house is. Once I am nearby, I might recall on which side of the street it lies, but I am certain that it is adjacent to a park." This sentence gives a glimpse of how our brain (mind) structures geographic space. We are terrible in estimating distances, maybe only slightly better in retaining direction and orientation, but (we are) fairly good when it comes to remembering *topological* relationships such as *adjacent, connected,* and *inside.*

Topology, a branch of mathematics, is exclusively devoted to the study of relationships which do not change due to elastic deformation of underlying space. For example, if there are two rectangles, one inside the other, or both adjacent to each other, drawn on a rubber sheet, and if it is stretched, twisted, or shrunk, the named relationships between the two rectangles will not change! Another clue about how our mind organizes space is to examine the language we speak: The shape of an object is a major determinant in an object's description. Is that the reason why we have trouble accepting a whale as a mammal and a sea horse as a fish? Objects are described by nouns, and we have as many nouns as different shapes. On the other hand, the spatial relationship between objects are described by prepositions and encode very weak descriptions of their shape. In the "Coffman Union is to the southeast of Vincent Hall," the shapes of the buildings

TABLE 1.2: Different Types of Spaces with Example Operations

Topological	Adjacent
Network	Shortest-path
Directional	North-of
Euclidean	Distance

play almost no role in the relationship "southeast." We could often replace the buildings with coarse rectangles without affecting the relationship.

Space taxonomy refers to the multitude of descriptions that are available to organize space: topological, network, directional, and Euclidean. Depending on why we are interested in modeling space in the first place, we can choose an appropriate spatial description. Table 1.2 shows one example of a spatial operation associated with a different model of space. It is important to realize that no single description (model) of space can answer all queries.

A data model is a rule or set of rules to identify and represent objects referenced by space. Minnesota is the "land of ten thousand lakes." How can these lakes be represented? An intuitive, direct way is to represent each lake as a two-dimensional region. Similarly a stream, depending on the scale, can be represented as a one-dimensional curved line, and a well-site by a zero-dimensional point. This is the *object* model. The object model is ideal for representing such non-amorphous spatial entities as lakes, road networks, and cities. The object model is conceptual; it is mapped onto the computer using the *vector* data structure. A vector data structure maps regions into polygons, lines into polylines, and points to points.

The *field* model is often used to represent continuous or amorphous concepts for example, the temperature or the clouds field. A field is a function that maps the underlying reference frame into an attribute domain. For temperature, popular attribute domains are Celsius and Fahrenheit. The *raster* data structure implements the *field* model on a computer. A raster data structure is a uniform grid imposed on the underlying space. Because field values are spatially autocorrelated (they are continuous), the value of each cell is typically the average of all the field points that lie within the cell. Other popular data structures for fields are TIN (triangulated irregular network), contour lines, and point grids. (More on this in Chapters 2 and 8.)

1.6.2 Query Language

From our discussion so far, it is obvious that the current functionality of relational query language (e.g., SQL2) has to be extended if it is to be a natural spatial query language. In particular, the ability to specify spatial ADT attributes and methods from within SQL is crucial. The industrywide endeavor to formulate a standard to extend SQL goes by the name SQL-3, the popular standard being SQL-2. SQL-3, provides support for ADTs and other data structures. It specifies the syntax and the semantics, giving freedom to vendors to customize their implementation.

For a spatial extension of SQL, a standard has already been agreed upon. The OGIS (Open GIS) consortium, led by major GIS and database vendors, has proposed a specification for incorporating 2D geospatial ADTs in SQL. The ADTs proposed are based on the *object* model and include operations for specifying topological and spatial analysis operations. In Chapter 2, we give a detailed description of the OGIS standard, along with an example to illustrate how spatial queries can be performed from within SQL.

1.6.3   Query Processing

As mentioned before, a database user interacts with the database using a declarative query language such as SQL. The user only specifies the result desired and not the algorithm to retrieve the result. The DBMS must automatically implement a plan to efficiently execute the query. Query processing refers to the sequence of steps that the DBMS will initiate to process the query.

Queries can be broadly divided into two categories: single-scan queries and multi-scan queries. In a single-scan query, a record (tuple) in the table (relation) being queried has to be accessed at most once. Thus the worst-case scenario, in terms of time, is that each record in the table will be accessed and processed to verify whether it meets the query criterion. The first spatial query we introduced in this chapter—*"List the names of all bookstores which are within ten miles of the Minneapolis downtown"*—is an example of a single-scan query. The result of this query will be all bookstores that intersect a circle of radius ten miles centered on the courthouse. This query is also an example of a *spatial-range* query, where the range refers to the query region. Here the query region is the circle of radius ten miles. If the query region is a rectangle, the spatial range query is often referred to as a *window* query.

A join query is a prototype example of a multiscan query. To answer a join query, the DBMS has to retrieve and combine two tables in the databases. If more than two tables are required to process the query, then the tables may be processed in pairs. The two tables are combined, or "joined," on a common attribute. Because a record in one table can be associated with more than one record in the second table, records may have to be accessed more than once to complete the join. In the context of SDBs, when the joining attributes are spatial in nature, the query is referred to as a *spatial-join* query. We now give an example to illustrate the difference between a nonspatial join and a spatial join.

Figure 1.7 illustrates the difference between a nonspatial and a spatial join. Consider the two relations shown in the figure: senator and business. The senator relation is characterized by three attributes: the name of the senator, his or her social security number, the senator's gender, and the district that the senator represents. The *district* is a spatial attribute and is represented by a polygon. The other relation, business, lists information about all the businesses: the business name, its owner, the owner's social security number, and the location of the business. The *location* is a spatial attribute represented as a point location. Consider the following query: *"Find the name of all female senators who own a business."* This example includes a nonspatial join, where the joining attributes are the social security number of the senator relation and the social security number of the business owner. In SQL, this query will be written as follows:

```
SELECT  S.name
FROM    Senator S, Business B
WHERE   S.soc-sec = B.soc-sec AND
        S.gender = 'Female'
```

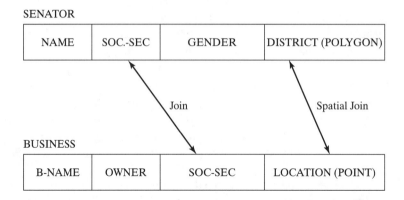

FIGURE 1.7. Two relations to illustrate the difference between join and spatial join.

Now consider the query, *"Find all senators who serve a district of area greater than 300 square miles and who own a business within the district."* This query includes a spatial-join operation on the attributes *location* and *district*. Thus, while in a nonspatial join the joining attributes must be of the same type, in a spatial join the attributes can be of different types: point and polygon, in this case. This is how the query will be expressed in SQL:

```
SELECT   S.name
FROM     Senator S, Business B
WHERE    S.district.Area() > 300 AND
         Within(B.location, S.district)
```

An SDBMS processes range queries using the filter-refine paradigm. This is a two-step process. In the first step, the objects to be queried are represented by their minimum bounding rectangles (MBRs). The rationale is that it is easier (computationally cheaper) to compute the intersection between a query region and a rectangle rather than between the query region and an arbitrary, irregularly shaped, spatial object. If the query region is a rectangle, then at most four computations are needed to determine whether the two rectangles intersect. This is called the filter-step, because many candidates are eliminated by this step. The result of the filter-step contains the candidates that satisfy the original query. The second step is to process the result of the filter-step using exact geometries. This is a computationally expensive process, but the input set for this step, thanks to the filter-step, has low cardinality. Figure 1.8 shows an example of the filter-refine strategy.

We now describe, with the help of an example, an algorithm to process the filter-step of a spatial-join query. This algorithm is based on the *plane sweep* technique, which is extensively used in computational geometry to compute the intersections of geometric objects.

The filter step of many spatial-join queries can be reduced to the problem of determining all pairs of intersecting rectangles. Consider two sets of rectangles (Figure 1.9[b]) $R = \{R_1, R_2, R_3, R_4\}$ and $S = \{S_1, S_2, S_3\}$, which represent the MBRs of the spatial attributes of two tables involved in a join. Each rectangle T can be identified by its lower-left corner, $(T.xl, T.yl)$ and its upper-right corner $(T.xu, T.yu)$, as shown in Figure 1.9(a). We sort all the rectangles in R and S according to the x values of their

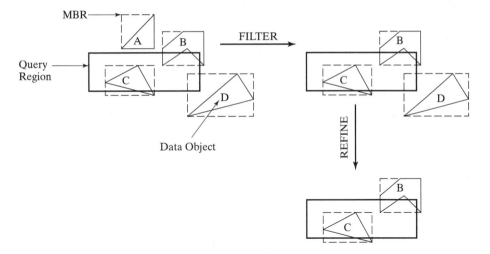

FIGURE 1.8. The filter-refine strategy for reducing computation time.

lower-left corners (i.e., on $T.xl$). The sorted rectangles are shown in Figure 1.9(c). We collect all of the (sorted) rectangles in R and S in the set $R \cup S$ and proceed as follows:

1. Move a *sweep line*, for example, a line perpendicular to the x-axis, from left to right, and stop at the first entry in $R \cup S$. This is the rectangle T with the smallest $T.xl$ value. In our example (see Figure 1.9[a]) this is the rectangle $R4$.

2. Search through the sorted rectangles of S until arriving at the first rectangle S^f such that $S^f.xl > T.xu$. Clearly, the relation $[T.xl, T.xu] \cap [S^j.xl, S^j.xu]$ holds (nonempty) for all $1 \le j < f$. In our example S^f is S^1. Note that the superscript is in the order of array index in Figure 1.9(c), i.e., $S^1 = S_2, S^2 = S_1, S^3 = S_3$. Thus S_2 is a candidate rectangle that may overlap R_4. This will be confirmed in the next step.

3. If the relation $[T.yl, T.yu] \cap [S^j.yl, S^j.yu]$ holds for any $1 \le j \le f$, then the rectangle S^j intersects T. Thus this step confirms that R_4 and S_2 indeed overlap, and $< R_4, S_2 >$ are part of the join result. Record all this information, and remove the rectangle T from the set $R \cup S$. R_4 is removed from the set $R \cup S$ because it cannot participate in any more pairs in the resulting set.

4. Move the sweep line across the set $R \cup S$ until it reaches the next rectangle entry. This is rectangle S_2 in our example. Now proceed as in steps 2 and 3.

5. Stop when the $R \cup S = \emptyset$.

The filter step of the spatial-join algorithm results in $< R_4, S_2 >$, $< R_1, S_2 >$, $< R_1, S_3 >$, $< R_2, S_3 >$, $< R_3, S_3 >$ as candidate pairs for the refinement step, based on the exact geometries of the objects. The refinement step may eliminate a few pairs from the final result if exact geometry computation shows that there is no overlap. The main purpose of the filter step is to reduce the computation cost of exact geometry computation by eliminating as many pairs as possible. Chapters 5 and 7 present more details of disk-based algorithms for processing spatial queries.

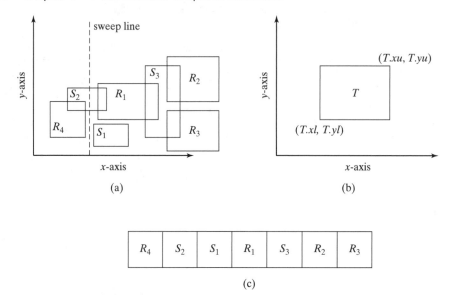

FIGURE 1.9. Determining pairs of intersecting rectangles: (a) two sets of rectangles: R and S; (b) a rectangle T with its lower-left and upper-right corners marked; and (c) the sorted set of rectangles with their joins. Note the filtering nature of the plane sweep algorithm. In the example, twelve possible rectangle pairs could be joined. The filtering step reduced the number of possibilities to five. An exact geometry test can be used to check which of the five pairs of objects satisfy the query predicate [Beckmann et al., 1990].

1.6.4 File Organization and Indices

DBMSs have been designed to handle very large amounts of data. This translates into a fundamental difference in how algorithms are designed in a GIS data analysis versus a database environment. In the former, the main focus is to minimize the computation time of an algorithm, assuming that the entire data set resides in main memory. In the latter, emphasis is placed on minimizing the sum of the computation and the I/O (input/output) time. The I/O time is the time required to transfer data from a disk (hard drive) to the main memory. This is because, despite falling prices, the main memory is not large enough to accommodate all the data for many large applications. This difference is conceptualized in the way one perceives the fundamental design of the computer. For many programmers, the computer essentially consists of two components: the CPU (central processing unit) and an infinite amount of main memory (Figure 1.10[a]). On the other hand, for many DBMS designers, the computer has three parts: the CPU, finite main memory, and infinite disk space (Figure 1.10[b]). Although a CPU can directly access data in the main memory, to access data on the disk, it first has to be transferred into the main memory. The difference in time between accessing data from random access memory (RAM) and disk is unbelievably large: a factor of a hundred thousand (year 2000). This ratio is getting worse every year because the CPU and memory are getting faster at a higher rate than disks and secondary storage devices.

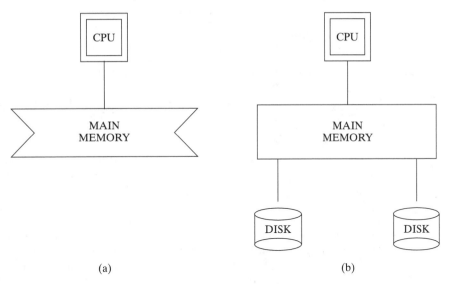

FIGURE 1.10. (a) Programmer's viewpoint; (b) DBMS designer's viewpoint.

At this moment (details in Chapter 4), it is worthwhile to view the secondary storage device (hard drive) as a book. The smallest unit of transfer between the disk and main memory is a page, and the records of tables are like structured lines of text on the page. A query issued by a user essentially causes a search about a few selected lines embedded in pages throughout the book. Some pages can reside in the main memory, and pages can be fetched only one at a time. To accelerate the search, the database uses an index. Thus in order to search for a line on a page, the DBMS can fetch all of the pages spanned by a table and scan them line by line until the desired record is found. The other option is to search in the index for a desired *key* word and then go directly to the page specified in the index. The index entries in a book are sorted in alphabetical order. Similarly, if the index is built on numbers, like the social security number, then they can be numerically ordered.

Spatial data can be sorted and ordered, but that comes at the loss of spatial proximity. What do we mean here? Consider Figure 1.11(a). Here we have a grid that is row-ordered. Now consider the neighbors of 4. On the grid the neighbors of 4 are 3, 7, and 8, but if stored in the way it is sorted, its neighbors will be 3 and 5. Thus, sorting has destroyed the original neighborhood relationship. Much research has been done to find better ways of ordering multidimensional data. Figure 1.11(b) shows another method. It is worth pointing out that no total ordering can preserve spatial proximity completely.

The *B-tree* (for balanced) index structure is arguably the most popular index employed by a relational DBMS. It is sometimes stated that the B-tree index structure is a major reason for the almost universal acceptance of relational database technology. The B-tree implementation crucially depends on the existence of an order in the indexing field. Figure 1.12 shows the crucial difference between a binary tree and a B-tree. Each node of a B-tree corresponds to a page of the disk. The number of entries in each node

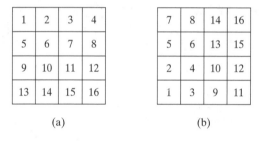

1	2	3	4
5	6	7	8
9	10	11	12
13	14	15	16

(a)

7	8	14	16
5	6	13	15
2	4	10	12
1	3	9	11

(b)

FIGURE 1.11. Different ways of ordering multidimensional data: (a) row order; (b) Z-order. If a line is drawn following the numbers in ascending order, the Z pattern will become obvious.

depends on the characteristics of the indexing field and the size of the disk page. If a disk page holds m keys, then the height of a B-tree is only $O(\log_m(n))$, where n is the number of total records. For trillon (10^{12}) records, one only requires a B-tree of height 6 for $m = 100$. Thus a record for a given key value can be retrieved in about half a dozen disk accesses even from such a large collection of records.

Because a natural order does not exist in multidimensional space, the B-tree cannot be used directly to create an index of spatial objects. The combination of spatial-order and B-tree is a common way to get around the lack of a natural order on spatial objects. Many commercial systems have adopted such an approach.

The R-tree data structure was one of the first index specifically designed to handle multidimensional extended objects. It essentially modifies the ideas of the B-tree to accommodate extended spatial objects. Figure 1.13 shows an example of how the R-tree organizes extended objects. More details follow in Chapter 4.

1.6.5 Query Optimization

One of the major strengths of relational database technology is how it efficiently executes a query by generating a sophisticated query evaluation plan. To explain this we revisit the query "*Find the names of all female senators who own a business.*" This query is actually a composition of two subqueries: a selection query and a join query. "*Name all*

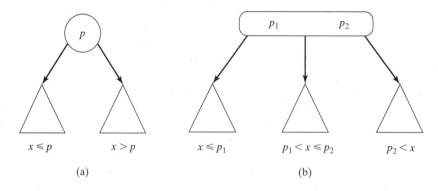

FIGURE 1.12. (a) Binary tree; (b) B-tree.

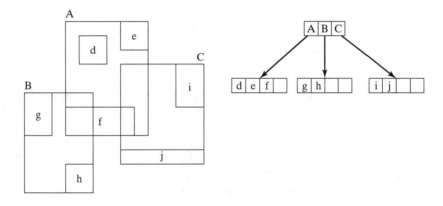

FIGURE 1.13. R-tree extends B-tree for spatial objects.

female senators" is a selection query because we select all of the female senators from a list of all senators. The query *"Find all senators who own a business"* is a join query because we combine two tables to process the query. The question is, in which order should these subqueries be processed: select before join or join before select? Remember a join is a multiscan query, and select is a single-scan query, so it is more important for a join operation to work on a smaller size table than the select operation. Now it is obvious that select should be done before join.

Consider the spatial query we have discussed before: *"Find all senators who serve a district of area greater than 300 square miles and who own a business within the district."* This query too is a composition of two subqueries: a range query and a spatial-join query. The range subquery is *"Name all senators who serve a district of area greater than 300 square miles."* The spatial-join query is *"Find all senators who own a business located in the district they serve."* Again, a range query is a single-scan and a join is a multiscan query, but there is one important difference. The single-scan query has to employ a potentially expensive function, *S.district.Area()*, to compute the area of each district. Of course, the join function also involves a computationally expensive function, *Within(B.location,S.district)*, but the point is that it is very difficult to assess how to order the processing of in spatial subqueries. This important step is taken up in Chapters 5 and 7.

1.6.6 Data Mining

Data mining, the systematic search for potentially useful information embedded in digital data, is now a hot topic of research inside and outside academia. Major corporations and government agencies have realized that the large amount of data that they have accumulated over the years, and are still gathering, can be systematically explored to provide a new perspective on their operations. Thus, data that was earlier considered a burden in terms of storage and management has suddenly become a source of wealth and profits. The story, now almost of mythic proportions, of how it was discovered by using data-mining tools that people who buy diapers in the afternoon are likely to buy beer too has fueled a massive effort to design and invent efficient tools for mining data. Until now most of the effort in data mining has focused on algorithm design and analysis. A database specialist can leverage his or her expertise on two fronts:

1. By designing algorithms that assume that the data sets are large or by designing general scaling tools that can be coupled with data-mining algorithms

2. By extending SQL with "mining" functionality, so that mining tools are callable from within SQL

Estimates showing that up to 80 percent of the data in digital form is actually spatial data have spawned efforts to invent mining techniques that take the special nature of spatial data into consideration. For example, random sampling is a common technique applied in data mining to cut down on the size of the data set being analyzed without significant loss of information. Traditional methods of sampling are not effective in the case of spatial data because of *spatial autocorrelation*. Thus techniques from spatial statistics should be incorporated into mining algorithms to deal with spatial data.

In GIS, data mining is not new. Map generalization and classification of remote sensing images are relatively mature fields and are clearly related to data mining. Famous historical examples of spatial data mining include identification of the contaminated water source responsible for the 1854 cholera epidemic in London [Griffith, 1999], as well as identification of fluoride in drinking water for good dental health. In Chapter 7 we make an effort to bridge this gap.

1.7 SUMMARY

Spatial data management is of use in many disciplines, including geography, remote sensing, urban planning, and natural resource management. Spatial database management plays an important role in the solution of grand challenge scientific problems such as global climate change and genomics.

There are three classes of users who can benefit from spatial database management systems. Business users are interested in using spatial data to augment other forms of information while deciding about marketing campaigns, distribution centers, and retail locations. For a business user, spatial data is an important source of secondary information.

For scientific users who specialize in the study of the environment, natural resources, and geography, spatial data is of paramount importance. Users in this group have been using GIS products for the analysis of spatial data, but with the size of data sets growing rapidly, there is a need for specialized data management techniques that address the distinguishing properties of spatial data.

Finally there is a third class of users who want to use spatial data to personalize their experience and interaction especially on the worldwide Web. For example, queries on a search engine can produce results that are spatially localized and more meaningful.

BIBLIOGRAPHIC NOTES

1.1 For a history of database technology and a general introduction to DBMS, see [Ramakrishnan, 1998; Elmasri and Navathe, 2000; Silberschatz et al., 1997]. For an overview of the shortcomings of RDBMS in handling spatial data and a general introduction to object-relational DBMS, see [Stonebraker and Moore, 1997].

1.2 For an overview of SDBs, see [Scholl et al., 2001; Shekhar et al., 1999a] and the special issue of very large databases (VLDB) journal and the overview in [Guting, 1994a] in particular.

1.3 For integrating a SDB into off-the-shelf databases systems for CAD applications, see [Kriegel et al., 2001]. For an example of SDBMS, see [de La Beaujardiere et al., 2000].

1.3.2 Spatial data models are covered in [Egenhofer, 1991b; Worboys, 1995] and [Laurini and Thompson, 1992; Price et al., 2000].

1.3.3 Extension of SQL for SDBs is discussed in [Egenhofer, 1994]. The OGIS specification for extending SQL for geospatial applications is described in [OpenGIS, 1998].

1.3.4 Representation of spatial data is covered extensively in [Laurini and Thompson, 1992; Worboys, 1995]. The filter-refine paradigm is discussed in [Chrisman, 1997].

1.3.5 The standard reference in spatial indexing is [Samet, 1990]. An up-to-date overview is in [Gaede and Gunther, 1998].

1.3.8 Issues related to the architectural design of SDBs are discussed in [Adam and Gangopadhyay, 1997; Worboys, 1995].

EXERCISES

Discussion

1. Discuss the differences between spatial and nonspatial data.
2. Geographic applications are a common source of spatial data. List at least four other important sources of spatial data.
3. What are the advantages of storing spatial data in a DBMS as opposed to a file system?
4. How can object-relational databases be used to implement an SDBMS?
5. List the differences and similarities between *spatial*, *CAD*, and *image* databases?
6. The interplay between the vector and raster data models has often been compared with the wave-particle duality in physics. Discuss.
7. Cognitive maps are described as "internal representations of the world and its spatial properties stored in memory." Do humans represent spatial objects as discrete entities in their minds? Is there a built-in bias against raster and in favor of vector representation?
8. Sorting is a popular method to access "traditional data" rapidly. Why is it difficult to sort spatial data?
9. Predicting global climate change has been identified as a premier challenge for the scientific community. How can SDBMS contribute in this endeavor?
10. E-commerce retailers reach customers all over the world via the Internet from a single facility. Some of them claim that geography and location are irrelevant in the Internet age. Do you agree? Justify your answer.
11. Define location-based and location independent services. Provide examples.
12. XML is emerging as a popular data interchange model on internet applications. Discusses the research impact of XML on spatial databases.
13. Compare and contrast:
    (i) GIS vs. SDBMS
    (ii) OODBMS vs. ORDBMS
    (iii) GI Systems vs. GI Services
    (iv) Data model vs. Query language
    (v) Query processing vs. File organization and indices
    (vi) Main memory vs. Disk
    (vii) Querying vs. Data mining
14. Define spatial databases. List a few applications of spatial databases beyond those listed in this chapter.

CHAPTER 2

Spatial Concepts and Data Models

2.1 MODELS OF SPATIAL INFORMATION

2.2 THREE-STEP DATABASE DESIGN

2.3 TRENDS: EXTENDING THE ER MODEL WITH SPATIAL CONCEPTS

2.4 TRENDS: OBJECT-ORIENTED DATA MODELING WITH UML

2.5 SUMMARY

This chapter presents techniques related to the modeling of spatial database applications. GIS is arguably the most popular spatial database application, and our discussion reflects this fact. Besides GIS, other applications with a definite spatial or geometric component, such as CAD and astronomy, can also benefit from the techniques described in this chapter.

Traditional database concerns have typically been dominated by business and administrative applications. There the focus had been to efficiently (and securely) process large numbers of relatively simple transactions. Falling prices of data-capturing devices such as the Global Positioning System (GPS), the easy availability of satellite and cartographic data over the Internet, and the increasing power of desktop computing have redefined the functionality of a database. A DBMS is no longer considered a distinct, isolated repository of data but an active component of a multisystem computing environment. In fact, the trend is to shift computationally intensive tasks directly to the DBMS. A GIS is a premier example of this trend.

An SDBMS integrates the special needs of modeling spatial data into the system. This is a nontrivial task because

- Spatial data is relatively more complex compared with traditional business data, and the old database constructs are not adequate for handling it.

- Database design and implementation are typically handled by computer scientists, while the handling of spatial data falls in the domain of geographers, environmentalists, and other physical scientists. Traditionally, these disciplines have evolved along different trajectories.

The remainder of the chapter is organized as follows. In Section 2.1 we describe the different models for processing spatial information. In Section 2.2 we provide general database design and modeling principles. Section 2.3 is devoted to the extensions of the entity-relationship (ER) model for SDBs, and Section 2.4 is devoted to the Unified

Modeling Language (UML), a conceptual model primarily designed for object-oriented databases. We close with a summary of the chapter.

2.1 MODELS OF SPATIAL INFORMATION

We introduce an example, `State-Park` SDB which will be used to illustrate the different concepts in spatial data modeling. A State-Park SDB consists of `forests` which are a collections of `forest-stands` that correspond to different species of trees. A State-Park is accessed by `roads` and has a `manager`. There are `fire-Stations` within a state-park which are exclusively responsible for monitoring and managing fires in the State-Park. The State-Park is also dotted with `facilities` such as camping groups and offices. Finally, there are `rivers` which pass through the state park and also supply water to the different facilities.

Models of spatial information are usually grouped into two broad categories: *field* and *object*. We illustrate this dichotomy with the help of an example shown in Figure 2.1. Consider an idealized forest partitioned into homogeneous areas, each with one (dominant) tree species. In this example there are three species, namely, Fir, Oak, and Pine.

There are two complementary ways of modeling the forest. In the *functional* viewpoint, the forest is modeled as a function where the *domain* is the underlying geographic space of the forest and the *range* is a set consisting of three elements—the names of the tree species. The function, say f, maps each point of the space occupied by the forest into exactly one element of the range. The function f is a step-function—constant where trees are alike and changing to a different value where the tree species changes. In GIS the functional model is called the *Field* model. In Figure 2.1(c), the field representation of the forest is shown using a piece-wise function. A different field representation can be defined on a grid with each cell specifying the name of the dominant tree species. This second representation may be preferred if the boundaries of forest-stand are highly irregular. Other field representation include iso-lines showing contours with fixed values of a physical variable, for example, temperature, pressure.

Now consider the places where the function f changes values. In an idealized setting where the demarcation between the tree species is clearly defined, we should get the boundaries of polygons. Each polygon can be assigned a unique identifier and a nonspatial attribute—the name of the tree species. Thus the forest can be modeled as a collection of polygons (i.e., forest-stands) each corresponding to a tree species. This is the *Object* viewpoint and is shown in Figure 2.1(b).

The decision to model a spatial application using a field or an object paradigm is based on the requirements of the application and tradition. Amorphous phenomena, for example, fire, flood, hazardous spills, are naturally modeled as fields the boundaries are fluid. Other spatial phenomena can also be modeled using fields. Field models are often used to model continuous spatial trends such as elevation, temperature, and soil variation. In fact, in the area of remote-sensing, where the earth's surface is mapped from satellite- and aircraft-based sensors, the field model is dominant. Object models are more common in modeling transportation networks (e.g., roads), land parcels for property tax, and legal ownership-related applications. It has been postulated that the object model may have originated from societal needs to demarcate ownerships viewing land as property [Couclelis, 1992].

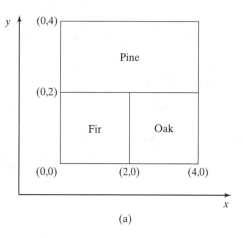

(a)

Object Viewpoint of Forest Stands

Area-ID	Dominant Tree Species	Area/Boundary
FS1	Pine	[(0,2),(4,2),(4,4),(0,4)]
FS2	Fir	[(0,0),(2,0),(2,2),(0,2)]
FS3	Oak	[(2,0),(4,0),(4,2),(2,2)]

(b)

Field Viewpoint of Forest Stands

$$f(x,y) = \begin{cases} \text{"Pine,"} & 2 \leqslant x \leqslant 4 \,;\, 2 < y \leqslant 4 \\ \text{"Fir,"} & 0 \leqslant x \leqslant 2;\, 0 \leqslant y \leqslant 2 \\ \text{"Oak,"} & 2 < x \leqslant 4;\, 0 \leqslant y \leqslant 2 \end{cases}$$

(c)

FIGURE 2.1. The object-field dichotomy. (a) A map showing three forest stands: *Pine, Fir, Oak*. (b) An *object* viewpoint representing the map as a collection of three objects. Each object has a unique identifier, a dominant tree species, and an area. The boundary of the area, a polygon, is specified by the coordinates. (c) A *field* viewpoint, where each point is mapped to the value of the dominant tree species.

2.1.1 Field-Based Model

Defining the field model for a spatial application requires that we determine three components: a *spatial framework*, *field functions*, and a set of relevant *field operations* [Worboys, 1995].

A spatial framework F is a finite grid imposed on the underlying space. All measurements are then based on this framework. The best-known example of a spatial framework is the system of latitude and longitude to reference the earth's surface. A spatial framework is a finite structure, and errors introduced due to discretization are unavoidable. A finite set of n computable functions or simple fields $\{f_i, \ 1 \leq i \leq n\}$,

$$f_i : \text{Spatial framework} \ \rightarrow \ \text{Attribute domain}(A_i)$$

map the spatial framework F onto different attribute domains A_i. The choice of the different field functions and the attribute domains is determined by the spatial application at hand. In the Forest example we had a single-field function, a step function, and the attribute domain was the set {fir, oak, pine}. For the special case when the functions are single-valued and the underlying space is the Euclidean plane, fields are naturally viewed as either surfaces or isolines, which are the locus of points that have the same attribute value. The third important component of field-based modeling is specification of the operations on the field functions.

Relationships and interactions between the different fields are specified by *field operations*. Field operations map a subset of fields onto other fields. Examples of field operations are union, $+$, and composition, $\circ$:

$$f + g : x \rightarrow f(x) + g(x)$$
$$f \circ g : x \rightarrow f(g(x))$$

Field operations can be classified into three categories [Worboys, 1995]: *local, focal,* and *zonal.*

Local Operations

For a local operation, the value of the new field at a given location in the spatial framework depends only on the value of the input field at that location. For example, consider an idealized State-Park which is completely partitioned into trees, lakes, and meadows. Define a function f and g as:

$$f(x) = \begin{cases} 1 & \text{if } x = \text{"tree"} \\ 0 & \text{otherwise} \end{cases}$$

and

$$g(x) = \begin{cases} 1 & \text{if } x = \text{"lake"} \\ 0 & \text{otherwise} \end{cases}$$

Then $f + g$, that is, the union of f and g is defined as

$$(f + g)(x) = \begin{cases} 1 & \text{if } x = \text{"tree" or "lake"} \\ 0 & \text{otherwise} \end{cases}$$

This is an example of a local operation.

Focal Operations

For a focal operation, the value of the resulting field at a given location depends on the values that the input field assumes in a small neighborhood of the location. The *limit* operation in calculus is an example of a focal operation. Let $E(x, y)$ be the elevation field of the State-Park. That is, E at (x, y) gives the value of the elevation at the location (x, y) in the spatial framework F. Then the operation that calculates the gradient of the elevation field, $\nabla \cdot E(x, y)$, is a focal operation, because the value of the gradient at (x, y) depends on the value of the elevation field in a "small" neighborhood of (x, y). Here we are assuming that the field varies smoothly and does not experience sharp jumps, as the step function did in the Forest example.

Zonal Operations

Zonal operations are naturally associated with aggregate operators or the integration function, $\int dx\, dy$ in calculus. In the `forest` example, the step function, which maps the forest onto the set of attributes {Oak, Fir, Pine}, also partitions the underlying space into three polygons, or *zones*. An operation that calculates the average height of the trees for each species is a zonal operation.

2.1.2 Object-Based Models

In object-based modeling, the focus is to abstract spatial information into distinct, identifiable, and relevant things, or entities, called *objects*. For example, we can characterize a park by the forest-stands, rivers, lakes, and roads that are contained in it. All these entities are clearly distinct and identifiable. Whether they are relevant or not depends on the application we are trying to model. Each object has a set of attributes that characterize it. The key difference between spatial objects and the objects/entities that are ubiquitous in traditional database modeling is that the attributes of spatial objects diverge into two distinct categories: spatial and nonspatial. It is through its spatial attributes that an object interacts with the underlying embedding space. In the `Forest` example, the forest-stand representing Fir is a spatial object, with the polygon that represents its spatial extent being its spatial attribute and the name Fir its nonspatial, alphanumeric attribute. A spatial object can have more than one spatial attribute representing, for instance, many levels of generalizations. A road on a map could be represented as a line or a polygon, depending on the scale of the map.

2.1.3 Spatial Data Types

A key issue in object-based models of spatial information is the choice of a basic set of spatial data types required to model common shapes on maps. Many proposals have been made over the years. A consensus is slowly emerging in terms of the OGIS standard [OGIS, 1999]. Figure 2.2 shows the fundamental building blocks of two-dimensional spatial geometry and their interrelationships in UML notation. We give a brief description of the UML notation in Section 2.4.

The most general shape is represented by "geometry" described via a "spatial representation system," which is a coordinate system like latitude/longitude or some other consensus framework. The "geometry" is subdivided into four categories, namely, *point*, *curve*, *surface*, and *geometry collection*. *Point* describes the shape of a zero-dimensional object, for example, city-centers in a map of the world. *Curve* describes the shapes of one-dimensional objects, for example, rivers in the map of a world. The *curve* objects are often approximated by a *linestring*, which is represented by two or more points. The simplest *linestring* is a straight line joining two or more *points*. The category *surface* describes the shape of two-dimensional objects, for example, countries on a map of the world. A *surface* is often modeled by a *polygon*. *Geometry collection* represents complex shapes, such as, collection of oil wells, a group of islands and so on. *Geometry collection* in turn is of three types, namely, *multipoint*, *multicurve*, and *multisurface*. The *geometry collection* spatial data types provide a "closure" property to OGIS spatial data types under geometric operations such as "geometric-union," "geometric-difference," or

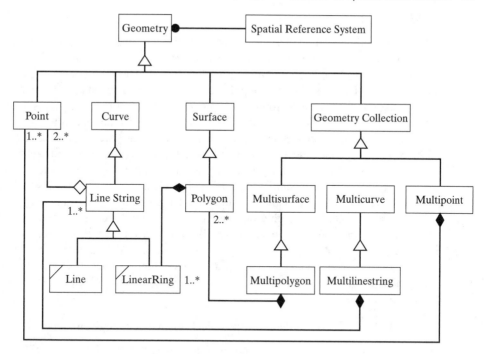

FIGURE 2.2. An OGIS proposal for building blocks of spatial geometry in UML notation [OGIS, 1999].

"geometric-intersection." For example, if one takes a geometric-difference of boundaries of Canada and Quebec, the result is a "multisurface" even if Canada and Quebec were of "surface" spatial data type. This property is useful to support multistep querying and data processing.

2.1.4 Operations on Spatial Objects

How do spatial objects interact with each other? In field-based modeling, the field function principally determines the type of operations allowed. After all, it would not be possible to apply a gradient operation on a nonsmooth field! In object-based modeling, the underlying embedding space determines the relationships that can exist between objects. We now describe a typology of the embedding space and associated relationships.

Set-Oriented

The simplest and most general of all embedding spaces is called set-oriented. Common relationships allowable in this setting are the usual set-based relationships of union, intersection, containment, and membership. Hierarchical relationships such as a forest-stand contained in a forest, a forest contained in a state park, and a state park contained within a state are adequately modeled by set theory.

Topological

To get an intuitive feeling of what a topological space is, imagine two polygons that touch (meet) each other and are drawn on a rubber sheet. Now if we deform the rubber sheet by stretching or bending but not cutting or folding it, the adjacency of the polygons remains intact. *Meet* is an example of a topological property, and the study of transformations (deformations) that preserve topological properties is called topology. Consider the map of the world with political boundaries of countries. The neighboring countries *meet* each other, whether the map is drawn on a sphere or on a flat space. The area of a polygon is clearly not a topological property. In fact, the relative areas of different countries are often not preserved in many maps. Areas of countries near the equator are reduced relative to the areas of countries near the poles in many planar maps. In Table 2.1 we list some common topological and nontopological properties [Worboys, 1995].

From a spatial/geographic database point of view, topological relationships such as *meet, within,* and *overlap* are most likely to be queried by a user of a spatial database management system. Is a given land parcel adjacent to a hazardous waste site? Does the river floodplain overlap a proposed highway network? All these are examples of topological relationships. Two common types of topological queries in spatial databases are:

- Find all objects that have a topological relation R to a given object.

- What is the topological relation between objects A and B?

The binary topological relationship between two objects, A and B, in a plane $\Re^2$ is based upon the intersection of A's interior ($A°$), boundary (∂A), and exterior (A^-) with B's interior ($B°$), boundary (∂B) and exterior (B^-) [Egenhofer, 1994]. The *nine-intersection* matrix between the six object parts defines a topological relationship and can be concisely represented using the following matrix:

$$\Gamma_9(A, B) = \begin{pmatrix} A° \cap B° & A° \cap \partial B & A° \cap B^- \\ \partial A \cap B° & \partial A \cap \partial B & \partial A \cap B^- \\ A^- \cap B° & A^- \cap \partial B & A^- \cap B^- \end{pmatrix}$$

By considering the values empty (0) and nonempty (1), one can distinguish between $2^9 = 512$ binary topological relationships. For a two-dimensional region embedded in $\Re^2$, eight relations can be realized, and they provide mutually exclusive complete coverage. These relations are *disjoint, meet, overlap, equal, contains, inside, covers,* and *covered by.*

Figure 2.3 shows how topological relations can be represented using the nine-intersection matrix. For example, the *disjoint* relationship is described in the nine-intersection model by the boolean matrix shown in the top-left corner of Figure 2.3. The zero entries indicate that *interior (A)* has no points in common with either *interior (B)* or *boundary (B)*. Similarly *interior (B)* has no point in common with *boundary (A)*. Similarly, *boundary (A)* and *boundary (B)* have no points in common.

The topological relationships on other pairs of spatial data types, for example *(point, surface), (point, curve)* can be defined in a similar manner. A point can be inside, outside, or on the boundary of a surface as listed in Table 2.1. A curve may *cross* the interior of a *surface* or may *meet* or be *disjoint* from a surface. A point may be an endpoint of a

TABLE 2.1: Examples of Topological and Nontopological Operations

Topological

endpoint(point, arc)	A point at the end of an arc.
simple-nonself-intersection (arc)	A nonself-intersecting arc does not cross itself.
on-boundary (point, region)	Vancouver is on the boundary of Canada and the United States.
inside (point, region)	Minneapolis is inside of Minnesota state.
outside (point, region)	Madison is outside of Minnesota state.
open (region)	Interior of Canada is an open region (excludes all its boundaries).
close (region)	Carleton County is a closed region (includes all its boundaries).
connected (region)	Switzerland is a connected region, whereas Japan is not (given any two points in the area, it is possible to follow a path from one point to the other such that the path is entirely within the area).
inside (point, loop)	A point is within the loop.
crosses (arc, region)	A road (arc) passes through a forest (region).
touches (region, region)	Minnesota (region) is a neighboring state of Wisconsin (region).
touches (arc, region)	Interstate freeway 90 (arc) passes by Lake Michigan (region).
overlap (region, region)	Land cover (region) overlaps with land use (region).

Nontopological

Euclidean-distance (point, point)	Distance between two points.
direction (point, point)	Madison city is east of Minneapolis city.
length (arc)	Length of a unit vector is one unit.
perimeter (area)	Perimeter of a unit square is 4 units.
area (region)	Area of unit square is one square unit.

curve, interior point of a curve, or off the curve as listed in Table 2.1. The relationships between curve are more complex and still an area of research [Clementini et al., 1993].

Directional

Directional relationships can be of three types, namely, absolute, object-relative, or viewer based. Absolute direction relationships are defined in the context to a global reference system, for example, north, south, east, west, northeast, and so on. Object-relative directions are defined, using the orientation of a give object. Example relationships include left, right, front, behind, above, below, and so on. Viewer relative directions are defined with respect to a specially designated reference object called the viewer.

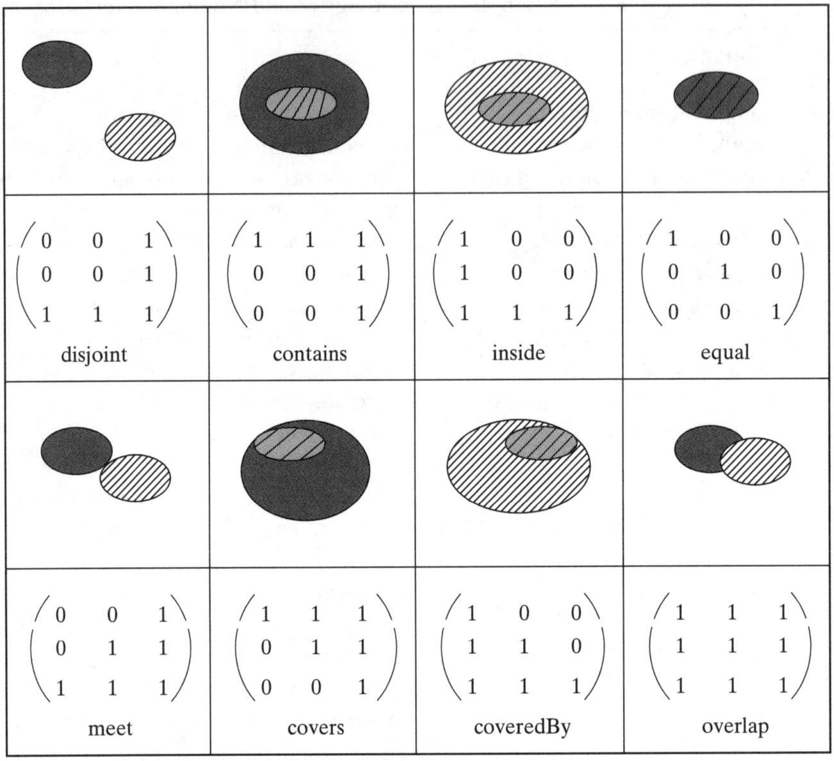

FIGURE 2.3. The nine-intersection model [Egenhofer et al., 1989].

Metric Space

Mathematically speaking, a set X is called a metric space if for any pair of points x and y of X, there is an associated real number $d(x, y)$, called the distance (also called a metric) from x to y, with the following properties:

1. $d(x, y) \geq 0$ and $d(x, x) = 0$
2. $d(x, y) = d(y, x)$
3. $d(x, y) \leq d(x, z) + d(z, y)$

for all x, y, z in X. Any function that satisfies these properties is called a metric on X.

In metric spaces the notion of distance is well defined. A distance function can be used to induce a topology on the space, and therefore every metric space is also a topological space. In network or graph settings, metric spaces play a crucial role. Optimal distance and shortest travel-time queries are ideally handled in a metric space setting.

Euclidean

Let R be the field of real numbers. A *vector space* V over R is a nonempty set V of objects v called *vectors*, together with two operations:

1. Addition: $u + v \in V$ for all $u\, v \in V$

2. Product: $\alpha u \in V$ for all $\alpha \in R, v \in V$.

Besides the existence of a special vector 0, there are other axioms that the two operations addition and product need to satisfy. For a complete discussion of vector space see [Blyth and Robertson, 1999].

If there exists a (minimal) finite set of vectors $\{e_1, e_2, \ldots, e_n\}$ such that any $v \in V$ can be expressed as a linear combination of the $e_i's$, that is, there exists $\alpha_1, \ldots \alpha_n \in R$ such that:

$$v = \alpha_1 e_1 + \ldots + \alpha_n e_n$$

then the vector space is finite dimensional. In a three-dimensional space, the $e_i's$ correspond to the familiar x, y, z coordinate axis. If we add the notion of inner product (angle) to vector space, we get a Euclidean space. In a Euclidean space setting, all spatial relationships, including set, topological, metric, and directional (north/south), can be defined.

2.1.5 Dynamic Spatial Operations

Most of the operations that we have discussed so far have been *static*, in the sense that the operands are not affected by the application of the operation. For example, calculating the length of a curve has no effect on the curve itself. *Dynamic* operations alter the objects upon which the operations act. The three fundamental dynamic operations are create, destroy, and update. All dynamic operations are variations upon one of these themes [Worboys, 1995]. In Table 2.2 some example of the create and update operations are listed.

An example of the *merge* operation is the "map-reclassification" operation supported by many GIS software products. Consider reclassification of the map of countries on the basis of the majority religion practiced in the countries, for example, *none, Islam, Christianity, Buddhism, and Hinduism*. The boundaries between neighboring countries with the same majority religion are removed via the *merge* operation in order to reclassify the maps. Similar examples of other dynamic spatial operations can be found in cartographic projections and map editing features in a GIS.

Additional classes of operations on spatial object exists. For example, operations can be defined on the shape of an extended object to ask queries, such as, which objects are squarish in shape? Which pair of objects fit like pieces of a jig-saw puzzle. The last

TABLE 2.2: Representative Example of Dynamic Spatial Operations [Worboys, 1995].

Create	reproduce (X)	Produces an exact replica of X.
	generate (X)	Generates an object that depends on but does not replicate X.
	split (X)	Creates objects whose aggregation is X.
	merge (X,Y,Z)	X, Y, and Z are merged to create a single object.
Update	translate	Shifts the position of the object in the plane.
	rotate	Changes the orientation without changing the shape.
	scale	The object size is changed, but the shape remains the same.
	reflect	The mirror reflection of an object in a straight line.
	shear	Deforms the object in a predefined fashion.

example is useful in designing new drugs (pharmaceutical) by finding molecules which can dock in certain areas of other molecules. Another family of spatial operations is based on visibility relationships to address queries like list the locations on a golf course to get best view of hole 9. We hope to see consensus mathematical frameworks for such families of operations in the near future.

2.1.6   Mapping Spatial Objects into Java

Having defined the spatial hierarchy (see Figure 2.2 and the corresponding array of spatial relationships), we can easily program these notions into an object-oriented programming language such as Java.

We give an example of how a specific query can be written in Java. The query is, *"Find all tourist offices within 10 miles of the Maple Campground."*

The java class `Facility` and `FacilitySet` are used to model the locations of tourist offices as well as the campgrounds. A separate class `Query` is used to model the distance computation and the query itself. The `Facility` class has three attributes, namely, *name*, *type*, and *location*. The *type* attribute is used to distinguish between tourist offices and campgrounds. The location of facilities is *point* spatial datatype. This program assumes that the spatial datatype *point* is available as part of a spatial library (e.g., SDE from ESRI). The library also provides a *distance* function on the *point* spatial datatypes. There are three methods in `FacilityClass`. The method *facility* is a constructor used to initialize new objects. Method *getName* is used to extract the *name* attribute and method; *withinDistance* is used to test if another facility is within a given distance.

Class `FacilitySet` is used to model a collection of facilities. For example, it can model a set of tourist offices. It has two attributes, *maxSize* and *FacilityTable*. maxSize designates the maximum size of the collection of facilities. The facilityTable is used to store information about each facility. There is only one method in `FacilitySet`. This method is used to read the information about various facilities from a file to initialize the attributes of an instance of `FacilitySet`.

The class `Query` implements a query to extract all the tourist offices within 10 miles of the Maple campground. This class has one method, named *main*, which loops through the list of tourist offices checking the distance to the Maple campground.

The key point of this discussion of the Java program is to show that the spatial datatypes and operations can be used from a host language different from SQL, which is used in the rest of the book. The second point is to compare the amount of programming effort required by spatial querying. SQL will greatly reduce the amount of code needed to specify simple spatial queries. It will also reduce the burden of performance tuning and data-structure selection. We encourage readers to compare SQL with Java in the coming chapters to revisit these points.

```
import java.lang.*;
import java.io.*;
import java.util.*;


/* assume class Point is given, which contains two attributes: x and y with
double type, and also some member functions, including distance (Point) */

/* Assume the original data is stored in file ``facilityFile''.
```

Each line in the file represents a facility; use @@ as its delimiter, e.g.
```
   Maple @@ campground @@ 2.0 @@ 3.0
   Office @@ Tourist-Office @@ 6.0 @@ 8.9
```

```java
public class Facility {
   protected String name;
   protected String type;
   protected Point  location;

   public Facility (String name, String type, Point location) {
     this.name = name;
     this.type = type;
     this.location = location;
   }

   public String getName() {
     return name;
   }

   public boolean withinDistance(Facility f, double d) {
     if (this.location.distance(f.location) < d)
       return true;
     else
       return false;
   }
}

public class FacilitySet {
   const maxSize = 50;
   protected Facility[maxSize] facilityTable;

   /* read from file filename and initialize the facility table */
   public FacilitySet(String filename) {
     BufferedReader in = new BufferedReader (new FileReader(filename));
     String inline;
     StringTokenizer strLine;
     int i=0 ;
     String token;

     while ((inline = in.readLine())!= null) {
       strLine = new StringTokenizer(inline, "@@");

        /* read name */
       token = strLine.nextToken();
       FacilityTable[i].name = token;

       /* read type */
       token = strLine.nextToken();
       FacilityTable[i].type = token;

       /* read x coordinate */
```

```
      token = strLine.nextToken();
      FacilityTable[i].location.x = Double.valueOf(token).doubleValue();

      /* read x coordinate */
      String type token = strLine.nextToken();
      FacilityTable[i++].location.y = Double.valueOf(token).doubleValue();

    }
  }
}

public class FacilityDemo {

  public static void main(String[] args) {

    Facility f = new Facility("Maple", "Campground", Point(2.0,4.0));
    Facility[] fTable = new FacilitySet("facilityFile");
    String[] resultTable = new string[fTable.length];

    int j=0;
    for (int i=0; i < fTable.length; i++) {
      if (f.withinDistance(fTable[i], 2.0)
        and fTable[i].type = "Tourist-Office")
          resultTable[j++] = fTable[i].name;
    }
  }
}
```

2.2 THREE-STEP DATABASE DESIGN

So far in this chapter we have described two models of spatial information: the object model and the field model. Our view of these models was from the perspective of data modeling involving concepts intrinsic to the spatial domain. We now introduce classical data modeling from the perspective of database design. Our ultimate goal is to "blend" the two families of concepts.

Database applications are modeled using a three-step [Elmasri and Navathe, 2000] design process. In the first step, all the available information related to the application is organized, using a high-level *conceptual data model*. At the conceptual level, the focus is on the datatypes of the application, their relationships and constraints. The actual implementation details are left out at this step of the design process. Plain text combined with simple but consistent graphic notation is often used to express the conceptual data model. The Entity Relationship (ER) model is one of the most prevalent of all conceptual design tools.

The second step, also called the logical modeling phase, is related to the actual implementation of the conceptual data model in a commercial DBMS. Data in a commercial database is organized using an implementation model. Examples of implementation models are hierarchical, network, and relational. The relational model is one of the most widely implemented models in current commercial databases. In the relational model, the datatypes, relationships, and constraints are all modeled as `Relations`. Tightly coupled with the relational model is the formal query language relational algebra (RA). The RA consists of simple operations that allow quering of the data organized as relations. RA is described in detail in Chapter 3.

The relational model does not fit the need of spatial data, as explained by [Herring, 1991]:

> Relational algebra characterizes the querying capabilities of relational databases. A relational database can answer any query expressible in relational algebra, which is universally accepted model of traditional applications of relational databases.
>
> In contrast, there is no universally accepted mathematical model of geographic information, making it difficult to design spatial query languages and spatial databases. In addition, there is a considerable semantic gap between GIS and relational databases, leading to complexities and inconveniences.

Chapter 7 provides a specific example to show that RA is not capable of expressing the *transitive closure*, an important graph operation, without additional assumptions. The transitive closure operation is closely linked to the *reclassification* operation [Delis et al., 1994], discussed in Section 2.1.5.

The third and final step, modeling of the physical design, deals with the nuts and bolts of the actual computer implementation of the database applications. Issues related to the storage, indexing, and memory management are handled at this level and will be the subject of discussion in subsequent chapters. We now introduce the ER model.

2.2.1 The ER Model

The first step in database design is to come up with the conceptual model of the "miniworld." The purpose of the conceptual model is to represent the miniworld in a manner devoid of computer metaphors. The motivation is to separate out the concepts of the application from the implementation detail. There are many design tools available for conceptual data modeling, but the ER model is one of the most popular. The ER model integrates seamlessly with the relational data model, which in turn is one of the most prevalent logical models, the second step in the three-step design paradigm. Besides the ER model and propelled by the success of the object-oriented design methodology, the UML is another popular conceptual modeling tool. We discuss the UML in some detail in the next section, but here we model the *State-Park* example using the ER model.

Entities and Attributes

In the ER model, the miniworld is partitioned into *entities* which are characterized by *attributes* and interrelated via *relationships*. Entities are things or objects that have an independent physical or conceptual existence. In the *State-Park* example, FOREST, RIVER, FOREST-STAND, ROAD, and FIRE-STATION are all examples of entities.

Entities are characterized by *attributes*. For example, *name* is an attribute of the entity FOREST. An attribute (or a set of attributes) that uniquely identifies instances of an entity is called the *key*. In our example the *name* attribute of the entity ROAD is a key, assuming it is not possible that two different roads have the same name. All instances of ROAD in our example database have unique names. Though not a conceptual design issue, a mechanism must exist in the DBMS to enforce this constraint.

Attributes can be single valued or multivalued. *Species* is a single-valued attribute of FOREST-STAND. We now explain the existence of a multivalued attribute in the context of our example. The FACILITY entity has an attribute Pointid, which is a unique identification for the spatial location of instances of the entity. We are assuming that the **map** scale predicates instances of FACILITY to be represented as points. It is possible that a given facility spans two distinct point locations, in which case the Pointid attribute is multivalued. A similar argument holds for other entities.

Suppose we want to store information about the *elevation* of a FOREST. Because *elevation* can change values within the FOREST entity, we model it as a multivalued attribute, since field data type is not available.

Relationships

Besides entities and attributes, the third construct in the ER model is the *relationship*. Entities interact or connect with each other through relationships. We have already noted spatial relationships in the previous section; here we focus on the general concept of relationships. Though many entities can participate in a given relationship, we will deal only with *binary* relationships, that is, those between two entities. There are three kinds of relationships based on cardinality constraints: one-one, many-one, and many-many.

One-One (1:1)
In a one-one relationship, each instance of one entity can relate to only one instance of the other participating entity. For example, the relationship *manages* between the entities MANAGER and FOREST is a one-one relationship; a FOREST can only have one MANAGER, and a MANAGER can manage only one FOREST.

Many-One (M:1)
A many-one relationship can potentially connect many instances of one entity with one instance of the other entity participating in the relationship. The *belongs_to* is a many-one relationship between the entities FACILITY and FOREST, assuming each facility belongs to only one forest but many facilities can belong to a forest.

Many-Many (M:N)
Sometimes many instances of one entity can be related to many instances of the other participating entity. The relationship supplies_water_to which connects the entities RIVER and FACILITY is such a relationship. Sometimes relationships can have attributes too. *supplies_water_to* has an attribute *Volume* which keeps track of the quantity of water supplied by a river to a facility.

ER Diagram

Associated with the ER model is the ER diagram, which gives a graphic representation to the conceptual model. In the ER diagram, entities are represented as *boxes*, attributes as *ovals* connected to the boxes with straight lines, and relationships as **diamond** boxes. The *cardinality* of the relationship, whether it is 1:1, M:1, or M:N, is shown around the diamonds. The key attribute is underlined, and multivalued attributes are represented as *double-ovals*. The ER diagram of the *State-Park* example is shown in Figure 2.4. There are seven entities, namely, FOREST-STAND, RIVER, ROAD, FACILITY, FOREST, FIRE-STATION, and MANAGER. The attributes of entity FOREST include *name*, *elevation*, and *polygonid*. *Name* is a unique id, that is, each forest has a unique name. The diagram

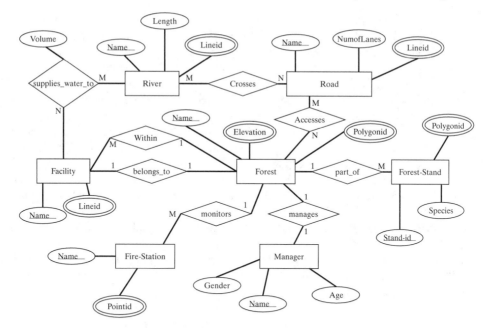

FIGURE 2.4. An ER diagram for the *State-Park* example.

also shows eight relationships. Entity FOREST participates in six relationships. Entity FIRE-STATION participates in only one relationship, namely, *monitors*. The cardinality constraints show that each fire station monitors one forest, but many fire stations can monitor a forest. Some of the relationships are spatial in nature. These include *crosses*, *within*, *part-of*. Many other spatial relationships are implicit in this diagram. For example, a river *crosses* a road is shown explicitly, but a river *crosses* a forest is implicit.

2.2.2 The Relational Model

The relational model to represent data was introduced by Codd in 1970. Since then, it has become one of the most popular logical data models. The popularity and power of this model is a consequence of the simplicity of its structure. We explain the terminology of the relational model in the context of the *State-Park* example. Suppose we wanted to organize available data of all the forests in state parks. Then we could organize the information in the form of a table, namely the table Forest, and list the array of the available information in columns. For the Forest table, the associated data consists of three things: the *Name* of the Forest, its *Elevation*, and spatial *Geometry*.

The table is called a *relation*, and the columns, *attributes*. Each different instance of Forest will be identified with a row in the table. A row is called a *tuple*, and the order in which the rows and columns appear in the table is unimportant. Thus a relation is an unordered collection of tuples. Together the table and column names constitute the *relation schema*, and a collection of rows or tuples is called a *relational instance*. The number of columns is called the degree of the relation. The Forest is a relation of degree three. Similarly, data about, for example, the different forest stands and rivers can be organized in separate tables.

What are the allowable values of the attributes? In traditional database applications the datatypes of the attributes, called `domains`, are limited, consisting of integers, floats, character strings, dates, and a few other domains. Furthermore, there is no provision for user-defined data types. In the `Forest` table, the attribute *name* fits nicely into this limited set but *elevation* and *geometry* do not. This is one of the reasons that traditional relational database technology is hard pressed to meet the requirements for SDBs. Despite that, we will show how spatial information can be mapped into a relational data model. In the object-relational data model, it would be justified to assume that we have added new basic domains or datatypes as specified in the OGIS standard. This is exactly what we will do in the next section.

Certain constraints on the relational schema must be maintained to ensure the logical consistency of the data. They are the *key, entity integrity*, and *referential integrity* constraints. The key constraint specifies that every relation must have a *primary key*. A key is a subset of the attributes of the relation whose values are unique across the tuples in a relation. There may be many keys in a relation, and the one that is used to identify the tuples in a relation is called the primary key. The entity integrity constraint states that no primary key can be null. This constraint is obvious; it would be impossible to uniquely identify tuples with a null value for its primary key. Logically consistent relationships between the different relations are maintained through the enforcement of referential integrity constraints. To explain the mechanism of referential integrity, we first describe the notion of a *foreign key*. A foreign key is a set of attributes in a relation which is duplicated in another relation. The referential integrity constraint stipulates that the value of the attributes of a foreign key either must appear as a value in the primary key of another relation or must be null. Thus a relation *refers* to another relation if it contains foreign keys.

2.2.3 Mapping the ER Model to the Relational Model

Many software packages, also called CASE tools, can translate an ER model to a relational schema. Example software packages include ERwin, Oracle Designer 2000, Rational Rose, and so on. This translation facility allows database designers to work with conceptual data models, focusing on the needs of application domain. If it were not for the spatial attributes, the ER model could be mapped seamlessly and intuitively into the relational model. There are six basic steps:

1. Map each entity into a separate relation. The attributes of the entity are mapped into the attributes of the relation. Similarly, the key of the entity is the primary key of the relation. The relational schema for ER diagram of Figure 2.4 is shown in Figure 2.5.
2. For relationships whose cardinality is 1:1, we place the key attribute of any one of the entities as a foreign key in the other relation. For example, the relation `Manager` has a foreign key attribute corresponding to the primary key, the *name*, of the `Forest`.
3. If the cardinality of the relationship is M:1, then place the primary key of $1-side$ relation as a foreign key in the relation of $M-side$. For example, the relation `Fire-Station` has a foreign key which is the primary key of the relation `Forest`.
4. Relationships with the cardinality M:N have to be handled in a distinct manner. Each M:N relationship is mapped onto a *new* relation. The name of the relation is

Forest-Stand

<u>Stand-id</u>	Species	Forest-name
(Integer)	(varchar)	(varchar)

Fstand-Geom

<u>Stand-id</u>	<u>Polygonid</u>
(Integer)	(Integer)

River

<u>Name</u>	Length
(varchar)	(Real)

River-Geom

<u>Name</u>	<u>Lineid</u>
(Integer)	(Integer)

Road

<u>Name</u>	NumofLanes
(varchar)	(Integer)

Road-Geom

<u>Rname</u>	<u>Lineid</u>
(varchar)	(Integer)

Facility

<u>Name</u>	Forest-name	Forest-name-2
(varchar)	(varchar)	(varchar)

Facility-Geom

<u>Name</u>	<u>Pointid</u>
(varchar)	(Integer)

Forest

<u>Name</u>
(varchar)

Forest-Geom

<u>Name</u>	<u>Polygonid</u>
(varchar)	(Integer)

Fire-Station

<u>Name</u>	ForName
(varchar)	(varchar)

Fstation-Geom

<u>Name</u>	<u>Pointid</u>
(varchar)	(Integer)

Supplies_Water_To

<u>FacName</u>	<u>RivName</u>	Volume
(varchar)	(varchar)	(Real)

Road-Access-Forest

<u>RoadName</u>	<u>ForName</u>
(varchar)	(varchar)

Manager

<u>Name</u>	<u>Age</u>	<u>Gender</u>	ForName
(varchar)	(Integer)	(varchar)	(varchar)

FIGURE 2.5. Relational schema for the State-Park example.

the name of the relationship, and the primary key of the relation consists of the pair of primary keys of the participating entities. If the relationship has any attributes then it becomes an attribute of the new relation. Supplies_Water_To is an example of an *M:N* relationship between the entities Facility and River. The river name and the facility name constitute the primary key, and the attribute *volume* becomes an attribute in the new table. Note that the M:N spatial relationship Road Crosses River results in a new table Road-Crosses-River.

5. For a multivalued attribute, a new relation is created that has two columns: one corresponding to the multivalued attribute and the other corresponding to the key of the entity that owns the multivalued attribute. Together the multivalued attribute and the key of the entity constitute the primary key of the new relation. For example, the Forest-Stand entity has a multivalued attribute *polygonid* which is an identification number (integer) for the geometric location of the city. *Pointid* is a multivalued attribute because a forest-stand may span two disjoint locations (e.g., a road may cut through a forest stand). We therefore have the relation Fstand-Geom. Similarly, we have relations Forest-Geom, River-Geom, Road-Geom, Facility-Geom, and Fstation-Geom.

6. The *elevation* attribute needs to be handled in a distinct manner. First, as we have pointed out, *elevation* is a multivalued attribute. Therefore we clearly need a new relation namely, Elevation. The attributes of this new relation are *Forest_Name*, *Elevation*, and *Pointid* as shown in Figure 2.6. The *elevation* attribute captures the height of the forest at the *pointid* location. In this table all three attributes constitute the primary key.

Spatial Tables

The spatial attributes and the space-varying attributes in the ER diagram have to be handled in a special way in the relational model. New domains, for example, spatial objects, are represented as new relations. The primary key for these relations is used as the foreign key in relations representing entities containing attributes typed using these domains. As described earlier, *pointid, lineid,* and *polygonid* are new domains and can be modeled as separate relations. Corresponding to each one of these attributes, there is a relation: Point, Line, and Polygon (see Figure 2.6).

Polygon

Polygonid	Seq-no	Pointid
(Integer)	(Integer)	(Integer)

Line

Lineid	Seq-no	Pointid
(Integer)	(Integer)	(Integer)

Point

Pointid	Latitude	Longitude
(Integer)	(Real)	(Real)

Elevation

Forest-name	Pointid (F.K.)	Elevation
(varchar)	(Integer)	(Real)

FIGURE 2.6. Schema for point, line, polygon, and elevation.

1. The `Point` table has three attributes: *pointid*, *latitude,* and *longitude*. Though there are many other reference systems, the latitude-longitude system is the most familiar, and all other reference systems can be derived from it.

2. A finite straight line can be defined in terms of two points. Therefore the *pointid* attribute in the `Line` table is a foreign key to the *point* table. The *seq-no* refers to the sequence number of the points that constitute a line identified by *lineid*.

3. The `Polygon` table is like the `Line` table with the constraint that the first and last sequence numbers refer to the same *pointid*.

2.3 TRENDS: EXTENDING THE ER MODEL WITH SPATIAL CONCEPTS

This translation of spatial attributes in an ER diagram to spatial table does not take full advantage of the spatial data types described in Section 2.1.3. It simply treats spatial attributes as any other nonspatial attributes. We now describe the emerging trend toward extending ER diagrams with pictograms to provide special treatment to spatial data types. This reduces clutter in ER diagrams, as well as in the resulting relational schema, while improving the quality of spatial modeling. The spatial relationships, for example, Road-Crosses-River can be omitted from the ER diagram and made implicit. The relations representing multivalued spatial attributes and M:N spatial relationships may not be needed in a relational schema.

As the earlier discussion shows, the ER model is unable, at least intuitively, to capture special semantics inherent in spatial modeling. Specifically, the shortcomings of the ER model are:

1. The ER model was originally designed with an implicit assumption of an object-based model. Therefore a field model cannot be naturally mapped using the ER model.

2. While in a traditional ER model, relations between entities are derived from the application under consideration, in spatial modeling there are always inherent relationships between spatial objects. For example, all the topological relationships discussed earlier are valid instances of relationships between two spatial entities. How should they be incorporated into the ER model without cluttering the diagram?

3. The type of entity used to model a spatial object depends on the scale of the "map." A city can be mapped as a point or a polygon depending on the resolution of the map. How should multiple representations of the same object be represented in a conceptual model?

2.3.1 Extending the ER Model with Pictograms

Many extensions have been proposed to the ER model to make the conceptual modeling of spatial applications easier and more intuitive. The idea is to add constructs that capture and convey the semantics of spatial reasoning and at the same time keep the graphical representation simple. Using *pictograms* to annotate and extend ER diagrams has been recently proposed.

Spatial relationships, including topological, directional, and metric relationships, are implicit between any two entities that have a spatial component. For example, it is natural to consider the topological relationship–*cross* between a `Forest` and `River` entity.

Including the *cross* relationship in an ER diagram does not convey added information about the structure of the application being modeled.

We will show how pictograms can be used to convey the spatial datatypes, the scale, and the implicit relationships of spatial entities. We will present the pictogram enhancement in the Bachus-Naur form (BNF) grammar notation, though it is not necessary to be familiar with the BNF notation to understand what follows. Information about the grammar notation can be found in any standard computer science text on compilers as well as many books on English grammar.

Entity Pictograms

Pictogram

A pictogram is a miniature representation of the object inserted inside of a box. These iconic representations are used to extend ER diagrams and are inserted at appropriate places inside the entity boxes. A pictogram can be a basic shape or a user-defined shape.

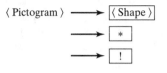

Grammar (for Pictogram)

Shape

Shape is the basic graphical element in the pictogram, which represents the elements in the spatial data model. A model element can be a basic shape, a multishape, a derived shape, or an alternate shape. Many of the objects have simple basic shapes.

⟨ Shape ⟩ ⟶ ⟨ Basic Shape ⟩

⟶ ⟨ Multi-Shape ⟩

⟶ ⟨ Derived Shape ⟩

⟶ ⟨ Alternate Shape ⟩

Grammar (for Shape)

Basic Shape

In a vector model, the basic elements are the point, line, and polygon. In a typical application, a majority of the spatial entities are represented as basic shapes. In the forest example, we had represented a facility as a point (0-D), a river or road network as lines (1-D), and forest areas as polygons (2-D).

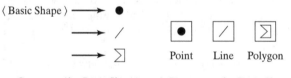

Grammar (for Basic Shape)   *Pictograms for Basic Shapes*

Multishape

To deal with objects that cannot be represented by one of the basic shapes, we have defined a set of aggregate shapes. Cardinality is used to quantify multiple shapes. For example, a river network will be represented as a concatenation of a line pictogram and its cardinality n. Similarly, some features cannot be depicted at a given scale, for which we use the cardinality of 0.

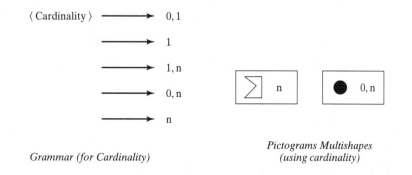

| Grammar (for Cardinality) | Pictograms Multishapes (using cardinality) |

Derived Shape

If the shape of an object is derived from the shape of other objects, then we represent the pictograms in italicized form. For example, we can derive the shape of the US from the shapes of its state boundaries.

Grammar (for Derived Shape)   *Pictograms for Derived Shapes*

Alternate Shape

Alternate shapes can be used for the same object based on certain conditions, for example, depending on the scale, a river can be represented as a polygon or a line.

⟨ Alternate Shape ⟩ ⟶ ⟨ Basic Shape ⟩ ⟨ Derived Shape ⟩
⟶ ⟨ Basic Shape ⟩ ⟨ Basic Shape ⟩

Grammar (for Alternate Shape)

Any Possible Shape

For a combination of shapes, we use a wild card * symbol, meaning that every geometric shape is possible. For example, an irrigation network consists of stations (point), canals (lines), and reservoirs (polygons).

Pictograms for Alternate Shapes

User-Defined Shape

Apart from the basic shapes of point, line, and polygon, users can define their own shapes. For example, in order to convey more information, a user might prefer to represent an irrigation network by using a pictogram other than the exclamation point.

Any Possible Shape   *User Defined Shape*

Relationship Pictograms

The relationship pictograms are used to model the relationships between the entities. For example, *part-of* is used to model the relationship between a route and a network, or it can be used to model the partitions of a forest into forest stands.

Part_of(Network)   Part_of(Partition)

Pictograms for Relationships

The pictogram-enhanced ER diagram is shown Figure 2.7. The `Facility` and `Fire-Station` entities are encoded with point pictograms, `River` and `Road` by line pictograms, and `Forest` and `Forest-Stand` by polygon pictograms. The *part_of* relationship between `Forest` and `Forest-Stand` is also shown. From the figure, it is clear that the pictograms enhance the spatial semantics conveyed by the ER diagram.

The *part_of* (partition) pictogram implies three spatial integrity constraints:

1. forest_stands are spatially "disjoint," i.e., any point in space is part of at most one forest_stand.
2. A forest_stand is spatially "inside" the forest it is part_of.
3. The geometric union of all forest_stands spatially "covers" the forest they belong to.

These spatial integrity constraints describe a spatial set-partition semantics.

It is useful to compare Figure 2.4 and Figure 2.7 to bring out the advantages of the pictogram enhanced ER model. Note that Figure 2.7 is less cluttered as it has fewer explicit relationships and attributes. Spatial relationships and attributes are implicit. Second, Figure 2.7 has more information about spatial relationships. For example, "river crosses forest" and "fire-station inside forest" are implied even though Figure 2.7 did not include those explicitly. The spatial integrity constraint implied by the part_of (partition) pictogram is also new. Last, the relational schema for Figure 2.7

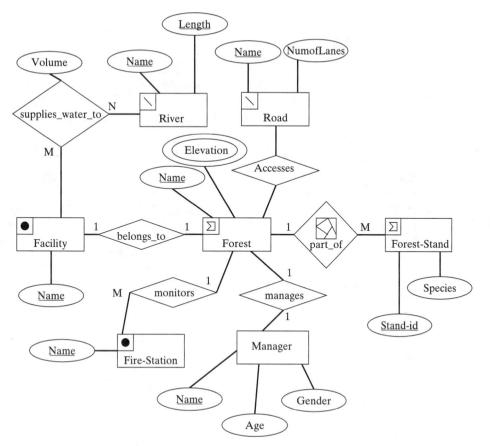

FIGURE 2.7. ER diagram for the *State-Park* example, with pictograms.

can be simpler than the relational schema for Figure 2.4. The relations for M:N spatial relationships as well as spatial data types were can be omitted.

2.4 TRENDS: OBJECT-ORIENTED DATA MODELING WITH UML

The popularity of object-oriented languages such as C++ and Java has encouraged the growth of OODBMS. The motivation behind the growing interest in OODBMS is that the direct mapping of the conceptual database schema into an object-oriented language leads to a reduction of impedance mismatch. Impedance mismatch is the degree of difficulty encountered when a model on one level is converted into a model on another level (for example, when the ER model is mapped onto the relational data model).

UML [Booch et al., 1999] is one of the emerging standards for conceptual level modeling for object-oriented software design. It is a comprehensive language to model the structural schema and dynamic behavior at conceptual level. As far as database design is concerned, we are only interested in modeling the static structure of the system. Instead

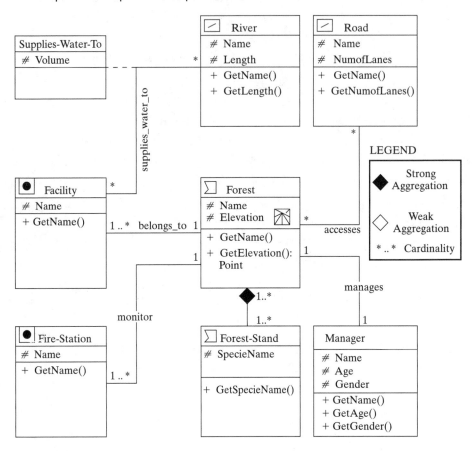

FIGURE 2.8. The State-Park example in UML class diagram.

of ER diagrams, we now have class diagrams. Figure 2.8 is the equivalent UML class diagram (UMLCD) representation of the *State-Park* example shown in Figure 2.4.

We briefly describe the UMLCD notations with reference to the State-Park example in the following list.

- Class is the encapsulation of all objects which share common properties in the context of the application. It is the equivalent of the entity in the ER model. For example, facility is an example of a class which, at least abstractly, captures functioning units within the state-park, such as restrooms, campsites, and tourist offices. We have extended the class diagrams with pictograms, as we did for the ER diagrams. This way it is clear that instances of the class Facility are spatial objects. More specifically, their spatial geometry is represented as points. This way all the spatial properties, relationships, and operations that are valid for point objects are applicable to the class Facility.

- Attributes characterize the objects of the class. Unlike ER notation, UMLCD has no notion of a key attribute. This is because in object oriented (OO) systems all objects have a system-generated unique identification. Attributes also have a scope or visibility associated with them. The scope regulates access to the attribute from within or outside of the class. This is essential for controlling the degree of modularity of the database design. There are three levels of scope, and each has a special symbol:

    1. + *Public*: This allows the attribute to be accessed and manipulated from any class.
    2. − *Private*: Only the class that owns the attribute is allowed to access the attribute.
    3. # *Protected*: Classes that are derived ("subtyped") from a parent class have access to the attribute. We have chosen to make all the attributes in the `State-Park` example *protected*.

- Methods are functions and are part of the class definition. They are responsible for modifying the behavior, or state of the class. The state of the class is embodied in the current values of the attributes. In object-oriented design, attributes should only be accessed through methods. In the `Facility` class, the *name* attribute of the class is accessed through the method *GetName( )*.

- Relationships relate one class to another or to itself. This is similar to the concept of relationship in the ER model. For database modeling, UMLCD has three important categories of relationships: aggregation, generalization, and association.

    1. Aggregation is a specific construct in UMLCD to capture the part-whole relationship. For example, the class `Forest-Stand` is engaged in a part-whole relationship with the class `Forest`. Sometimes a class can be part of more than one other classes. To distinguish the two cases, the former is called *strong* aggregation and the latter *weak*.
    2. Generalization is best described in the context of the spatial hierarchy shown in Figure 2.2. For example, the class `Geometry` is a generalization of its *subclasses* `Point`, `Line`, and `Polygon`.
    3. Associations show how objects of different classes are related. Like relationships in the ER model, associations can be *binary* if they connect two classes or *ternary* if they connect three classes. The relation *supplies_water_to* is an example of an association between the classes `Facility` and `River`. Notice that there is a class `SuppliesWaterTo` connected to the *supplies_water_to* association via a dotted line. This is because the association itself has an attribute *Volume*.

2.4.1   Comparison between ER and UML

The main constructs in ER and UMLCD are summarized in Table 2.3. The preceding discussion has shown that there are many similarities between these two modeling paradigms. However, there are a few differences between ER and UMLCD.

TABLE 2.3: ER and UMLCD Concepts

Concepts from ER	Concepts from UML
Entity	Class
Attribute	Attribute
Key attribute	
	Methods
Inheritance	Inheritance
Aggregation	Aggregation
Weak entity	

The concept of "entities" in ER diagrams corresponds closely with the concept of "classes" in class diagrams of UML. Both entities and classes have attributes, and may participate in relationships, such as inheritance and aggregation. Classes can also include "methods" besides attributes. Methods are procedures or functions encapsulating logic and computational recipes which are usually not part of entities in the ER model. Class diagrams can model the attributes as well as methods from the classes from object-oriented programming languages, for example, Java.

In UMLCD there is a notion of *methods* which can be used to modify the behavior of the state of the classes.

Some concepts from the ER model are not available in class diagrams. One such concept is weak entities, which depend on another entity for unique identification. Consider electronic mail addresses consisting of a user name and a domain name. For example, root@cs.umn.edu has a user name "root" and a domain name "cs.umn.edu." Clearly, user name "root" is not unique and depends on the domain name for unique identification. Class diagrams and object-oriented paradigms assume a unique id for all objects and do not support the notion of weak entities.

In ER each entity instance is characterized by a user-defined explicit identity, while in UMLCD it is assumed that a system will generate a unique identity for the instantiated classes.

2.5 SUMMARY

Spatial information modeling can be categorized into two groups: *field* and *object*. The *field* model is useful for modeling amorphous spatial constructs which vary smoothly in space, for example, rainfall, cloud cover, smoke, aerosol. The *object* is useful for modeling discrete, identifiable constructs, example, countries.

Associated with each model are a set of operations that characterize the model. Operations associated with the field model are grouped into three categories: *local*, *focal*, and *zonal*. Operations associated with the object model are categorized on the basis of their mathematical properties: *set-oriented, Euclidean, topological*, and *metric*.

The *ER* model is widely used for the conceptual level modeling of data. Though the ER model is not designed for any specific form of data, it is primarily used for simple data types and constructs. The ER model can be mapped to the database *relational* model by following a sequence of well laid-out steps.

The ER and the relational model have to be extended to incorporate the special characteristics of spatial data. The ER model can be extended by introducing *pictograms* that symbolize different spatial data types and relationships. Similarly, the relational model can be extended by incorporating new data types and their associated operations. For example, three well-known data types used in spatial applications are point, line, and polygon. UML, which is one of popular conceptual modeling language for OODBMS, can also be extended with pictograms for spatial data modeling.

BIBLIOGRAPHIC NOTES

2.1 The object-field dichotomy is a recurring subject of debate in GIS and spatial modeling. While database models have a bias toward the object viewpoint, most data collection is geared towards field-type analysis. For a historical and psychological background to the object-field debate, see [Couclelis, 1992].

2.1.1 Our discussion of field-based modeling follows [Worboys, 1995].

2.1.2 Topological aspects of the object-based spatial data model have been pioneered in [Egenhofer, 1991a] and rigorously extended in [Clementini et al., 1993].

2.1.4 For further discussion on an object model of direction, see [Shekhar et al., 1999a].

2.2 Database design and related issues are covered in any introductory text on databases. See, for example [Elmasri and Navathe, 2000; Ramakrishnan, 1998].

2.3.1 Our discussion of extending ER models with pictograms follows [Shekhar et al., 1999c]. This paper presents a logical data model for spatial databases by extending the ER model with spatial pictograms (PEER) and provides a mapping to translate PEER into logical data model.

2.4 Extensions of ER modeling for spatial data have been explored in [Hadzilacos and Tryfona, 1997; Shekhar et al., 1997]. A consensus is still lacking. For further discussion on modeling geospatial application databases using UML-based repositories, see [Brodeur et al., 2000].

EXERCISES

1. Discuss "Scientific rigor and rationality favor the field model, but the human mind prefers the object model."
2. Weather forecasting is an example where the variables of interest—pressure, temperature, and wind—are modeled as fields. But the public prefers to receive information in terms of discrete, entities. For example, "The front will stall," or "This high will weaken" [Goodchild, 1986] Can you cite another example where this field-object dichotomy is apparent?
3. A lake is sometimes modeled as an object. Can you give an example in which it might be useful to model a lake as a field? Are lake boundaries are well defined?
4. Match the columns:

Nominal	Temp. in Celsius
Ordinal	Temp. in Kelvin
Interval	Social security #
Ratio	Color spectrum

5. Design an ER diagram to represent the geographic and political features of the World. The World consists of three entities: country, city, and river. On the basis of these three entities answer the following questions:

- If two countries have diplomatic ties between them, they are related by the relation *diplomatic_ties*. Draw this relationship on an ER diagram and label its cardinality.

- Water is often described as the hot issue for the twenty-first century. If two countries share a river, that does not necessarily mean they both have rights to access its water. Represent the relation *river_owned_by* between the Country and River entity.

- In many instances the capital city of a country is not its official business center. For example, New York is the business capital of the US, Shanghai of China, and Sydney of Australia. Represent the relationship *business_capital* between the City and Country entities.

6. Consider the problem of representing the OGIS hierarchy in an OO language such as Java. How would you model inheritance? For example, MultiPoint inherits properties from both the Point and GeometryCollection classes. How will you model associations and cardinality constraints? Where will you use abstract classes?

7. Study UML [Booch et al., 1999] for data modeling. Which UML diagrams are relevant for data modeling? Do they offer any advantage over ER? How will you represent the following concepts in UML: primary key, foreign key, entities, relationships, cardinality constraints, participation constraints, and pictograms?

8. Model the State-Park example using UML.

9. Classify the following operations into local, focal, zonal: (a) slope, (b) snow-covered park, (c) site selection for a new facility, (d) average population, and (e) total population.

10. Many spatial data types in OGIS refer to a planar world. These include line string and polygons. These may include large approximation errors while modeling the shapes of long river or large counties on the spherical surface of earth. Propose a few spherical spatial data types to better approximate large objects on a sphere. Which spatial relationships (e.g., topological, metric) are affected by planar approximations?

11. Revisit the Java program implementing the query about tourist-offices within ten miles of camp ground "Maple." The main() method in class FacilityDemo will slow down linearly as the number of tourist-offices increases. Device a variation of plane-sweep algorithm from Chapter 1 to speed up the search algorithm.

12. Develop translation rules to convert pictograms in a conceptual data model (e.g., ERD) to OGIS spatial data types embedded in a logical data model (e.g., Java, SQL) or physical data model.

13. Consider a few 3×3 boolean matrices other than the eight shown in Figure 2.3. Why are those matrices not interesting in defining topological relationships among 2-d surfaces embedded in R^2? Provide an example topological relationship between surfaces in 3-d, which is not modeled by eight operators in Figure 2.3.

14. Spatial data is sometimes considered a special case of multidimensional data, that is, data embedded in multidimensional space (e.g., temperature, pressure, volume, time). Compare and contrast spatial data embedded in Euclidean space (e.g., latitude, longitude) with other multidimensional data.

15. Compare the primitive spatial data types in OGIS type hierarchy (2.2) and pictograms defined in section 2.1.6. Provide pictograms for the following OGIS data types: point, line string, polygon, multipoint, multiline string, multipolygon.

16. Both OGIS and pictograms include a set of six spatial data types: point, line string, polygon, multipoint, multiline string, multipolygon.

(a) Sketch an argument to show this set of six data types is closed under basic geometric operations such as geometric-union, geometric-intersection, geometric-difference, and so forth. A set S of data types is closed under operation O if the resultant data type from applying O on elements in S is also in S.

(b) Why is closure an interesting property for query languages?

17. Consider the basic set S of six spatial data types. Select the most "natural" data type for representing the shape of the following entities on a map of the world/nation. Identify your assumptions: countries, rivers, lakes, highways, cities. How will the choices of spatial data types change as the scale of the map changes? How would you represent scale dependence in pictograms?

18. Study the ER diagrams in Figure 2.4. What does it specify about the following questions:

   (i) How many forests can a manager manage?
   (ii) How many forest-stands can a manager manage?
   (iii) How many fire-stations can monitor a forest?
   (iv) How many facilities can belong to a forest?
   (v) What are the spatial relationships between rivers and forests?
   (vi) What are the spatial relationships among forest-stands in a forest?

19. Study the ER diagrams with pictograms in Figure 2.7. Which questions listed in Exercise 18 will have different answers? Create a relational schema for Figure 2.7.

20. Study the relational schema in Figure 2.5 and identify any missing tables for M:N relationships. Also identify any missing foreign keys for 1:1 and 1:N relationships in Figure 2.4. Should the spatial tables in Figure 2.6 include additional tables for collections of points, line-strings or polygons?

21. Revise the ER diagram with pictograms in Figure 2.7 to allow the following requirements:

   (i) Roads may have a spatial representation of line-strings (e.g., center-line) or polygons (e.g., land parcel occupied).
   (ii) Facilities may have a spatial representation of point collection or polygon collection?
   (iii) Roads are parts of a road network.
   (iv) Manager have a mailing address and a map location.

22. Study some of the public-domain digital spatial data sets (e.g., census, TIGER files). Develop conceptual data models (e.g., ER model and diagrams) for these data sets.

23. Suppose one wants to revise the data model for State-Park example to allow a Fire-Station to monitor multiple forests. List revisions to ER diagrams (Figure 2.4 and Figure 2.7) and relational schema (Figure 2.5).

24. Left and right sides of an object are inverted in mirror image, however top and bottom are not. Explain using absolute and relative diagrams.

C H A P T E R   3

Spatial Query Languages

A query language, the principal means of interaction with the database, is a core requirement of a DBMS. A popular commercial query language for relational database management systems (RDBMS) is SQL. It is partly based on the formal query language, relational algebra (RA) and it is easy to use, intuitive, and versatile. Because SDBMSs are an example of an *extensible* DBMS and deal with both spatial and nonspatial data, it is natural to seek for an extension of SQL to incorporate spatial data.

As shown in the previous chapter, the relational model has limitations in effectively handling spatial data. Spatial data is "complex," involving a melange of polygons, lines, and points, and the relational model is geared for dealing with simple data types such as integers, strings, dates, and so forth.

Constructs from object-oriented programming, such as user-defined types and data and functional inheritance, have found immediate applications in the modeling of complex data. The widespread use of the relational model and SQL for applications involving simple datatypes combined with the functionality of the object-oriented model has led to the birth of a new "hybrid" paradigm for database management systems, the OR-DBMS.

A corollary to this newfound interest in OR-DBMS is the desire to extend SQL with object functionality. This effort has materialized into a new OR-DBMS standard for SQL:SQL3. Because we are dealing with spatial data, we examine the spatial extensions and libraries for SQL3.

A unique feature of spatial data is that the "natural" medium of interaction with the user is visual rather than textual. Hence any spatial query language should support a sophisticated graphical-visual component. Having said that, we focus here on the nongraphical spatial extensions of SQL. In Section 3.1, we introduce the World database, which will form the basis of all query examples in the chapter. Sections 3.2 and 3.3 provide a brief overview of RA and SQL, respectively. Section 3.4 is devoted to a discussion on the spatial requirements for extending SQL. We also introduce the OGIS standard for extending SQL for geospatial data. In Section 3.5, we show how common spatial queries can be posed in OGIS extended SQL. In Section 3.6, we introduce SQL3 and Oracle8's implementation of a subset of SQL3.

3.1   STANDARD DATABASE QUERY LANGUAGES

Users interact with the data embedded in a DBMS using a query language. Unlike traditional programming languages, database query languages are relatively easy to learn and use. In this section we describe two such query languages. The first, RA, is the more formal of the two and typically not implemented in commercial databases. The importance of RA lies in the fact that it forms the core of SQL, the most popular and widely implemented database query language.

3.1.1   World Database

We introduce RA and SQL with the help of an example database. We introduce a new example database here to provide some diversity in examples and exercises. The `World` database consists of three entities: `Country`, `City`, and `River`. The pictogram-enhanced ER diagram of the database and the example tables are shown in Figure 3.1 and Table 3.1, respectively. The schema of the database is shown below. Note that an underlined attribute is a primary key. For example, Name is a primary key in Country table, City table, and River table.

Country(*Name*: varchar(35), *Cont*: varchar(35), *Pop*: integer,
        GDP: Integer, *Life-Exp*: integer, *Shape*: char(13))
City(*Name*: varchar(35), *Country*: varchar(35), *Pop*: integer,
        Capital: char(1), *Shape*: char(9))
River(*Name*: varchar(35), *Origin*: varchar(35), *Length*: integer,
        Shape: char(13))

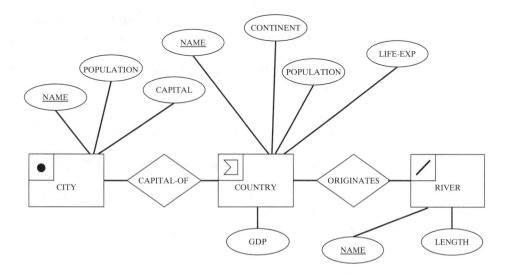

FIGURE 3.1. The ER diagram of the `World` database.

TABLE 3.1: The Tables of the World Database with Sample Records

COUNTRY	Name	Cont	Pop (millions)	GDP (billions)	Life-Exp	Shape
	Canada	NAM	30.1	658.0	77.08	Polygonid-1
	Mexico	NAM	107.5	694.3	69.36	Polygonid-2
	Brazil	SAM	183.3	1004.0	65.60	Polygonid-3
	Cuba	NAM	11.7	16.9	75.95	Polygonid-4
	USA	NAM	270.0	8003.0	75.75	Polygonid-5
	Argentina	SAM	36.3	348.2	70.75	Polygonid-6

(a) Country

CITY	Name	Country	Pop (millions)	Capital	Shape
	Havana	Cuba	2.1	Y	Pointid-1
	Washington, D.C.	USA	3.2	Y	Pointid-2
	Monterrey	Mexico	2.0	N	Pointid-3
	Toronto	Canada	3.4	N	Pointid-4
	Brasilia	Brazil	1.5	Y	Pointid-5
	Rosario	Argentina	1.1	N	Pointid-6
	Ottawa	Canada	0.8	Y	Pointid-7
	Mexico City	Mexico	14.1	Y	Pointid-8
	Buenos Aires	Argentina	10.75	Y	Pointid-9

(b) City

RIVER	Name	Origin	Length (kilometers)	Shape
	Rio Parana	Brazil	2600	LineStringid-1
	St. Lawrence	USA	1200	LineStringid-2
	Rio Grande	USA	3000	LineStringid-3
	Mississippi	USA	6000	LineStringid-4

(c) River

The Country entity has six attributes. The *Name* of the country and the continent (*Cont*) it belongs to are character strings of maximum length thirty-five. The population (*Pop*) and the gross domestic product (*GDP*) are integer types. The GDP is the total value of goods and services produced in a country in one fiscal year. Life-Exp attribute represents the life expectancy in years (rounded to the nearest integer) for residents of a country. The *Shape* attribute needs some explanation. The geometry of a country is represented in the *Shape* column of Table 3.1. In relational databases, where the datatypes are limited, the *Shape* attribute is a foreign key to a shape table. In an object-relational or object-oriented database, the *Shape* attribute will be a polygon abstract datatype (ADT). Because, for the moment, our aim is to introduce basic RA and SQL, we will not query the *Shape* attribute until Section 3.4.

The City relation has five attributes: *Name, Country, Pop, Capital,* and *Shape.* The *Country* attribute is a foreign key into the Country table. *Capital* is a fixed character type of length one; a city is a capital of a country, or it is not. The *Shape* attribute is a foreign key into a point shape table. As for the Country relation, we will not query the *Shape* column before learning about OGIS data types for SQL3.

The four attributes of the River relation are *Name, Origin, Length,* and *Shape.* The *Origin* attribute is a foreign key into the Country relation and specifies the country where the river originates. The *Shape* attribute is a foreign key into a line string shape table. To determine the country of origin of a river, the geometric information specified in the *Shape* attribute is not sufficient. The overloading of name across tables can be resolved by a qualifying attribute with tables using a dot notation table.attribute. County.Name, city.Name, and river.Name uniquely identify the Name attribute inside different tables. We also need information about the direction of the river flow. In Chapter 7 we discuss querying spatial networks where directional information is important.

3.2   RA

RA is a formal query language associated with the relational model. An *algebra* is a mathematical structure consisting of two distinct sets of elements, $(\mathbf{\Omega_a}, \mathbf{\Omega_o})$. Ω_a is the set of *operands* and Ω_o is the set of *operations*. An algebra must satisfy many axioms, but the most crucial is that the result of an *operation* on an *operand* must remain in Ω_a. A simple example of an algebra is the set of integers. The *operands* are the integers, and the *operations* are addition and multiplication. In Chapter 8 we discuss other kinds of algebra associated with raster and image objects.

In RA there is only one type of operand and six basic operations. The operand is a relation (table), and the six operations are *select, project, union, cross-product, difference,* and *intersection*. We now introduce some of the basic operations in detail.

3.2.1   The Select and Project Operations

To manipulate data in a single relation, RA provides two operations: *select* and *project*. The select operation retrieves a subset of rows of the relational table, and the project operation extracts a subset of the columns. For example, to list all the countries in the Country table which are in *North-America* (NAM), we use the following relational algebra expression:

$$\sigma_{\text{cont=NAM}}(Country).$$

The result of this operation is shown in Table 3.2(a). The rows retrieved by the select operation σ are specified by the comparison selection operator, which in this example is *cont= 'North-America'*. The schema of the input relation is not altered by the select operator. The formal syntax of the select operation is

$$\sigma_{<\text{selection operator}>}(\text{Relation}).$$

Subsets of columns for all rows in a relation are extracted by applying the *project* operation, π. For example, to retrieve the names of all countries listed in the Country table, we use the following expression:

$$\pi_{\text{Name}}(Country).$$

The formal syntax of the project operation is

$$\pi_{<\text{ list of attributes }>}(\text{Relation})$$

We can combine the select and the project operations. The following expression yields the names of countries in North America. See Table 3.2(c) for the result.

$$\pi_{\text{Name}}(\sigma_{\text{Cont=NAM}}(Country))$$

TABLE 3.2: Results of Two Basic Operations in RA Select and Project

Name	Cont	Pop (millions)	GDP (billions)	Life-Exp	Shape
Canada	NAM	30.1	658.0	77.08	Polygonid-1
Mexico	NAM	107.5	694.3	69.36	Polygonid-2
Cuba	NAM	11.7	16.9	75.95	Polygonid-4
USA	NAM	270.0	8003.0	75.75	Polygonid-5

(a) Select

Name
Canada
Mexico
Brazil
Cuba
USA
Argentina

(b) Project

Name
Canada
Mexico
Cuba
USA

(c) Select and project

3.2.2 Set Operations

At its most fundamental level a relation is a set. Thus all set operations are valid operations in the relational algebra. Set operations are applied to relations that are *union-compatible*. Two relations are union-compatible if they have the same number of columns, share the same domain, and if the columns appear in the same order from left to right.

- **Union:** If R and S are relations, then $R \cup S$ returns all tuples which are either in R or S. For example, we can use the union operation to list the countries which are either in North America or have a river originating in them:

  1. $R = \pi_{\text{Name}}(\sigma_{\text{Cont=NAM}}(\text{Country}))$
  2. $S = \pi_{\text{Origin}}(\text{River})$
  3. $R \cup S$.

  The resulting relation is shown in Table 3.4(a). Notice that the attributes *R.Name* and *S.Origin* have the same domain, as *R.Origin* refers to County.Name. This is sufficient for R and S to be union-compatible.

- **Difference:** $R - S$ returns all tuples in R that are not in S. The difference operation can be used, for example, to list all countries in North America that have no river (listed in the River table) originating in them. The resulting relation is shown in Table 3.4(b).

  1. $R = \pi_{\text{Name}}(\sigma_{\text{Cont=NAM}}(\text{Country}))$
  2. $S = \pi_{\text{Origin}}(\text{River})$
  3. $R - S$.

TABLE 3.3: The Cross-Product of Relations R and S

R	R.A	R.B
	A_1	B_1
	A_2	B_2

(a) Relation R

S	S.C	S.D
	C_1	D_1
	C_2	D_2

(b) Relation S

$R \times S$	R.A	R.B	S.C	S.D
	A_1	B_1	C_1	D_1
	A_1	B_1	C_2	D_2
	A_2	B_2	C_1	D_1
	A_2	B_2	C_2	D_2

(c) $R \times S$

- **Intersection:** For two union-compatible relations R and S, the intersection operation $R \cap S$ returns all tuples which occur both in R and S. Note that this operation, though convenient, is redundant: it can be derived from the difference operation, $R \cap S = R - (R - S)$. To list countries that are in South America and also have an originating river, we use the intersection operation. The result is shown in Table 3.4(c).

  1. $R = \pi_{\text{Name}}(\sigma_{\text{Cont=SAM}}(\text{Country}))$
  2. $R = \pi_{\text{Origin}}(\text{River})$
  3. $R \cap S$.

- **Cross-Product:** This operation applies to any pair of relations, not just those that are union-compatible. $R \times S$ returns a relation whose schema contains all the attributes of R followed by those of S. For simplicity, an abstract example is shown in Table 3.3. Notice the use of the cascading dot notation to distinguish the attributes of the two relations.

3.2.3 Join Operation

The select and project operations are useful for extracting information from a single relation. The *join* operation is used to query across different relational tables. A join operation can be thought of as a cross-product followed by the select operation. The general join operation is called the *conditional* join. An important and special case of the conditional join is called the *natural* join.

TABLE 3.4: The Results of Set Operations

NAME
Canada
Mexico
Brazil
Cuba
USA

(a)
Union

NAME
Canada
Mexico
Cuba

(b)
Difference

NAME
Brazil

(c)
Intersection

Conditional Joins

The general conditional join, $\bowtie_c$, between two relations R and S is expressed as follows:

$$R \bowtie_c S = \sigma_c(R \times S).$$

The c condition usually refers to the attributes of both R and S. For example, we can use the join operation to query for the names of the countries whose population is greater than Mexico's (see Table 3.5):

1. $R = \pi_{\text{Name, Pop}}(\text{Country})$
2. $S = R$. (S is duplicate copy of R)
3. Form the cross-product $R \times S$. The schema of the $R \times S$ relation is

$R \times S$	R.Name	R.Pop	S.Name	S.Pop

4. Apply condition, that is, the population of a country in relation S is greater than the population of Mexico.

$$U = R \bowtie S = \sigma_{(\text{R.Name = 'Mexico'}) \wedge (\text{R.Pop} > \text{S.Pop})}(R \times S)$$

Natural Join

An important special case of the conditional join is the *natural join*. In a natural join, only the *equality* selection condition is applied to the common attributes of the two relations and only one column in result represents common equi-join attribute. For example, a natural join can be used to find the populations of countries where rivers originate. The steps follow:

TABLE 3.5: Steps of the Conditional Join Operation

$R \times S$	R.Name	R.Pop	S.Name	S.Pop
	⋮	⋮	⋮	⋮
	Mexico	107.5	Canada	30.1
	Mexico	107.5	Mexico	107.5
	Mexico	107.5	Brazil	183.3
	Mexico	107.5	Cuba	11.7
	Mexico	107.5	USA	270.0
	Mexico	107.5	Argentina	36.3
	⋮	⋮	⋮	⋮

(a) A portion of $R \times S$

R.Name	R.Pop	S.Name	S.Pop
Mexico	107.5	Canada	30.1
Mexico	107.5	Cuba	11.7
Mexico	107.5	Argentina	36.3

(b) The select operation on $R \times S$

1. Rename the `Country` relation C and the `River` relation R.
2. Form the cross-product $C \times R$.
3. Join the two relations on the attributes *C.Name* and *R.Origin*. The domains of these two attributes are identical,

$$C \bowtie_{\text{C.Name = R.Origin}} R.$$

4. In a natural join, the selection condition is unambiguous; therefore, it does not have to be explicitly subscripted in the join formula.
5. The final result is obtained by projecting onto the *Name* and *Pop* attributes:

$$\pi_{\text{Name, Pop}}(C \bowtie R).$$

3.3   BASIC SQL PRIMER

SQL is a commercial query language first developed at IBM. Since then, it has become the standard query language for RDBMS. SQL is a declarative language, that is, the user only has to specify the answer rather than a procedure to retrieve the answer.

The SQL language has at least two separate components: the data definition language (DDL) and the data modification language (DML). The DDL is used to create, delete, and modify the definition of the tables in the database. In the DML, queries are posed and rows inserted and deleted from tables specified in the DDL. SQL also have other statements for data control language. We now provide a brief introduction to SQL. Our aim is to provide enough understanding of the language so that readers can appreciate the spatial extensions that we discuss in Section 3.4. A more detailed and complete exposition of SQL can be found in any standard text on databases [Elmasri and Navathe, 2000; Ullman and Widom, 1999].

3.3.1   DDL

The creation of the relational schema and the addition and deletion of the tables are specified in the DDL component of SQL. For example, the `City` schema introduced in Section 3.2 is defined below in SQL. The `Country` and `River` tables are defined in Table 3.6.

```
CREATE   TABLE CITY {
         Name   VARCHAR(35),
         Country   VARCHAR(35),
         Pop   INT,
         Capital   CHAR(1),
         Shape   CHAR(13),
         PRIMARY KEY   Name }
```

The **CREATE TABLE** statement is used to define the relations in a relational schema. The name of the table is **CITY**. The table has four columns, and the name of each column and its corresponding datatype must be specified. The *Name* and *Country* attributes must be ASCII character strings of less than thirty-five characters. *Population*

TABLE 3.6: The Country and River Schema in SQL

CREATE TABLE Country { Name VARCHAR(35), Cont VARCHAR(35), Pop INT, GDP INT, Shape CHAR(15), PRIMARY KEY (Name) }	CREATE TABLE River { Name VARCHAR(35), Origin VARCHAR(35), Length INT, Shape CHAR(15), PRIMARY KEY (Name) }
(a) Country schema	(b) River schema

is of the type integer, and *Capital* is an attribute which is a single character *Y* or *N*. In SQL92 the possible datatypes are fixed and cannot be user defined. We do not list the complete set of datatypes, which can be found in any text on standard databases. Finally, the *Name* attribute is the primary key of the relation. Thus each row in the table must have a unique value for the *Name* attribute. Tables no longer in use can be removed from the database using the DROP TABLE command. Another important command in DDL is ALTER TABLE for modifying the schema of the relation.

3.3.2 DML

After the table has been created as specified in DDL, it is ready to accept data. This task, which is often called "populating the table," is done in the DML component of SQL. For example, the following statement adds one row to the table River:

```
INSERT INTO River(Name, Origin, Length)
    VALUES('Mississippi','USA', 6000)
```

If all the attributes of the relation are not specified, then default values are automatically substituted. The most often used default value is NULL. An attempt to add another row in the River table with Name = 'Mississippi' will be rejected by the DBMS because of the primary key constraint specified in the DDL.

The basic form to remove rows from the table is as follows:

```
DELETE FROM TABLE WHERE < CONDITIONS >
```

For example, the following statement removes the row from the table River that we inserted above.

```
DELETE  FROM  River
        WHERE  Name = 'Mississippi'
```

3.3.3 Basic Form of an SQL Query

Once the database schema has been defined in the DDL component and the tables populated, queries can be expressed in SQL to extract relevant subsets of data from the database. The basic syntax of an SQL query is extremely simple:

```
SELECT   column-names
FROM     relations
WHERE    tuple-constraint
```

This form is equivalent to the RA expression consisting of π, σ, and $\bowtie$. SQL SELECT statement has more clauses related to aggregation (e.g., GROUP BY, HAVING), ordering results (e.g., ORDER BY), and so forth. In addition, SQL allows the formulation of nested queries. We illustrate these with a set of examples.

3.3.4   Example Queries in SQL

We now give examples of how to pose different types of queries in SQL. Our purpose is to give a flavor of the versatility and power of SELECT statement. All the tables queried are from the WORLD example introduced in Section 3.1.1. The results of the different queries can be found in Tables 3.7 and 3.8.

1. **Query:** List all the cities and the country they belong to in the CITY table.

```
SELECT   Ci.Name, Ci.Country
FROM     CITY Ci
```

Comments: The SQL expression is equivalent to the project operation in RA. The WHERE clause is missing in the SQL expression because there is no

TABLE 3.7: Tables from the Select, Project, and Select and Project Operations

Name	Country	Pop(millions)	Capital	Shape
Havana	Cuba	2.1	Y	Point
Washington, D.C.	USA	3.2	Y	Point
Brasilia	Brazil	1.5	Y	Point
Ottawa	Canada	0.8	Y	Point
Mexico City	Mexico	14.1	Y	Point
Buenos Aires	Argentina	10.75	Y	Point

(a) Query 2 Select

Name	Country
Havana	Cuba
Washington, D.C.	USA
Monterrey	Mexico
Toronto	Canada
Brasilia	Brazil
Rosario	Argentina
Ottawa	Canada
Mexico City	Mexico
Buenos Aires	Argentina

(b) Query 1 Project

Name	Life-exp
Mexico	69.36
Brazil	65.60

(c) Query 3: Select and project

TABLE 3.8: Results of Example Queries

Ci.Name	Co.Pop
Brasilia	183.3
Washington, D.C.	270.0

(a) Query 4

Ci.Name	Ci.Pop
Washington, D.C.	3.2

(b) Query 5

Average-Pop
2.2

(c) Query 6

Cont	Continent-Pop
NAM	2343.05
SAM	676.1

(d) Query 7

Origin	Min-length
USA	1200

(e) Query 8

Co.Name
Mexico
Brazil
USA

(f) Query 9

equivalent of the `select` operation in RA required in this query. Also notice the optional cascading dot notation. The `CITY` table is renamed `Ci`, and its attributes are referenced as `Ci.Name` and `Ci.Country`.

2. **Query:** List the names of the capital cities in the `CITY` table.

```
SELECT   *
FROM     CITY
WHERE    CAPITAL='Y'
```

Comments: This SQL expression is equivalent to the **select** operation in RA. It is unfortunate that in SQL the select operation of RA is specified in the `WHERE` and not the `SELECT` clause! The * in `SELECT` means that all the attributes in the `CITY` table must be listed.

3. **Query:** List the attributes of countries in the `Country` relation where the life-expectancy is less than seventy years.

```
SELECT   Co.Name, Co.Life-Exp
FROM     Country Co
WHERE    Co.Life-Exp < 70
```

Comments: This expression is equivalent to $\pi \circ \sigma$ in RA. The projected attributes, `Co.Name` and `Co.Life-Exp` in this example are specified in the `SELECT` clause. The selection condition is specified in the `WHERE` clause.

4. **Query:** List the capital cities and populations of countries whose GDP exceeds one trillion dollars.

```
SELECT  Ci.Name, Co.Pop
FROM    City Ci, Country Co
WHERE   Ci.Country = Co.Name AND
        Co.GDP > 1000.0 AND
        Ci.Capital= 'Y'
```

Comments: This is an implicit way of expressing the `join` operation. SQL2 and SQL3 also support an explicit JOIN operation. In this case the two tables `City` and `Country` are matched on their common attributes `Ci.country` and `Co.name`. Furthermore, two selection conditions are specified separately on the `City` and `Country` table. Notice how the cascading dot notation alleviated the potential confusion that might have arisen as a result of the attribute names in the two relations.

5. **Query:** What is the name and population of the capital city in the country where the St. Lawrence River originates?

```
SELECT  Ci.Name, Ci.Pop
FROM    City Ci, Country Co, River R
WHERE   R.Origin = Co.Name AND
        Co.Name = Ci.Country AND
        R.Name = 'St. Lawrence' AND
        Ci.Capital= 'Y'
```

Comments: This query involves a join among three tables. The `River` and `Country` tables are joined on the attributes *Origin* and *Name*. The `Country` and the `City` tables are joined on the attributes *Name* and *Country*. There are two selection conditions on the `River` and the `City` tables respectively.

6. **Query:** What is the average population of the noncapital cities listed in the `City` table?

```
SELECT  AVG(Ci.Pop)
FROM    City Ci
WHERE   Ci.Capital= 'N'
```

Comments: The `AVG` (Average) is an example of an aggregate operation. These operations are not available in RA. Besides `AVG`, other aggregate operations are `COUNT`, `MAX`, `MIN`, and `SUM`. The aggregate operations expand the functionality of SQL because they allow computations to be performed on the retrieved data.

7. **Query:** For each continent, find the average GDP.

```
SELECT    Co.Cont, Avg(Co.GDP) AS Continent-GDP
FROM      Country Co
GROUP BY  Co.Cont
```

Comments: This query expression represents a major departure from the basic SQL query format. This is because of the presence of the GROUP BY clause.

The GROUP BY clause partitions the table on the basis of the attribute listed in the clause. In this example there are two possible values of *Co.cont*: NAM and SAM. Therefore the Country table is partitioned into two groups. For each group, the average *GDP* is calculated. The average value is then stored under the attribute *Continent-GDP* as specified in the SELECT clause.

8. **Query:** For each country in which at least two rivers originate, find the length of the smallest river.

```
SELECT      R.Origin, MIN(R.length) AS Min-length
FROM        River R
GROUP BY    R.Origin
HAVING      COUNT(*) > 1
```

Comments: This is similar to the previous query. The difference is that the HAVING clause allows selection conditions to be enforced on the different groups formed in the GROUP BY clause. Thus only those groups are considered which have more than one member.

9. **Query:** List the countries whose GDP is greater than that of Canada.

```
SELECT   Co.Name
FROM     Country Co
WHERE    Co.GDP      > ANY   ( SELECT   Co1.GDP
                              FROM      Country Co1
                              WHERE     Co1.Name = 'Canada' )
```

Comments: This is an example of a nested query. These are queries which have other queries embedded in them. A nested query becomes mandatory when an intermediate table, which does not exist, is required before a query can be evaluated. The embedded query typically appears in the WHERE clause, though it can appear, albeit rarely, in the FROM and the SELECT clauses. The ANY is a set comparison operator. Consult a standard database text for a complete overview of nested queries.

3.3.5 Summary of RA and SQL

RA is a formal database query language. Although it is typically not implemented in any commercial DBMS, it forms an important core of SQL. SQL is the most widely implemented database language. SQL has two components: the DDL and DML. The schema of the database tables are specified and populated in the DDL. The actual queries are posed in DML. We have given a brief overview of SQL. More information can be found in any standard text on databases.

3.4 EXTENDING SQL FOR SPATIAL DATA

Although they are powerful query-processing languages, RA and SQL have their short-comings. The main one is that these languages traditionally provided only simple datatypes, for example, integers, dates, and strings. SDB applications must handle complex datatypes such as points, lines, and polygons. Database vendors have responded in two ways: They have either used *blobs* to store spatial information, or they have created a hybrid system in which spatial attributes are stored in operating-system files via a GIS. SQL cannot process data stored as blobs, and it is the responsibility of the application techniques to handle data in blob form [Stonebraker and Moore, 1997]. This solution is neither efficient nor aesthetic because the data depends on the host-language application code. In a hybrid system, spatial attributes are stored in a separate operating-system file and thus are unable to take advantage of traditional database services such as query language, concurrency control, and indexing support.

Object-oriented systems have had a major influence on expanding the capabilities of DBMS to support spatial (complex) objects. The program to extend a relational database with object-oriented features falls under the general framework of OR-DBMS. The key feature of OR-DBMS is that it supports a version of SQL, SQL3/SQL99, which supports the notion of user-defined types (as in Java or C++). Our goal is to study SQL3/SQL99 enough so that we can use it as a tool to manipulate and retrieve spatial data.

The principle demand of spatial SQL is to provide a higher abstraction of spatial data by incorporating concepts closer to our perception of space [Egenhofer, 1994]. This is accomplished by incorporating the object-oriented concept of user-defined ADTs. An ADT is a user-defined type and its associated functions. For example, if we have land parcels stored as polygons in a database, then a useful ADT may be a combination of the type *polygon* and some associated function (method), say, `adjacent`. The `adjacent` function may be applied to `land parcels` to determine if they share a common boundary. The term *abstract* is used because the end user need not know the implementation details of the associated functions. All end users need to know is the interface, that is, the available functions and the data types for the input parameters and output results.

3.4.1 The OGIS Standard for Extending SQL

The OGIS consortium was formed by major software vendors to formulate an industry wide standard related to GIS interoperability. The OGIS spatial data model can be embedded in a variety of programming languages, for example, C, Java, SQL, and so on. We focus on SQL embedding in this section.

The OGIS is based on a geometry data model shown in Figure 2.2. Recall that the data model consists of a base-class, `GEOMETRY`, which is noninstantiable (i.e., objects cannot be defined as instances of `GEOMETRY`), but specifies a spatial reference system applicable to all its subclasses. The four major subclasses derived from the `GEOMETRY` superclass are `Point, Curve Surface` and `GeometryCollection`. Associated with each class is a set of operations that acts on instances of the classes. A subset of important operations and their definitions are listed in Table 3.9.

The operations specified in the OGIS standard fall into three categories:

1. Basic operations apply to all geometry datatypes. For example, `SpatialReference` returns the underlying coordinate system where the geometry of the object was defined. Examples of common reference systems include the well-known *latitude* and *longitude* system and the often-used Universal Traversal Mercator (UTM).

2. Operations test for topological relationships between spatial objects. For example, `overlap` tests whether the interior (see Chapter 2) of two objects has a nonempty set intersection.

TABLE 3.9: A Sample of Operations Listed in the OGIS Standard for SQL [OGIS, 1999]

Basic Functions	SpatialReference()	Returns the underlying coordinate system of the geometry
	Envelope()	Returns the minimum orthogonal bounding rectangle of the geometry
	Export()	Returns the geometry in a different representation
	IsEmpty()	Returns true if the geometry is a null set
	IsSimple()	Returns true if the geometry is simple (no self-intersection)
	Boundary()	Returns the boundary of the geometry
Topological/ Set Operators	Equal	Returns true if the interior and boundary of the two geometries are spatially equal
	Disjoint	Returns true if the boundaries and interior do not intersect
	Intersect	Returns true if the geometries are not disjoint
	Touch	Returns true if the boundaries of two surfaces intersect but the interiors do not
	Cross	Returns true if the interior of a surface intersects with a curve
	Within	Returns true if the interior of the given geometry does not intersect with the exterior of another geometry
	Contains	Tests if the given geometry contains another given geometry
	Overlap	Returns true if the interiors of two geometries have nonempty intersection
Spatial Analysis	Distance	Returns the shortest distance between two geometries
	Buffer	Returns a geometry that consists of all points whose distance from the given geometry is less than or equal to the specified distance
	ConvexHull	Returns the smallest convex geometric set enclosing the geometry
	Intersection	Returns the geometric intersection of two geometries
	Union	Returns the geometric union of two geometries
	Difference	Returns the portion of a geometry that does not intersect with another given geometry
	SymmDiff	Returns the portions of two geometries that do not intersect with each other

3. General operations are for spatial analysis. For example, distance returns the shortest distance between two spatial objects.

3.4.2   Limitations of the Standard

The OGIS specification is limited to the *object* model of space. As shown in the previous chapter, spatial information is sometimes most naturally mapped onto a field-based model. OGIS is developing consensus models for field datatypes and operations. In Chapter 8 we introduce some relevant operations for the field-based model which may be incorporated into a future OGIS standard.

Even within the *object* model, the OGIS operations are limited for simple SELECT-PROJECT-JOIN queries. Support for spatial aggregate queries with the GROUP BY and HAVING clauses does pose problems (see Exercise 4). Finally, the focus in the OGIS standard is exclusively on basic topological and metric spatial relationships. Support for a whole class of metric operations, namely, those based on the *direction* predicate (e.g., north, south, left, front), is missing. It also does not support dynamic, shape-based, and visibility-based operations discussed in Section 2.1.5.

3.5   EXAMPLE QUERIES THAT EMPHASIZE SPATIAL ASPECTS

Using the OGIS datatypes and operations, we formulate SQL queries in the World database which highlight the spatial relationships between the three entities: Country, City, and River. We first redefine the relational schema, assuming that the OGIS datatypes and operations are available in SQL. Revised schema is shown in Table 3.10.

1. **Query:** Find the names of all countries which are neighbors of the United States (USA) in the Country table.

```
SELECT   C1.Name AS "Neighbors of USA"
FROM     Country C1, Country C2
WHERE    Touch(C1.Shape, C2.Shape) = 1 AND
         C2.Name = 'USA'
```

Comments: The Touch predicate checks if any two geometric objects are adjacent to each other without overlapping. It is a useful operation to determine neighboring geometric objects. The Touch operation is one of the eight topological predicates specified in the OGIS standard. One of the nice properties

TABLE 3.10: Basic Tables

```
CREATE   TABLE   Country(
         Name    varchar(30),
         Cont    varchar(30),
         Pop     Integer,
         GDP     Number,
         Shape   Polygon);

            (a)
```

```
CREATE   TABLE   River(
         Name    varchar(30),
         Origin  varchar(30),
         Length  Number,
         Shape   LineString);

            (b)
```

```
CREATE   TABLE   City (
         Name      varchar(30),
         Country   varchar(30),
         Pop       integer,
         Shape     Point );

            (c)
```

of topological operations is that they are invariant under many geometric transformations. In particular the choice of the coordinate system for the World database will not affect the results of topological operations.

Topological operations apply to many different combinations of geometric types. Therefore, in an ideal situation these operations should be defined in an "overloaded" fashion. Unfortunately, many object-relational DBMSs do not support object-oriented notions of class inheritance and operation overloading. Thus, for all practical purposes these operations may be defined individually for each combination of applicable geometric types.

2. **Query:** For all the rivers listed in the `River` table, find the countries through which they pass.

```
SELECT  R.Name C.Name
FROM    River R, Country C
WHERE   Cross(R.Shape, C.Shape) = 1
```

Comments: The `Cross` is also a topological predicate. It is most often used to check for the intersection between a `LineString` and `Polygon` objects, as in this example, or a pair of `LineString` objects.

3. **Query:** Which city listed in the `City` table is closest to each river listed in the `River` table?

```
SELECT C1.Name, R1.Name
FROM   City C1, River R1
WHERE  Distance (C1.Shape, R1.Shape)  <
               ALL (SELECT Distance(C2.Shape, R1.Shape)
               FROM        City C2
               WHERE       C1.Name <> C2.Name
               )
```

Comments: The `Distance` is a real-valued binary operation. It is being used once in the `WHERE` clause and again in the `SELECT` clause of the subquery. The `Distance` function is defined for any combination of geometric objects.

4. **Query:** The St. Lawrence River can supply water to cities that are within 300 km. List the cities that can use water from the St. Lawrence.

```
SELECT  Ci.Name
FROM    City Ci, River R
WHERE   Overlap(Ci.Shape, Buffer(R.Shape,300)) = 1 AND
        R.Name = 'St. Lawrence'
```

Comments: The `Buffer` of a geometric object is a geometric region centered at the object whose size is determined by a parameter in the `Buffer` operation. In the example the query dictates the size of the buffer region. The buffer operation is used in many GIS applications, including floodplain management and urban and rural zoning laws. A graphical depiction of the buffer operation

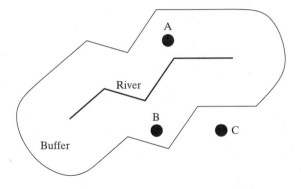

FIGURE 3.2. The buffer of a river and points within and outside.

is shown in Figure 3.2. In the figure, Cities A and B are likely to be affected if there is a flood on the river, whereas City C will remain unaffected.

5. **Query:** List the name, population, and area of each country listed in the Country table.

```
SELECT   C.Name, C.Pop, Area(C.Shape) AS "Area"
FROM     Country C
```

Comments: This query illustrates the use of the Area function. This function is only applicable for Polygon and MultiPolygon geometry types. Calculating the Area clearly depends upon the underlying coordinate system of the World database. For example, if the shape of the Country tuples is given in terms of latitude and longitude, then an intermediate coordinate transformation must be be performed before the Area can be calculated. The same care must be taken for Distance and the Length function.

6. **Query:** List the length of the rivers in each of the countries they pass through.

```
SELECT   R.Name, C.Name, Length(Intersection(R.Shape, C.Shape))
         AS "Length"
FROM     River R, Country C
WHERE    Cross(R.Shape, C.Shape) = 1
```

Comments: The return value of the Intersection binary operation is a geometry type. The Intersection operation is different from the Intersects function, which is a topological predicate to determine if two geometries intersect. The Intersection of a LineString and Polygon can either be a Point or LineString type. If a river does pass through a country, then the result will be a LineString. In that case, the Length function will return non-zero length of the river in each country it passes through.

7. **Query:** List the GDP and the distance of a country's capital city to the equator for all countries.

TABLE 3.11: Results of Query 7

Co. Name	Co. GDP	Dist-to-Eq (in Km).
Havana	16.9	2562
Washington, D.C.	8003	4324
Brasilia	1004	1756
Ottawa	658	5005
Mexico City	694.3	2161
Buenos Aires	348.2	3854

```
SELECT   Co.GDP, Distance(Point(0,Ci.Shape.y),Ci.Shape)
         AS "Distance"
FROM     Country Co, City Ci
WHERE    Co.Name = Ci.Country AND
         Ci.Capital = 'Y'
```

Comments: Searching for implicit relationships between datasets stored in a database is outside the scope of standard database functionality. Current DBMSs are geared toward on-line transaction processing (OLTP), while this query, as posed, is in the realm of on-line analytical processing (OLAP). OLAP itself falls under the label of data mining, and we explore this topic in Chapter 8. At the moment the best we can do is list each capital and its distance to the equator.

Point(0, Ci.Shape.y) is a point on the equator which has the same longitude as that of the current capital instantiated in Ci.Name. Results are shown in Table 3.11

8. **Query:** List all countries, ordered by number of neighboring countries.

```
SELECT     Co.Name, Count(Co1.Name)
FROM       Country Co, Country Co1
WHERE      Touch(Co.Shape, Co1.Shape)
GROUP BY   Co.Name
ORDER BY   Count(Co1.Name)
```

Comments: In this query all the countries with at least one neighbor are sorted on the basis of number of neighbors.

9. **Query:** List the countries with only one neighboring country. A country is a neighbor of another country if their land masses share a boundary. According to this definition, island countries, like Iceland, have no neighbors.

```
SELECT     Co.Name
FROM       Country Co, Country Co1
WHERE      Touch(Co.Shape, Co1.Shape))
GROUP BY   Co.Name
HAVING     Count(Co1.Name) = 1
```

```
SELECT   Co.Name
FROM     Country Co
WHERE    Co.Name IN
         (SELECT   Co.Name
         FROM      Country Co, Country Co1
         WHERE     Touch(Co.Shape, Co1.Shape)
         GROUP BY  Co.Name
         HAVING    Count(*) = 1)
```

Comments: Here we have a nested query in the FROM clause. The result of the query within the FROM clause is a table consisting of pairs of countries which are neighbors. The GROUP BY clause partitions the new table on the basis of the names of the countries. Finally the HAVING clause forces the selection to be paired to those countries that have only one neighbor. The HAVING clause plays a role similar to the WHERE clause with the exception that it must include such aggregate functions as count, sum, max, and min.

10. **Query:** Which country has the maximum number of neighbors?

```
CREATE VIEW Neighbor AS
SELECT              Co.Name, Count(Co1.Name) AS num_neighbors
FROM                Country Co, Country Co1
WHERE               Touch(Co.Shape, Co1.Shape)
GROUP BY            Co.Name


SELECT   Co.Name, num_neighbors
FROM     Neighbor
WHERE    num_neighbor = (SELECT Max(num_neighbors)
         FROM Neighbor)
```

Comments: This query demonstrates the use of views in simplifying complex queries. First query (view) computes the number of neighbors for each country. This view creates a virtual table which can be used as a normal table in subsequent queries. The second query selects the country with the largest number of neighbors from the Neighbor view.

3.6   TRENDS: OBJECT-RELATIONAL SQL

The OGIS standard specifies the datatypes and their associated operations which are considered essential for spatial applications such as GIS. For example, for the Point datatype an important operation is Distance, which computes the distance between two points. The length operation is not a semantically correct operation on a *Point* datatype. This is similar to the argument that the concatenation operation makes more sense for Character datatype than for, say, the Integer type.

In relational databases the set of datatypes is fixed. In object-relational and object-oriented databases, this limitation has been relaxed, and there is built in support for user-defined datatypes. Even though this feature is clearly an advantage, especially when dealing with nontraditional database applications such as GIS, the burden of constructing syntactically and semantically correct datatypes is now on the database application developer. To share some of the burden, commercial database vendors have introduced application-specific "packages" which provide a seamless interface to the database user. For example, Oracle markets a GIS specific package called the Spatial Data Cartridge.

SQL3/SQL99, the proposed SQL standard for OR-DBMS allows user-defined datatypes within the overall framework of a relational database. Two features of the SQL3 standard that may be beneficial for defining user-defined spatial datatypes are described below.

3.6.1   A Glance at SQL3

The SQL3/SQL99 proposes two major extensions to SQL2/SQL92, the current accepted SQL draft.

1. *ADT:* An ADT can be defined using a CREATE TYPE statement. Like classes in object-oriented technology, an ADT consists of attributes and member functions to access the values of the attributes. Member functions can potentially modify the value of the attributes in the datatype and thus can also change the database state.

    An ADT can appear as a column type in a relational schema. To access the value that the ADT encapsulates, a member function specified in the CREATE TYPE must be used. For example, the following script creates a type Point with the definition of one member function Distance:

    ```
    CREATE TYPE   Point   (
              x   NUMBER,
              y   NUMBER,

       FUNCTION   Distance(:u Point,:v Point)
                  RETURNS NUMBER
                          );
    ```

    The colons before u and v signify that these are local variables.

2. *Row Type:* A row type is a type for a relation. A row type specifies the schema of a relation. For example the following statement creates a row type Point.

    ```
    CREATE ROW TYPE   Point   (
              x   NUMBER,
              y   NUMBER );
    ```

    We can now create a table that instantiates the row type. For example:

    ```
    CREATE TABLE Pointtable of TYPE Point;
    ```

In this text we emphasize the use of ADT instead of row type. This is because the ADT as a column type naturally harmonizes the definition of an OR-DBMS as an extended relational database.

3.6.2 Object-Relational Schema

Oracle8 is an OR-DBMS introduced by the Oracle Corporation. Similar products are available from other database companies, for example, IBM. OR-DBMS implements a part of the SQL3 Standard. The ADT is called the "object type" in this system.

Below we describe how the three basic spatial datatypes: Point, LineString, and Polygon are constructed in Oracle8.

```
CREATE   TYPE Point AS OBJECT (
         x   NUMBER,
         y   NUMBER,
         MEMBER FUNCTION Distance(P2   IN Point) RETURN NUMBER,
         PRAGMA RESTRICT_REFERENCES(Distance, WNDS));
```

The Point type has two attributes, x and y, and one member function, Distance. PRAGMA alludes to the fact that the Distance function will not modify the state of the database: WNDS (Write No Database State). Of course in the OGIS standard many other operations related to the Point type are specified, but for simplicity we have shown only one. After its creation the Point type can be used in a relation as an attribute type. For example, the schema of the relation City can be defined as follows:

```
CREATE   TABLE     City (
         Name      varchar(30),
         Country   varchar(35),
         Pop       int,
         Capital   char(1),
         Shape     Point  );
```

Once the relation schema has been defined, the table can be populated in the usual way. For example, the following statement adds information related to Brasilia, the capital of Brazil, into the database

```
INSERT INTO CITY('Brasilia', 'Brazil', 1.5, 'Y',
                 Point(-55.4,-23.2));
```

The construction of the LineString datatype is slightly more involved than that of the Point type. We begin by creating an intermediate type, LineType:

```
CREATE TYPE LineType AS VARRAY(500) OF Point;
```

Thus LineType is a variable array of Point datatype with a maximum length of 500. Type specific member functions cannot be defined if the type is defined as a Varray. Therefore we create another type LineString

```
CREATE   TYPE LineString AS OBJECT (
         Num_of_Points INT,
         Geometry LineType,
         MEMBER FUNCTION Length(SELF IN) RETURN NUMBER,
         PRAGMA RESTRICT_REFERENCES(Length, WNDS));
```

The attribute Num_of_Points stores the size (in terms of points) of each instance of the LineString type. We are now ready to define the schema of the River table

```
CREATE  TABLE  River(
        Name    varchar(30),
        Origin  varchar(30),
        Length  number,
        Shape   LineString  );
```

While inserting data into the River table, we have to keep track of the different datatypes involved.

```
INSERT INTO RIVER('Mississippi', 'USA', 6000,
                LineString(3, LineType(Point(1,1),Point(1,2),
                Point(2,3)))
```

The Polygon type is similar to LineString. The sequence of type and table creation and data insertion is given in Table 3.12.

TABLE 3.12: The Sequence of Creation of the Country Table

```
CREATE TYPE PolyType AS VARRAY(500) OF Point
```

(a)

```
CREATE  TYPE Polygon AS OBJECT (
        Num_of_Points INT,
        Geometry PolyType ,
        MEMBER FUNCTION Area(SELF IN) RETURN NUMBER,
        PRAGMA RESTRICT_REFERENCES(Length, WNDS));
```

(b)

```
CREATE  TABLE   Country(
        Name    varchar(30),
        Cont    varchar(30),
        Pop     int,
        GDP     number,
        Life-Exp number,
        Shape   LineString  );
```

(c)

```
INSERT INTO   Country('Mexico', 'NAM', 107.5, 694.3, 69.36,
              Polygon(23, Polytype(Point(1,1), ..., Point(1,1)))
```

(d)

3.6.3   Example Queries

1. Query: List all the pairs of cities in the `City` table and the distances between them.

```
SELECT  C1.Name, C1.Distance(C2.Shape) AS ''Distance''
FROM    City C1, City C2
WHERE   C1.Name <> C2.Name
```

Comments: Notice the object-oriented notation for the `Distance` function in the `SELECT` clause. Contrast it with the test notation used in Section 3.5: `Distance(C1.Shape, C2.Shape)`. The predicate in the `WHERE` clause ensures that the `Distance` function is not applied between two copies of the same city.

2. Query: Validate the length of the rivers given in the `River` table, using the geometric information encoded in the `Shape` attribute.

```
SELECT  R.Name, R.Length, R.Length() AS ''Derived Length''
FROM    River R
```

Comments: This query is being used for data validation. The length of the rivers is already available in the `Length` attribute of the `River` table. Using the `Length()` function we can check the integrity of the data in the table.

3. Query: List the names, populations, and areas of all countries adjacent to the USA.

```
SELECT  C2.Name, C2.Pop, C2.Area() AS ''Area''
FROM    Country C1, Country C2
WHERE   C1.Name = 'USA' AND
        C1.Touch(C2.Shape) = 1
```

Comments: The `Area()` function is a *natural* function for the Polygon ADT to support. Along with `Area()`, the query also invokes the `Touch` topological predicate.

3.7   SUMMARY

In this chapter we discussed database query languages, covering the following topics.

RA is the formal query language associated with the relational model. It is rarely, if ever, implemented in a commercial system but forms the core of SQL.

SQL is the most widely implemented query language. It is a declarative language, in that the user only has to specify the result of the query rather than means of a arriving at the result. SQL extends RA with many other important functions, including aggregate functions to analytically process queried data.

The *OGIS* standard recommends a set of spatial datatypes and functions that are considered crucial for spatial data querying.

SQL3/SQL 1999 is the standardization platform for the object-relational extension of SQL. It is not specific to GIS or spatial databases but covers general object-relational databases. The most natural scenario is that the OGIS standard recommendations will be implemented in a subset of SQL3.

BIBLIOGRAPHIC NOTES

3.1, 3.2, 3.3   A complete exposition of relational algebra and SQL can be found in any introductory text in databases, including [Elmasri and Navathe, 2000; Ramakrishnan, 1998; Ullman and Widom, 1999].

3.4, 3.5   Extensions of SQL for spatial applications are explored in [Egenhofer, 1994]. The OGIS document [OpenGIS, 1998] is an attempt to harmonize the different spatial extensions of SQL. For an example of query languages in supporting spatial data analysis, see [Lin and Huang, 2001].

3.6   SQL 1999/SQL3 is the adopted standard for the object-relational extension of SQL. Subsets of the standard have already been implemented in commercial products, including Oracle's Oracle8 and IBM's DB2.

EXERCISES

For all queries in Exercises 1 and 2 refer to Table 3.1.

1. Express the following queries in relational algebra.
   (a) Find all countries whose GDP is greater than $500 billion but less than $1 trillion.
   (b) List the life expectancy in countries that have rivers originating in them.
   (c) Find all cities that are either in South America or whose population is less than two million.
   (d) List all cities which are not in South America.
2. Express in SQL the queries listed in Exercise 1.
3. Express the following queries in SQL.
   (a) Count the number of countries whose population is less than 100 million.
   (b) Find the country in North America with the smallest GDP. Do not use the MIN function. Hint: nested query.
   (c) List all countries that are in North America or whose capital cities have a population of less than 5 million.
   (d) Find the country with the second highest GDP.
4. The Reclassify (see Section 2.1.5) is an aggregate function that combines spatial geometries on the basis of nonspatial attributes. It creates new objects from the existing ones, generally by removing the internal boundaries of the adjacent polygons whose chosen attribute is same. Can we express the Reclassify operation using OGIS operations and SQL92 with spatial datatypes? Explain.
5. Discuss the geometry data model of Figure 2.2. Given that on a "world" scale, cities are represented as point datatypes, what datatype should be used to represent the countries of the world. Note: Singapore, the Vatican, and Monaco are countries. What are the implementation implications for the spatial functions recommended by the OGIS standard.
6. [Egenhofer, 1994] proposes a list of requirements for extending SQL for spatial applications. The requirements are shown below. Which of these the recommendations have been accepted in the OGIS SQL standard? Discuss possible reasons for postponing the others.
7. The OGIS standard includes a set of *topological* spatial predicates. How should the standard be extended to include directional predicates such as East, North, North-East, and so forth. Note that the directional predicates may be fuzzy: "Where does North-East end and East begin?"
8. This exercise surveys the dimension-extended nine-intersection model: DE-9IM. The DE-9IM extends Egenhofer's nine-intersection model introduced in Chapter 2. The

Spatial ADT	An abstract data type spatial hierarchy with associated operations
Graphical presentation	Natural medium of interaction with spatial data
Result combination	Combining the results of a sequence of queries
Context	Place result in context by including information not explicitly requested
Content examination	Provide mechanisms to guide the evolution of map drawing
Selection by pointing	Pose and constraints by pointing to maps
Display manipulations	Varying graphical presentation of spatial objects and their parts
Legend	Descriptive legend
Labels	Labels for understanding of drawings
Selection of map scale	Produced map should allow user to continue applying their skills on interpreting actual size of objects drawn and the selection of a specific scale of rendering
Area of interest	Tools to restrict the area of interest to a particular geography

template matrix of `DE-9IM` is shown below.

$$\Gamma_9(A, B) = \begin{pmatrix} dim(A^\circ \cap B^\circ) & dim(A^\circ \partial B^\circ) & dim(A^\circ \cap B^-) \\ dim(\partial A \cap B^\circ) & dim(\partial A \cap \partial B) & dim(\partial A \cap B^-) \\ dim(A^- \cap B^\circ) & dim(A^- \cap \partial B) & dim(A^- \cap B^-) \end{pmatrix}$$

The key difference between `9IM` and `DE-9IM` is that instead of testing whether each entry in the matrix is empty or nonempty; in the `DE-9IM` only the dimension of the geometric object is required. The dimension of planar two-dimensional objects can take four values: -1 for empty-set, 0 for points, 1 for lines, and 2 for nonzero area objects. In many instances the value of the matrix entry does not matter. The following is the list of values that the matrix entries can span.

T: X and Y must intersect. $dim(X \cap Y) = 0, 1, 2$. X and Y are either the interior, exterior, or boundary of A and B respectively.

F: $dim(X \cap Y) = -1$. X and Y must not intersect.

$*$: It does not matter if the intersection exists. $dim(X \cap Y) = \{-1, 0, 1, 2\}$

0: $dim(X \cap Y) = 0$

1: $dim(X \cap Y) = 1$

2: $dim(X \cap Y) = 2$

Below is the *signature* matrix of two equal objects.

$$\begin{pmatrix} T & * & F \\ * & * & F \\ * & * & * \end{pmatrix}$$

(a) What is the signature matrix (matrices) of the touch and cross topological operations? Note that the signature matrix depends on the combination of the datatypes. The signature matrix of a point/point combination is different from that of a multipolygon/multipolygon combination.

(b) What operation (and combination of datatypes) does the following signature matrix represent?

$$\begin{pmatrix} 1 & * & T \\ * & * & F \\ T & * & * \end{pmatrix}$$

(c) Consider the sample figures shown Figure 3.3. What are signature matrices in 9IM and DE-9IM. Is DE-9IM superior to 9IM? Discuss.

9. Express the following queries in SQL, using the OGIS extended datatype and functions.

(a) List all cities in the City table which are within five thousand miles of Washington, D.C.

(b) What is the length of Rio Paranas in Argentina and Brazil?

(c) Do Argentina and Brazil share a border?

(d) List the countries that lie completely south of the equator.

10. Given the schema:

> RIVER(NAME:char, FLOOD-PLAIN:polygon, GEOMETRY:linstring)
> ROAD(ID:char, NAME:char, TYPE:char, GEOMETRY:linstring)
> FOREST(NAME:char, GEOMETRY:polygon)
> LAND-PARCELS(ID:integer, GEOMETRY:polygon, county:char)

Transform the following queries into SQL using the OGIS specified datatypes and operations.

(a) Name all the rivers that cross Itasca State Forest.

(b) Name all the tar roads that intersect Francis Forest.

(c) All roads with stretches within the floodplain of the river Montana are susceptible to flooding. Identify all these roads.

(d) No urban development is allowed within two miles of the Red River and five miles of the Big Tree State Park. Identify the landparcels and the county they are in that cannot be developed.

(e) A river defines part of boundary of a country.

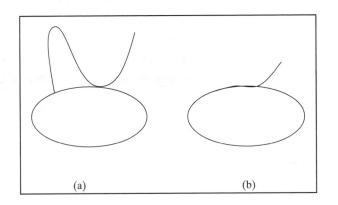

FIGURE 3.3. Sample objects [Clementini and Felice, 1995]

11. Study the compiler tools such as YACC (Yet Another Compiler Compiler). Develop a syntax scheme to generate SQL3 data definition statements from an Entity Relationship Diagram (ERD) annotated with pictograms.

12. How would one model the following spatial relationships using 9-intersection model or OGIS topological operations?

    (a) A river (LineString) originates in a country (Polygon)

    (b) A country (e.g., Vatican city) is completely surrounded by another (e.g., Italy) country

    (c) A river (e.g., Missouri) falls into another (e.g., Mississippi) river

    (d) Forest stands partition a forest

13. Review the example RA queries provided for state park database in Appendix. Write SQL expressions for each RA query.

14. Redraw the ER diagram provided in Figure 3.4 using pictograms. How will one represent Fishing-Opener and Distance attributes in the new ER diagram. Generate tables by translating the resulting ER diagram using SQL3/OGIS constructs.

15. Consider the table-designs in Figure 1.3 and 1.4. Describe SQL queries to compute spatial properties (e.g. area, perimeter) of census blocks using each representation. Which representation lead to simple queries?

16. Revisit the Java program in Section 2.1.6. Design Java programs to carry out the spatial queries listed in Section 3.6.3. Compare and contrast querying spatial dataset using Java with querying using SQL3/OGIS.

17. Define user defined data types for geometry aggregation data types in OGIS using SQL3.

18. Revisit relational schema for state park example in Section 2.2.3. Outline SQL DML statements to create relevant tables using OGIS spatial data type.

19. Consider shape-based queries, for example, list countries shaped like ladies boot or list squarish census blocks. Propose extensions to SQL3/OGIS to support such queries.

20. Consider visibility-based queries, for example, list objects visible (not occluded) from a vista-point and viewer orientation. Propose a set of data types and operations for extending SQL3/OGIS to support such queries.

3.8 APPENDIX: *STATE PARK DATABASE*

The `State Park` database consists of two entities: `Park` and `Lake`. The attributes of these two entities and their relationships are shown in Figure 3.4. The ER diagram is mapped into the relational schema shown below. The entities and their relationships are materialized in Table 3.13.

```
StatePark(Sid: integer, Sname: string, Area: float, Distance: float)
  Lake(Lid: integer, Lname: string, Depth: float, Main-Catch: string)
     ParkLake(Lid: integer, Sid: integer, Fishing-Opener: date)
```

The above schema represents three entities: `StatePark`, `Lake`, and `ParkLake`. `StatePark` represents all the state parks in Minnesota, and its attributes are a unique national identity number, `Sid`; the name of the park, `Sname`; its area in sq. km., `Area`; and the distance of the park from Minneapolis, `Distance`. The `Lake` entity also has a unique id, `Lid`, a name, `Lname`; the average depth of the lake, `Depth`; and the primary fish in the lake, `Main-catch`. The `ParkLake` entity is used to integrate queries across the two entities `StatePark` and `Lake`. `ParkLake` identifies the lakes that are in the state parks. Its attributes are `Lid`, `Sid`, and the date the fishing season commences on the

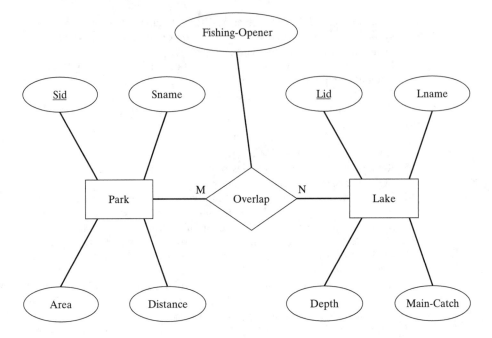

FIGURE 3.4. The ER diagram of the StatePark database.

given lake, Fishing-Opener. Here we are assuming that different lakes have different Fishing-Openers.

3.8.1 Example Queries in RA

We now give examples that show how the relational operators defined earlier can be used to retrieve and manipulate the data in a database. Our format is as follows: We first list the query in plain English; then we give the equivalent expression in RA, and finally we make comments about the algebraic expression, including an alternate form of the algebraic expression.

TABLE 3.13: Tables for the StatePark Database

Park	Sid	Sname	Area	Distance
	S1	Itasca	150.0	52
	S2	Woodbury	255.0	75
	S3	Brighton	175.0	300

(a) Park

Lake	Lid	Lname	Depth	Main-Catch
	100	Lino	20.0	Walleye
	200	Chaska	30.0	Trout
	300	Sussex	45.0	Walleye
	400	Todd	28.0	Bass

(b) Lake

ParkLake	Lid	Sid	Fishing-Opener
	100	S1	05/15
	200	S1	05/15
	300	S3	06/01

(c) ParkLake

Query: Find the name of the `StatePark` which contains the `Lake` with `Lid` number 100.

$$\pi_{\text{Spname}}(\text{StatePark} \bowtie \sigma_{\text{Lid} = 100}(\text{ParkLake}))$$

Comments: We begin by selecting the set of tuples in `ParkLake` with Lid 100. The resultant set is naturally joined with the relation `StatePark` on the key `Sid`. The result is projected onto the `StatePark` name, `Spname`. This query can be broken into parts using the renaming operator ρ. The renaming operator is used to name the intermediate relations that arise during the evaluation of a complex query. It can also be used to rename the attributes of a relation. For example,

$$\rho(\text{Newname}(1 \rightarrow Att1), \text{Oldname})$$

renames the relation `Oldname` to the `Newname`. Also the first attribute, counting from left to right, of the `Newname` is called `Att1`.

With this naming convention, we can break up this query into parts as follows:

$$\rho(Temp1, \sigma_{Lid=100}(ParkLake))$$
$$\rho(Temp2, Temp1 \bowtie StatePark)$$
$$\pi_{Spname}(Temp2)$$

An alternate formulation of the query is

$$\pi_{spname}(\sigma_{Lid=100}(ParkLake \bowtie StatePark))$$

From the point of view of implementation, this query is more expensive than the previous one because it is performing a join on a larger set, and join is the most expensive of all the five operators in relational algebra.

1. **Query:** Find the names of the `StateParks` with `Lakes` where the `MainCatch` is `Trout`.

$$\pi_{\text{Spname}}(\text{StatePark} \bowtie (\text{ParkLake} \bowtie \sigma_{\text{Main-Catch} = \text{'Trout'}}(\text{Lake})))$$

Comments: Here we are applying two join operators in succession. But first we reduce the set size by first selecting all `Lakes` with `Main-Catch` of `Trout`. Then we join the resultant on the `Lid` key with `ParkLake`. This is followed by another join with `StatePark` on `Sid`. Finally we project the answer on the `StatePark` name.

2. **Query:** *Find the* `Main-Catch` *of the lakes that are in Itasca State Park*

$$\pi_{\text{Main-Catch}}(\text{Lake} \bowtie (\text{ParkLake} \bowtie \sigma_{\text{Spname}= \text{'Itasca'}}(\text{StatePark})))$$

Comments: This query is very similar to the one above.

Query: *Find the names of* `StateParks` *with at least one lake.*

$$\pi_{\text{Spname}}(\text{StatePark} \bowtie \text{ParkLake})$$

Comment: The join on `Sid` creates an intermediate relation in which tuples from the `StatePark` relation are attached to the tuples from `ParkLake`. The result is then projected onto `Spname`.

3. **Query:** *List the names of* StateParks *with lakes whose main catch is either bass or walleye.*

$$\rho(\text{TempLake}, \sigma_{\text{Main-Catch} = \text{`Bass'}}(Lake) \cup \sigma_{\text{Main-Catch} = \text{`Walleye'}}(Lake)$$
$$\pi_{\text{spname}}(\text{TempLake} \bowtie \text{ParkLake} \bowtie StatePark)$$

Comments: Here we use the union operator for the first time. We first select lakes with Main-Catch of bass or walleye. We then join on Lid with ParkLake and join again on Sid with StatePark. We get the result by projecting on Spname.

4. **Query:** *Find the names of* StateParks *that have both bass and walleye as the* Main-Catch *in their lakes.*

$$\rho(TempBass, \pi_{Spname}(\sigma_{Main-Catch=\text{`Bass'}} \bowtie ParkLake \bowtie StatePark))$$
$$\rho(TempWall, \pi_{Spname}(\sigma_{Main-Catch=\text{`Walleye'}} \bowtie ParkLake \bowtie StatePark))$$
$$TempBass \cap TempWall$$

Comment: This query formulation is barely right!

5. **Query:** *Find the names of the* StateParks *that have at least two lakes.*

$$c\rho(Temp, \pi_{Sid,Spname,Lid}(StatePark \bowtie ParkLake))$$
$$\rho(Temppair, Temp \times Temp)$$
$$\pi_{Spname}\sigma_{(Sid1=Sid2) \wedge (Lid1 \neq Lid2)}Temppair.$$

6. **Query:** *Find the identification number,* Sid, *of the* StateParks *that are at least fifty miles away from Minneapolis with lakes where the* Main-Catch *is not trout.*

$$\pi_{sid}(\sigma_{distance>50}StatePark) \quad -$$
$$\pi_{sid}((\sigma_{main-catch=\text{'}Trout\text{'}}Lake \quad \bowtie \quad ParkLake \bowtie StatePark$$

C H A P T E R   4

Spatial Storage and Indexing

In this chapter we describe efficient ways of retrieving data from a spatial database. This is often done through the use of *indexes*. Like the index in the back of a book, a database index can be used to quickly access data requested by a particular query without stepping through the entire database. We describe indexes which are particularly suited for spatial databases. So far our discussion about SDBs has been largely confined to high-level issues related to the modeling and querying of spatial data. In this chapter we explore the physical database design and, in a manner of speaking, "go under the hood."

Physical database design is critical to ensure reasonable performance for various queries written in an elegant but high-level logical language like SQL, which provides no hints about implementation algorithms and data structures. Naive physical database design may make the response time for answering even the simplest SQL queries unacceptable to end users. Historically, physical database design techniques such as the B+ tree indexes are credited for the large-scale adoption of relational database technology by providing reasonable response time for SQL queries of many kinds. For example, searching a record matching a given key in a collection of 10 billion records can be carried out by using ten-disk accesses in a fraction of a second, even when the entire dataset is on a magnetic disk. Developments in query processing techniques (discussed in Chapter 5) have continued to improve performance at a rate higher than the improvements in hardware performance.

DBMSs systems are designed to handle large volumes of data. In order to understand how data is stored, we need to explore briefly the design and geometry of typical *secondary storage* devices. Familiarity with the characteristics of secondary storage will help us design strategies for storing data so that it can be retrieved in an efficient manner. The fundamental insight at the physical design level is that datasets are often too large to fit in the primary memory of the computer and secondary storage access time is several orders of magnitude slower than main memory. This is a performance bottleneck because data has to be shipped back and forth between primary memory and secondary storage. Thus the goal of good physical database design is to keep this amount of data transfer to an absolute minimum.

The purpose of a spatial storage structure is to facilitate spatial selection and join queries. That is, in response to a query the spatial access method will only search through a relevant subset of objects embedded in the space to retrieve the query answer set.

A fundamental idea for spatial indexing and, in fact, for all spatial query processing, is the use of approximations. This allows index structures to manage an object in terms of one or more spatial keys, which are much simpler geometric objects than the object itself. The prime example is the bounding box (the smallest axis-parallel rectangle enclosing the object). For grid approximations, space is divided into cells by a regular grid, and the object is represented by the set of cells that it intersects. The use of approximations leads to a filter and refine strategy for query processing: First based on the approximations, a filtering step is executed; it returns a set of candidates that is a superset of the objects fulfilling a predicate. Second, for each candidate (or a pair of candidates in case of a spatial join) in a refinement step the exact geometry is checked. Due to the use of bounding boxes, most spatial data structures are designed to store either a set of points (for point values) or a set of rectangles (for line or region values).

The operations offered by such structures are *insert, delete,* and *member* (find a stored point or a rectangle) to manage the set as such. Apart from that, one or more query operations are supported. For stored rectangles and points, some important operations are:

- *Point query:* Find all rectangles containing a given point.

- *Range query:* Find all points within a query rectangle.

- *Nearest neighbor:* Find the point closest to a query point.

- *Distance scan:* Enumerate points in increasing distance from a query point.

- *Intersection query:* Find all the rectangles intersecting a query rectangle.

- *Containment query:* Find all the rectangles completely within a query rectangle.

- *Spatial join query:* Find all pairs of rectangles that overlap each other.

In Section 4.1 we give a detailed description of physical storage requirements of spatial data, including the geometry of storage devices, buffer management strategies, file structure concepts, clustering, and space-filling curves. In Section 4.2 we describe indexing strategies for spatial data. In Section 4.3 we focus on related issues about concurrency control and spatial-join indexes.

4.1 STORAGE: DISKS AND FILES

The requirements of a traditional database transaction and a programming language application are in some sense *orthogonal.* For example, a C program that computes the inverse of a matrix is a CPU-intensive operation, involving complex formulas and calculations. In the beginning of the program, the actual matrix data is pulled into the primary memory. The dataset that the function operates on will be small enough to fit, all at once, in the primary memory. The CPU's access to the primary memory is quite fast (order of nanoseconds), and thus the efficiency of a program is directly related to the CPU speed. Traditional database applications involve large amounts of data, and, despite falling memory prices, it is still prohibitive to store all the data in the primary memory. The DBMS has to arrange for portions of data to be shipped back and forth from the main to a secondary storage device, typically a disk drive. This is a severe bottleneck, because the access to secondary storage is relatively slow (order of milliseconds). Once the data is in main memory, the functions that operate on the data are simple, involving operators such as ($<$, $=$, $>$, *MIN, MAX, AVG*). Thus, for a traditional database application, the

TABLE 4.1: The Characteristics of a Traditional DBMS, a Programming Application, and an SDBMS on the Basis of Relative CPU and I/O Costs

	CPU Cost	I/O Cost
DBMS	Low	High
C Program	High	Low
SDBMS	High	High

cost of transferring data from secondary to primary memory, the I/O cost, is the right measure of efficiency.

For spatial databases, the situation is more complex. First, the computational complexity of functions involved in a spatial application is comparable to those in a programming language application. Second, the storage requirements of a spatial database are generally more severe than those of a traditional database. For example, one low-resolution satellite image of the United States can consume as much as 30Mb of disk space! As shown in Table 4.1 the difference between a traditional DBMS application, a programming application, and an SDBMS application can be characterized on the basis of the relative CPU and I/O costs.

In fact, a spatial database is typically too large to even fit on an average-sized secondary storage device, and data spills over to *tertiary* storage, for example, a tape drive. Tapes are sequential devices; to access the last byte of data on the disk, the whole tape has to be wound, and they are usually off-line. The cost of off-loading data from a tape is not included while measuring the performance of a DBMS. Secondary storage (and of course the primary memory), on the other hand, is an example of random access devices, very much like a CD-ROM.

4.1.1   Disk Geometry and Implications

To understand the geometry of the disk drive, the CD-ROM player analogy is a good one to keep in mind. Metallic disks or platters are arranged and rotate on a spindle. Magnetic tracks, where potential data resides, are marked on the platter in concentric circles spreading out toward the edge of the platter. Because there are multiple platters, all the tracks with the same diameter constitute a `cylinder`.

Each track is partitioned into sectors, and the size of a sector may be fixed by the manufacturer of the drive. A disk block is an integer multiple of the sector, and this multiple can be set at the time the disk is initialized. The disk block or simply the page is the *smallest unit of transfer* between the disk and the main memory. Because the blocks are laid out on tracks, a disk is a logical one-dimensional device. Data is transferred from the disk to the primary memory using an array of disk heads, one per platter. When instructed by the DBMS to fetch a block on the disk, the heads mechanically move, in unison, and park themselves just above the track on which the block resides. All the heads are in identical positions with respect to the tracks of their platters. Also, the heads never touch the actual platters—that would be a disk *crash!* resulting in loss of data. Once the head has moved to the correct track, the targeted block rotates under the head, and the magnetized information on the block is copied through the disk head into the main memory. Thus the whole process can be divided into three parts, each with their

TABLE 4.2: Physical and Performance Parameters
of the Western Digital AC36400 Disk Drive

Formatted Capacity	6448 MB
Cylinders	13,328
Sector/Track	63
Bytes per sector	512
Platters	3 double-sided
Seek time	9.5 ms
Latency time	5.5 ms

characteristic (averaged) time. The first, seek time (t_s), is a measure of how long the disk heads take to arrive at a particular track. The second, latency (t_l), is the time it takes for the block to rotate under the head. Finally, there is the transfer time (t_t) to actually read or write data in the block once the head is correctly positioned. Thus the total access time (t_a) is given by

$$t_a = t_s + t_l + t_t$$

and typically the following inequality holds true:

$$t_s > t_l > t_t.$$

Though the transfer time, t_t, is fixed at the time of disk initialization, a strategic placement of data on the disk can considerably lower t_s and t_l, the seek and latency time, respectively. Table 4.2 shows the typical physical and performance specifications of a Western Digital Caviar AC36400 disk drive.

4.1.2 Buffer Manager

The buffer manager is a software module within the DBMS with the sole task of managing the transfer of data between main and secondary memory. Because the quantity of data that a typical database transaction interacts with is much larger than the capacity of the main memory, the buffer manager has to implement a protocol for the efficient processing of the transaction. In particular, it must ensure that the transaction is not suspended because a piece of data is not available in the main memory. The protocols that the manager implements are called replacement policies because they deal with replacing pages in the main memory with those from the secondary memory. Conventional virtual memory page replacement algorithms like least recently used (LRU) may not be sufficient for buffer management in relational databases.

Buffer management in a relational database management system is primarily based on relational query behavior. A set of pages which is accessed frequently is called a *hot set*. This behavior is typical for loops (e.g., nested loops). In this scheme, a query is given a local buffer pool of a size equal to its hot set size, and new queries are allowed into the system only if its hot set fits in memory. Even though hot set provides an accurate model of page access (reference) patterns for relational databases, it is based on LRU replacement scheme. DBMIN algorithm [Chou and DeWitt, 1985] is based on the query locality set model (QLSM). The page reference model of QLSM does not depend on any particular page replacement scheme (e.g., LRU as in the case of the hot set model). QLSM characterizes the reference patterns of a database operation into sequential, random, and hierarchical references. Buffers are allocated and managed on a per file instance (table) basis. The set of buffered pages associated with a file instance is referred to as its locality set. Locality set sizes are estimated from a query plan and database statistics. Bookkeeping is done by maintaining a global page table and global free list. If the requested page is found in the locality set and global page table, the page is directly returned, and usage statistics for that page are updated. If the page is not found, then the page is read into the (one of the free pages) locality set. If a free page is not available (i.e., size of the locality set is bigger than the maximum threshold), then one of the existing pages is replaced according to a locality set specific page replacement policy. A detailed simulation study shows that DBMIN provides 7 to 13 percent more throughput than the hot set algorithm.

4.1.3   Field, Record, and File

The concept of a page is a useful abstraction for understanding the movement of data between different memory devices. At a higher level of interaction, though, it is more efficient to perceive data as organized in a hierarchy of file, record, and field. A `file` is a collection of records spanning (possibly) multiple pages. A page is a collection of slots, where each slot contains a record, and each `record` is a collection of `fields` of the same or different types.

The size of a record in the `COUNTRY` table is size(name) + size(cont) + size(pop) + size(GDP) + size(life-exp) + size(shape) $\leq 30 + 30 + 4 + 4 + 4 + 8 = 80$ bytes. This is assuming that four bytes of storage is assigned to an integer data type and eight bytes of storage for a pointer to the actual storage location for a shape spatial datatype. This calculation assumes that varchar (N) datatype will be given N bytes for simplicity even though in reality it may use less space. There are six records in the `COUNTRY` table, which translates into a storage requirement of 480 bytes. This can be fitted into a single sector of a disk as shown in Figure 4.1. Similarly, the size of the records for the `CITY` table is seventy three bytes, and the storage needed for the nine records is 657 bytes, which can fit into two sectors of the disk assuming 512 bytes sectors. Each sector also contains format information to identify free space, the beginning of each record and possible fields, the address of the next sector, and so forth. Special sectors may be used as a directory to find the first sectors of various tables. Figure 4.1 simplifies many details of actual storage but has the basic information to show how tables are stored physically on secondary storage.

Within these broad parameters, there are many ways of specifically organizing fields, records, and files to suit a particular application. For example, the fields of a record can be of fixed or variable length; the records within a file can be ordered or unordered; and the file can be organized as a linked list or directory of pages. The pros and cons of each type of organization have been thoroughly examined and can be found in any introductory book on databases [Ramakrishnan, 1998].

The binary large object (BLOB) field type has played an important role in the development of spatial databases. Traditional databases cannot explicitly handle complex datatypes like point, line, and polygon, but they do provide support for converting a complex object into a binary representation and storing it in the BLOB field. This way an RDBMS can manage and provide transactional support for complex datatypes. For example, the `Oracle` RDBMS provides a `LONG RAW` field for storing byte strings which

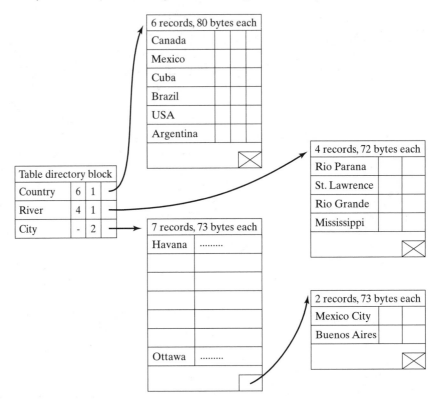

FIGURE 4.1. Mapping the records from Country, City, and River tables to disk pages.

are larger than 256 bytes. Despite this, the BLOB field cannot technically be regarded as a datatype because the RDBMS treats a BLOB as unformatted data with no structure. In particular, no query operations are available for the BLOB field.

4.1.4   File Structures

File structure refers to the organization of records in a file. The simplest form of organization is an unordered file, also called a heap, where records are in no particular order. The file storing the RIVER table in Figure 4.1 is an example of an unordered file. Searching for a record given a key (e.g., name) requires scanning the records in the file. In the worst case, all records must be checked by fetching all the disk pages holding data for the file. On average half the disk pages need to be retrieved. The main advantage of an unordered file is in the insert operation, which can simply add a new record to the end of the file.

More sophisticated file organizations include hashed file and ordered files. Hashed file organization divides the records into a set of buckets using a function called the hash function. Hash functions maps values for a chosen key field, for example, *city.name*, onto one of the buckets using a very simple computation. Figure 4.2 shows a hashed file with four buckets, each stored on a separate disk page. The hash function returns 1 for names with less than or equal to 6 characters, returns 2 for names with 7 or 8 characters, returns 3 for names with 9 or 10 characters and returns 4 for names with 11 or more characters.

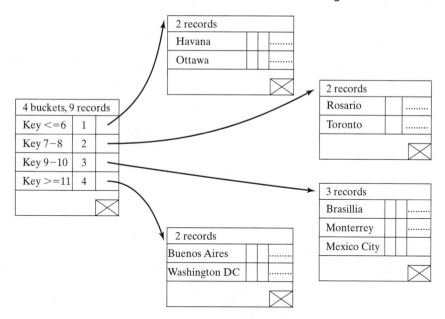

FIGURE 4.2. Hashed file organization for City table.

The names of cities are mapped to buckets 1 through 4 via the hash function. It is desirable that the hash function maps roughly an equal number of records to each bucket. Hashed file organization is very efficient for point search, insert, and delete operations which can be carried out in a constant time (e.g., two disk accesses) independent of the number of records in the file given a perfect hash function. Hashed file organization is not suited for range searches, for example, retrieve details of all cities whose name begins with the letter "B," since all buckets can contain the qualifying records.

Ordered files organize the records by sorting them based on a given key field. Figure 4.3 shows a sorted file organization for the record of city table with *city.name* as key field. Binary search algorithms can be used to search for the record with the given

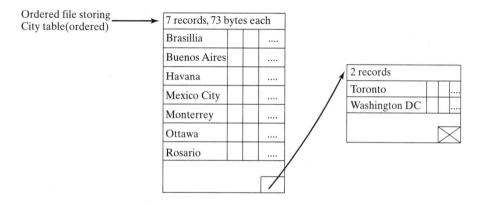

FIGURE 4.3. Ordered file organization for City table.

value of key attribute. Range queries can also be processed with a binary search for first qualifying records and scanning the following records. The cost of a binary search grows logarithmically with the number of records in the file. A file with 1 million records can be searched for the record containing a unique city name in about $log_2(10^6) = 20$ disk accesses. The actual cost may be lower as each disk page contains multiple records.

We note that ordered file organization cannot be applied directly to a spatial field, for example, location of a city, unless a total order is defined on points in a multidimensional space. Ordered file organization can also be generalized to spatial clustering based file organizations for spatial data sets.

4.1.5 Clustering

In its most abstract form, the goal of clustering is to reduce seek (t_s) and latency (t_l) time in answering common large queries. For spatial databases, this implies that objects that are adjacent in space and are commonly requested jointly by queries should be stored physically together in secondary memory. There are three types of clustering [Brinkhoff and Kriegel, 1994] that an SDBMS may support in order to provide efficient query processing:

1. *Internal clustering:* In order to speed up an access to a single object, the complete representation of one object is stored in one disk page, assuming its size is smaller than the free space on the page. Otherwise, the object is stored on multiple, physically consecutive pages. In this case, the number of pages occupied by the object is at most one higher than the minimum number of pages necessary to store the object.

2. *Local clustering:* In order to speed up access to several objects, a set of spatial objects (or their approximations) is grouped onto *one* page. This grouping may be performed according to the location of the objects (or approximations) in data space.

3. *Global clustering:* In contrast to local clustering, a set of spatially adjacent objects is stored not on one but on several physically consecutive pages which can be accessed by a single read request.

The design of spatial clustering techniques is more difficult compared with traditional clustering because there is no natural order in multidimensional space where spatial data resides. This is complicated by the fact that the storage disk is a logical one-dimensional device. Thus, what is needed is a mapping from a higher dimensional space to a one-dimensional space which is *distance-preserving*, so that elements close in space are mapped onto nearby points on the line, and *one-to-one*: no two points in the space are mapped onto the same point on the line. Several mappings, none of them ideal, have been proposed to accomplish this. The most prominent ones include the *Z-order*, *Gray code*, and *Hilbert curve*. For simplicity, we postpone the discussion of more sophisticated spatial clustering methods such as min-cut graph-partitioning (Section 6.5.2) and geometric methods (Section 4.2.2), which are computationally more expensive but may provide better clustering during bulk-loading.

We now show how Z-curve and the Hilbert curve can be uniformly generated by using replacement rules [Asano et al., 1997]. The construction is shown in Figures 4.4 and 4.5. We begin by representing the area of an $N \times N$ grid as a single cell. We iterate, and in the ith iteration, $i = 0, \ldots, n-1$ (for $N = 2^n$), we partition the area of the $N \times N$ grid into $2^i \cdot 2^i$ blocks, each of size $2^{n-1} \times 2^{n-1}$.

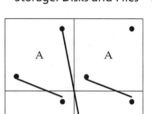

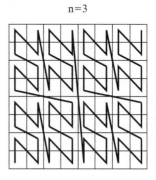

FIGURE 4.4. Generating a Z-curve [Asano et al., 1997].

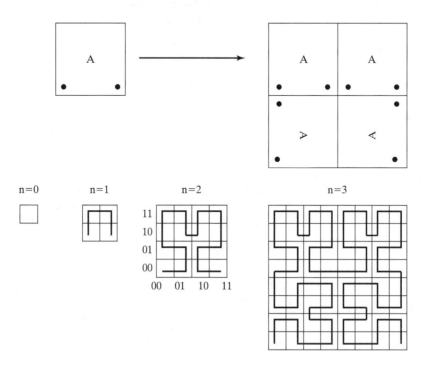

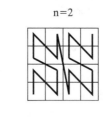

FIGURE 4.5. Generating a Hilbert curve [Asano et al., 1997].

Thus, in each iteration, all cells are replaced by four blocks of size $2^{n-i-1} \times 2^{n-i-1}$. Furthermore, the rotation of blocks is allowed. Two dots denote the entry and exit points of the curve into a cell. In a cell that is not refined further, both dots coincide at the center of the cell; in each refinement, the dots lie at the corresponding corner cells of the refined partition. Finally, lines between dots on the right side of the productions represent subsequent blocks in the numbering.

Algorithm for the Z-Curve and Hilbert Curve

The path of the space-filling curve imposes a linear order in space that can be obtained by following the curve from one end to the other. See Figure 4.4.

We now give an algorithm for generating the values of the Z-curve and Hilbert curve [Faloutsos and Roseman, 1989].

Z-Curve

1. Read the binary representation of the x and y coordinates.
2. Interleave the bits of the binary numbers into one string. See Figure 4.6 for an example.
3. Calculate the decimal value of the resulting binary string.

Figure 4.7 shows additional examples to find the z-values, given x, y coordinates.

Hilbert Curve

1. Read in the n-bit binary representation of the x and y coordinates.
2. Interleave bits of the two binary numbers into one string.
3. Divide the string from left to right into 2-bit strings, s_i, for $i = 1, \ldots, n$.
4. Give a decimal value, d_i, for each 2-bit string, as follows: "00" equals 0, "01" equals 1; "10" equals 3; "11" equals 2.
5. For each number j in the array, if

$j = 0$ then switch every following occurrence of 1 in the array to 3 and every following occurrence of 3 in the array to 1;

$j = 3$ then switch every following occurrence of 0 in the array to 2 and every following occurrence of 2 in the array to 0;

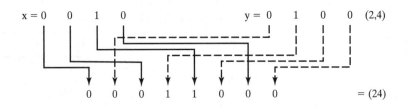

FIGURE 4.6. Example to calculate the z-value.

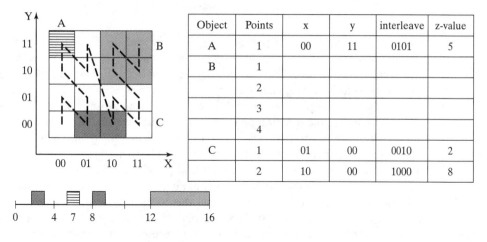

Object	Points	x	y	interleave	z-value
A	1	00	11	0101	5
B	1				
	2				
	3				
	4				
C	1	01	00	0010	2
	2	10	00	1000	8

FIGURE 4.7. A trace for finding z-values.

6. Convert each number in the array to its binary representation (2-bit strings), concatenate all the strings in order from left to right, and calculate the decimal value.

Figure 4.8 shows an example translation using the above algorithm.

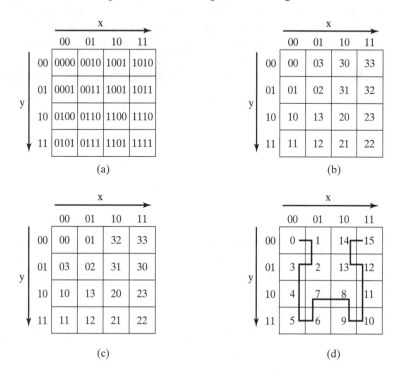

FIGURE 4.8. Example showing Hilbert curve translation.

A Measure of Disk Accesses

To analyze the clustering properties of the Z-curve and the Hilbert curve, we assume a multidimensional space with finite granularity (number of cells), where each point corresponds to a grid cell. The curves assign a single integer value to each cell. Ideally, it is desirable to have mappings that result in fewer disk accesses. The number of disk accesses, however, depends on several factors, such as the capacity of the disk pages, the splitting algorithm, the insertion order, and so on. Here we shall use instead the average number of *clusters*, or *continuous runs*, or *buckets* of grid points within a subspace represented by a given query as the measure of clustering performance of the space-filling curves [Moon et al., 1996]. If each grid point is mapped to one disk block, this measure exactly corresponds to the number of nonconsecutive disk accesses that involved additional seek time. For instance, say that the 10 buckets accessed to answer a query are 2, 4-8, 10-14, 16. In this case there are four clusters; on the other hand, if the buckets to be accessed are numbered 9-13, 15-19, this corresponds to only two clusters. From a clustering point of view, the second arrangement is 50 percent better than the first one. See Figure 4.9 for an illustration.

Note that the Hilbert curve method is slightly better than the Z-curve because it does not have any diagonal lines. However the Hilbert algorithm and the computation of precise entry and exit points are more complex than the Z-curve.

Handling Regions

We can map ranges in N-dimensional space to points in twice as many (2N) dimensions using the Z-curve for the minimum orthogonal bounding rectangle of extended objects. A region typically breaks into one or more pieces (blocks), each of which can be described by a z-value. A *block* is a square region that is the result of one or more quadtree subdivisions of the original image. A quadtree subdivision recursively divides space into four equal parts. Pixels are clearly 1×1 blocks. For example, the region labeled C in Figure 4.7 breaks into two pixels, C_1 and C_2, with z-values

$$z_{C_1} = 0010 = (2)_{10}$$
$$z_{C_2} = 1000 = (8)_{10}$$

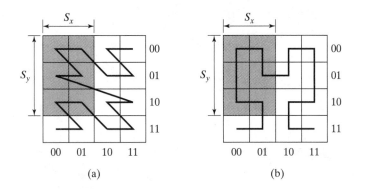

FIGURE 4.9. Illustration of clusters: (a) two clusters for the Z-curve; (b) one cluster for the Hilbert curve.

The region labeled B in Figure 4.7 consists of four pixels, which have the common prefix 11 in their z-values; in this case, the z-value of B is exactly this common prefix,

$$z_B = 11$$

or, using "∗" as the "don't care" character,

$$z_B = 11 ∗ ∗$$

A large region may be decomposed into many pieces; for efficiency, we typically approximate such a region with a coarser-resolution region.

In conclusion, each object (and range query) can be uniquely represented by the z-values of its blocks (or by the minimum and maximum z-values of its blocks). Each such z-value can be treated as a primary key of a record of the form (z-value, object-id, other attributes, . . .), and it can be inserted in a primary-key file structure, such as a B+ tree. Additional objects in the same address space can be handled in the same way; their z-values will be inserted into the same B+ tree. These blocks are used for efficient processing of range queries.

Algorithms for Access Methods

The Z-ordering method can handle all the queries that we have listed earlier:

- *Point queries:* Binary search on a given Z value in a sorted file, or use a B-tree search on Z-value-based B-tree index.

- *Range queries:* The query shape is translated into a set of z-values as if it were a data region. Typically, we opt for an approximate representation of it, trying to balance the number of z-values and the amount of extra area in the approximation. Then we search with the z-values of the data regions for matching z-values. The matching is done efficiently because of the following observation: Let z_1 and z_2 be two z-values, and let z_1 be the shorter one, without loss of generality; then, for the corresponding regions (i.e., blocks) r_1 and r_2, there are only two possibilities: (1) either r_1 completely contains r_2, if z_1 is the prefix of z_2 (e.g., $z_1 = 1^{***}$, $z_2 = 11^{**}$ or $z_1 = {}^*1^{**}$, $z_2 = 11^{**}$), or (2) the two regions are *disjoint* (e.g., $z_1 = {}^*0^{**}$, $z_2 = 11^{**}$).

- *Nearest-neighbor queries:* The distance in Z-order space does not correspond well to the distance in the original X-Y coordinate space. To handle the nearest neighbor query using Z-order B-tree, first, we compute the z−value of the query point p_i and search the data point p_j with the closest z−value from the B-tree. Then we compute the distance r between p_i and p_j and issue a range query centered at p_i with radius r. We check all the retrieved points and return the one with the shortest distance to the query point.

- *Spatial joins:* The algorithm for spatial joins is a generalization of the algorithm for the range query. Let S be a set of spatial objects (e.g., lakes) and R be another set (e.g., railway-line segments). The spatial join "Find all the railways that cross lakes" is handled as follows. The elements of set S are translated into z-values and sorted; the elements of set R are also translated into a sorted list of z-values; the two lists of z-values are then merged. The "don't care" character ∗ has to be treated carefully to determine overlap.

There are some disadvantages with using a Z-order B-tree. One problem is with respect to join operations: index partitions cannot be directly joined if the grid structures are not compatible, and we have to recompute the indexes in order to facilitate the spatial join. Another disadvantage of a Z-order as the space filling curve is the long diagonal jumps where the consecutive z-values connecting these jumps are far apart in X-Y coordinate space. The spatial clustering of Z-ordering can be improved by using the Hilbert curve.

4.2   SPATIAL INDEXING

Index files are auxiliary files used to speed up the searching of a data file. The records in an index file have only two fields, namely, the key-value and the address of a page in the data file. Records in an index file are often ordered (possibly using a space filling curve) and may be further organized using specialized search data-structures such as B tree, R-tree, Grid file, and so on. Figure 4.10 shows a secondary index file of city table on the key field name. Because the records in index files are only thirty eight bytes, assuming eight byte addresses for disk pages, all nine index records fit in a single disk page. The index records are sorted and contain addresses of disk pages in the data file containing appropriate records. The data file itself may be unordered with respect to the key field.

If the records in the data file were ordered by the key field, then the index need only keep the first key field value for each disk page of the data file as shown in Figure 4.11. This kind of index is called the primary index.

Because the records in the index file are ordered, binary search can be used for searching index files even if the data file is not ordered. In addition, the index file tends to be smaller (in terms of number of disk pages) and thus is faster to search. Once an

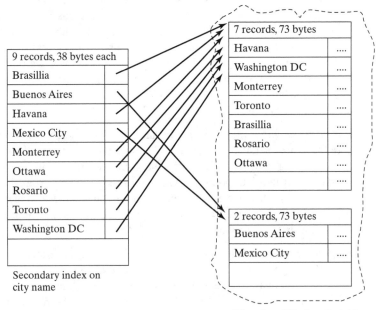

FIGURE 4.10. Secondary index on the City table.

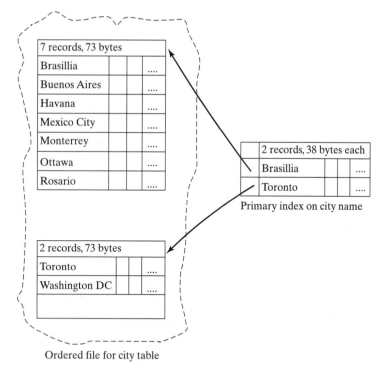

FIGURE 4.11. Primary index on the City table.

appropriate index record is found, the data record is extracted by fetching the data file disk page pointed to by the index record.

A spatial index structure organizes objects with a set of buckets (which normally correspond to pages of secondary memory). Each bucket has an associated bucket region, a part of space containing all objects stored in the bucket. Bucket regions are usually rectangles. For point data structures, these regions are normally disjoint, and they partition the space so that each point belongs to precisely one bucket. For some rectangle data structures, bucket regions may overlap.

There are essentially two ways of providing a spatial index:

1. Dedicated external spatial data structures are added to the system, offering for spatial attributes what a B-tree does for linear attributes.

2. Spatial objects are mapped into a 1-D space using a space filling curve (e.g., Z-order, Hilbert-curve) so that they can be stored within a standard 1-D index such as the B-tree.

Apart from spatial selection, spatial indexing also supports other operations such as spatial join, finding the object closest to a query value, and so on.

4.2.1   Grid Files

One of the simplest methods to access multidimensional points is the *fixed grid* access structure (e.g., latitude-longitude grid). As illustrated in Figure 4.12, the fixed-grid method

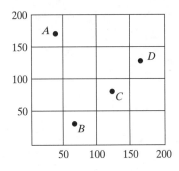

FIGURE 4.12. A fixed-grid structure for points (A, B, C, D).

divides the embedding n-dimensional hyperspace into equal-size buckets. The data structure that implements the fixed grid is an n-dimensional array. The points that lie in a cell can be stored in a dynamic structure (such as a linked list) to handle overflows. This structure is useful for static uniformly distributed data (e.g., satellite imagery). However, the fixed-grid structure is rigid, and its directory can be sparse and large.

To achieve more flexibility and better performance, [Nievergelt et al., 1984] introduced the *grid file*. The grid file has relatively good I/O performance for exact-match and partial-match retrieval. The grid file multiattribute indexing technique splits the embedding n-dimensional space. However, in terms of locality, it uses a grid method, that is, it partitions all regions in the splitting direction. With grid files, the goal is to achieve the two disk-access principle: one access to get the directory entry and the other to get the actual buckets to retrieve the record. More specifically, there are two parts to the grid file. One part consists of an n-dimensional *grid directory*, where each entry in the directory points to a data bucket. Figure 4.13 shows an n-dimensional grid directory where $n = 2$. The second structure consists of one-dimensional arrays that are *linear scales*. These arrays are used to identify the index of the grid directory that references the block or bucket containing the objects (records).

To illustrate searching with grid files, consider the structure in Figure 4.14. Here the buckets are $A, B, C, D, E, F, G, H, I, J, K, L, M$. Note that grid directory entries $(1, 1)$ and $(1, 2)$ "share" the same bucket. This means points or records belonging to these regions are stored in the same bucket. The same is true for entries $(2, 3)$ and $(3, 3)$, as well as entries $(1, 4)$ and $(2, 4)$. Now suppose we are given a point such as $(60, 80)$, and we want to locate the bucket that stores the record/object with $X = 60$ and $Y = 80$. The linear scale corresponding to the x-axis yields the index $3(X = 60)$, and the linear scale corresponding to the y-axis has index $4(Y = 80)$. The $(3, 4)$ entry of the grid directory is bucket C. Therefore, the object with $X = 60$ and $Y = 80$ is located in bucket C.

In terms of dimensionality and locality, the partitioning is done with only one hyperplane (or along one of the dimensions), but the *split extends to all the regions in the splitting direction*. The search time for the grid file is good. For exact-match queries, it takes one disk access to the directory and one access to the data. However, the nature of the grid file makes the directory quite sparse, leading to wastage of main memory buffers as well secondary storage. In other words, hypercubes may have very few or no records, and adjacent directory entries may point to the same data block. The implication of this statement is that for partial-match and range queries, many directory entries, but only a few data blocks, may have to be scanned.

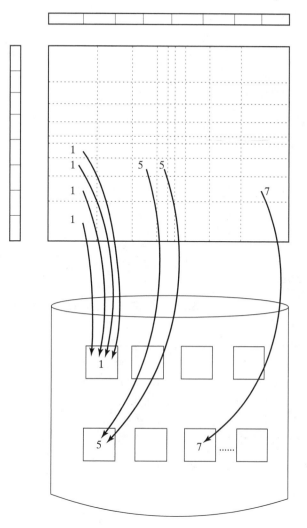

FIGURE 4.13. A two-dimensional grid directory and data pages.

4.2.2 R-Trees

One of the first access methods created to support extended objects was Guttman's R-tree [Guttman, 1984]. The R-tree is a height-balanced tree which is the natural extension of the B-tree for k-dimensions. Objects are represented in the R-tree by their minimum bounding rectangle (MBR). R-trees are characterized by the following properties:

1. Every leaf node contains between m and M index records, unless it is the root (where $m \le M/2$).

2. For each index record *(I, tuple-identifier)* in a leaf node, I is the minimum bounding rectangle that spatially contains the k-dimensional data object represented by the indicated tuple.

3. Every nonleaf node has between m and M children, unless it is a root.

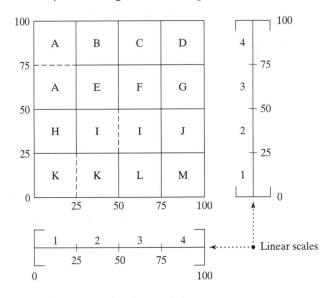

FIGURE 4.14. Grid file with linear scales.

4. For each entry *(I, child-pointer)* in a nonleaf node, *I* is the minimum bounding rectangle that spatially contains the rectangles in the child node.
5. The root node has at least two children, unless it is a leaf.
6. All leaves appear on the same level.
7. All MBRs have sides parallel to the axis of a global coordinate system as shown in Figure 4.15.

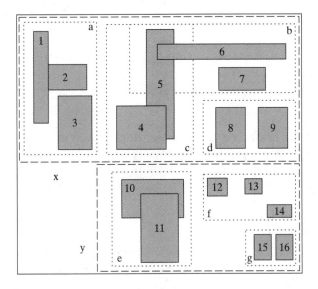

FIGURE 4.15. A collection of spatial objects.

Each node in the tree corresponds to a disk page. A leaf node consists of a number of entries with format *(I, tuple-id)*, where *I* is an MBR, and *tuple-id* is the unique identifier for the tuple in the database holding the object corresponding to that MBR. *I* is represented as $I = (I_0, \ldots, I_{k-1})$, where I_i is a closed, bounded interval $[a, b]$ along direction i. Nonfinite intervals can also be considered, by having a, b, or both equal to infinity.

Nonleaf nodes are composed of a number of entries of the format *(I, child-pointer)* where *I* is the MBR for all rectangles in the lower node entries pointed to by *child-pointer*. Each node in the tree can have a maximum of *M* entries and a minimum (where $m \leq M/2$) entry, unless it is the root. The root node has at least two children, unless it is a leaf.

In Figure 4.15, a set of spatial objects (MBRs) in a two-dimensional space is shown. Figure 4.16 shows an R-tree for the set of MBRs of Figure 4.15. Each node of the tree has a maximum of three entries. The objects are shown on the leaf nodes of the tree in dark shading.

Point and range queries can be processed in a top-down recursive manner on R-tree. The query point (or region) is tested first against each entry (I, child-pointer) in the root. If the query point is inside (or query region overlaps with) I, then the search algorithm is applied recursively on entries in the R-tree node pointed to by the child-pointer. This process stops after reaching the leaves of R-tree. The selected entries in leaves are used to retrieve the records associated with the selected spatial keys.

Example: Consider the search for objects overlapping with rectangle 5 in Figure 4.16. Entry x in root overlaps with the rectangle 5 and the search will be continued along that branch of R-tree. The entries b and c in x are overlapping with rectangle 5, thus are searched next. Finally the rectangles 4, 5 and 6 are identified as leaf entries that overlap the query rectangle 5.

Because the R-tree is a balanced tree, an insertion may propagate node splits toward the root in case the leaf node for the inserted object is already filled. The page-split algorithm is rather complex; however, R-tree has been implemented in many commercial relational database systems that support conventional access methods and disk pages of reasonable size (1024 bytes).

The maximum number of levels in an R-tree is $\lfloor \log_m N \rfloor - 1$, where N is the total number of entries of the tree. In the worst case, there will be a node-space utilization of m/M, except for the root. If m is greater than 3 or 4, the tree will spread horizontally, so that almost all space is used for leaf nodes containing index records. Typically the value of m is large, and the depth of the R-tree is relatively small. For example, an R-tree indexing 100 million rectangles may have a depth of 5 given $m = 100$. The R-tree is

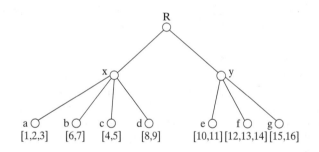

FIGURE 4.16. R-tree hierarchy.

a dynamic structure and also allows the storage of heterogeneous objects: for instance, points, lines, and nonzero-area objects, as shown in Figure 4.15.

Search performance depends on two parameters: *coverage* and *overlap*. *Coverage* of a level of the tree is the total area covered by all MBRs of all nodes at that level. This way, coverage is an indirect measure of dead space area, or empty space covered by the tree. *Overlap* of a level of the tree is the total area of space covered by more than one rectangle associated with nodes at that level. Overlap may make it necessary to visit more than one node of the tree to find an object. This problem associated with the R-tree means that a worst case performance of search operations cannot be estimated, even if an attempt is made to minimize overlap.

From the previous discussion, we can see that in order to have an efficient R-tree, both coverage and overlap should be minimized, and the overlap minimization is even more critical than coverage. This problem has led to the development of other variations and alternative structures based on the R-tree. The packed R-tree, the R^*-tree, and the R+ tree are such examples.

The packed R-tree approach assumes that data is relatively static and that data objects are known before tree construction. The first time the database is created, it is efficiently organized in order to minimize overlap and coverage. Further insertions and deletions are treated just as in Guttman's original R-tree structure. The R^*-tree is a variation that relies on a combined optimization of area, margin, and overlap of each minimum bounding rectangle in intermediate nodes of the tree.

In R+ trees, the MBRs of spatial objects may be split by rectangles in nonleaf nodes of the tree. The properties of an R+ tree follows:

1. For each entry *(I, child-pointer)* in an intermediate node, the subtree rooted at the node pointed to by *child-pointer* contains a rectangle *R* if and only if *R* is covered by *I*. The only exception is when *I* is a rectangle at a leaf node. In that case *R* must just overlap with *I*.

2. For any two entries $(I_1, child-pointer_1)$ and $(I_2, child-pointer_2)$ of an intermediate node, the overlap between I_1 and I_2 is zero.

3. The root has at least two children, unless it is a leaf.

4. All leaves are at the same level.

All rectangles in an intermediate node are disjoint, thus yielding zero overlap among intermediate node entries. If an object MBR is split by two or more rectangles in higher level nodes of the R+ tree, each of the entries associated with those rectangles in nonleaf nodes will have a descendant leaf node that points to that object. This way, the height of the tree may increase (although only slightly), but search operations will be performed more efficiently.

Figure 4.17 shows an R+ tree for the set of spatial objects shown previously in Figure 4.15. The new MBRs are shown in Figure 4.18. A maximum of three entries per node is assumed. Pointers to two objects are duplicated as each of the corresponding object overlap two leaf nodes rectangles. Please note that the bounding rectangles should touch each other when they enclose a common object, for example, object 5 is common for MBRs b and c. However they are shown as disjoint in Figure 4.18 for clarity.

R+ trees are better than packed R-trees for highly dynamic data because they ensure continued efficiency. A packing algorithm can also be applied to R+ trees, in

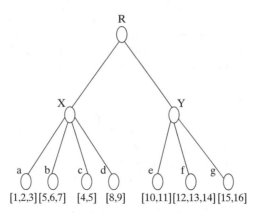

FIGURE 4.17. R+ tree hierarchy.

order to achieve an initial, efficient arrangement of data in the tree. Contrary to the R-tree, downward propagation of splitting may be necessary because of Property 1 of R+ trees. For that reason, the choice of node splits is very important.

When a node overflows, the respective rectangle is split by a hyperplane. The hyperplane is parallel to one of the k directions (in a k-dimensional space), and may have different positions. The choice of the hyperplane can be based on several criteria, such as the reduction of coverage or height of the tree. For the latter, the hyperplane must be chosen to minimize the number of rectangle splits.

4.2.3 Cost Models

R-trees are one of the popular indexing structures used in spatial databases. We can find several variants of R-trees in the literature so one natural question arises: which one is

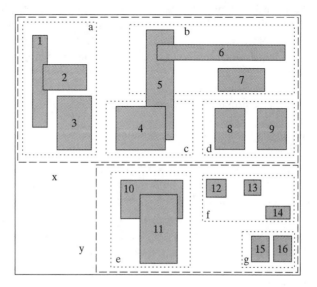

FIGURE 4.18. Rectangles for interior nodes of a R+ tree.

better or more efficient? In order to compare these variants, first we need accurate cost models. Selection query performance over R-trees and $R+$ trees can be found in [Faloutsos and Sellis, 1987]. This model assumes that the data is uniformly distributed, and all nodes of the tree are fully populated (packed trees). Analytical cost models for predicting query performance as a function of the average node size and query window size can be found in [Kamel and Faloutsos, 1993; Pagel et al., 1993b]. These models capture the quantitative relationship between area, perimeter and the number of objects, as a function of performance of a R-tree. Most of these models estimate the performance as a function of the number of nodes accessed alone, ignoring the buffer usage. Buffer based cost prediction models were simultaneously and independently introduced in [Leutenegger and Lopez, 2000; Theodoridis et al., 2000a]. [Leutenegger and Lopez, 2000] extends the model described in [Kamel and Faloutsos, 1993; Pagel et al., 1993b], taking into account the existence of a buffer. They provide cost models for both uniform access and data driven access. Experimental evaluation shows that small amounts of buffer can superlinearly improve the performance of point queries over well-structured R-trees and provide linear improvements for poorly structured R-trees. [Theodoridis et al., 2000a] provides cost models for selection and join queries as a function of data properties based on path buffer for join queries. Experimental evaluation shows that performance gain for join queries is about 10–30 percent for one-dimensional data and about 50 percent for two-dimensional data.

4.3   TRENDS

4.3.1   TR*-Tree for Object Decomposition

Object approximations are used to reduce the number of exact geometry tests of polygons. Object decompositions are used to speed-up such tests. Consider a point-in-polygon test. This test is rather time-consuming for polygons with thousands of vertices. On the other hand, only a small local part of the object is actually relevant for deciding whether an object contains a point. This leads to the idea of object decompositions, where the objects are divided into a number of simple and local components (e.g., triangles, trapezoids, convex polygons, etc.) which satisfy some quantitative constraint.

Using object decompositions, geometric tests are applied only to the object components, which is much more efficient than testing the whole polygon. To decide which components are relevant for a particular test, the components of one object are organized in specific spatial structures.

A decomposition strategy can be organized as follows:

1. In a preprocessing step, polygonal objects can be decomposed into a minimum set of disjoint trapezoids, using a plane-sweep algorithm (see Figure 4.19).

2. Because a complete spatial order cannot be defined on the set of trapezoids that are generated by this decomposition process, a binary search on these trapezoids is not possible. Therefore, the R-tree can be used for the spatial search.

3. In order to speed up the geometric test, [Schneider and Kriegel, 1991] have developed the TR*-tree, a variant of the R-tree, designed to minimize the main memory operations and to store the trapezoids of the decomposed objects. The main characteristic of the structure of the TR*-tree is its small maximum number of entries per node. The TR*-tree representation of an accessed object is completely loaded into main memory for spatial query processing.

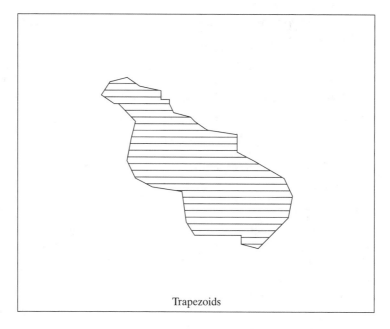

Trapezoids

FIGURE 4.19. Trapezoids to decompose the object.

4.3.2 Concurrency Control

A DBMS is designed to provide simultaneous, or *concurrent,* access by multiple user programs to a shared database. To understand how the DBMS manages concurrent operations, it is convenient to view a database as a collection of objects, and an execution of a user program, or *transaction* as a series of *reads* and *writes* of database objects. For efficiency, the actions of a transaction are allowed to be *interleaved* but under the constraint that a logical partial order or serializability between transactions is maintained.

Important differences between a transaction in a DBMS and, say, a C program executing on an operating system are summarized by the acronym *ACID. Atomicity* guarantees that either all the actions of a transaction are carried out, or none are. *Consistency* implies that a transaction cannot violate data consistency constraints predefined on a database. *Isolation* refers to the property that actions of a transaction can be understood without the knowledge of concurrently executing transactions. *Durability* ensures that the effects of a transactions persist across system crashes.

A DBMS typically employs a concurrency control technique, for example, a *locking protocol*, to provide concurrent access to a database. Two rules define the widely used, strict two-phase locking (Strict 2PL) protocol:

1. For a *read* action on an object, a transaction acquires a *shared* lock on the object. An *exclusive* lock is provided for a *write* action.

2. All locks associated with a transaction are released when the transaction is completed.

For hierarchical index structures, particularly for the B+ tree, the locking protocol described earlier has been adapted to take advantage of the tree structure. For the *search* and *insert* operations, the following observations have provided the insight for modification:

- The function of the nonleaf nodes is to direct the search toward the leaf nodes where the actual data is stored. Thus, a search operation does not need any locks if nodes in the B-tree index are threaded at every level.

- The insert operation needs an exclusive lock only on one node at any time if index nodes are threaded at each level.

For R-trees, the search and the update operations are different from those of B-trees because (1) keys in an R-tree are multidimensional MBRs that have no linear order defined on them, and (2) the keys can overlap. For search operations, this implies that the query rectangle has to descend all subtrees that intersect or fully contain the range specification. Furthermore, there is no guarantee that the child node contains any keys of interest, even if its bounding rectangle intersects the search range. For update operations, in R-trees, upward propagation can occur not only when a node is split but also when a bounding rectangle is modified.

A strategy to increase degree of concurrency in B-trees by guaranteeing that only one node needs to be locked at a given time has been proposed by [Lehman and Yao, 1981]. This strategy has been subsequently adapted for R-trees by [Kornacker and Banks, 1995]. Other concurrency control techniques for R-tree are proposed by [Chakrabarti and Mehrotra, 1999].

The B-link tree adds a right-link pointer from a node to its right sibling on the same level to order the nodes by their keys. Even if a node is split, a B-tree search process can still traverse through it. A search process can identify a node that has been split, as splits may lead to the highest key on the node being smaller than the query key. The search process can follow the right-link pointer to look at new pages added by the split. The traversal of the right-link ends when the search process reaches a node whose highest key is larger than the query key. Similarly, an insertion process can avoid lock coupling during the initial search to reach the correct leaf. If the page is split, the insertion process can release the lock on the node after inserting a right sibling into the linked list at that level. It may need to follow the right-link due to concurrent splits.

The B-link strategy depends on the linear order among the keys to determine when a child node was split and also how far right the search process had to traverse. The keys in an R-tree are MBRs which do not exhibit a natural linear order.

The R-link tree assigns a unique logical sequence number (LSN) to each node. LSNs monotonically increase with time. The search and insertion operations use the LSNs to identify split nodes and to end traversal of the right-link chain. Entries in each node of an R-link tree consist of a key MBR, a pointer to the child node, and the expected LSN number for the child node. When a node is split, the old LSN is assigned to the new (right sibling) node, and a new LSN is generated for the old node! A process descending down the tree can detect the split by comparing the node's LSN with that of the expected LSN of the node in the parent. In case of a split, the search follows the right-link pointer until it reaches at a node with a matching LSN.

An R-link tree is a balanced tree. Its index nodes contain a set of entries and a right-link r. The nodes at each level of the tree form a single-linked list via the right-links.

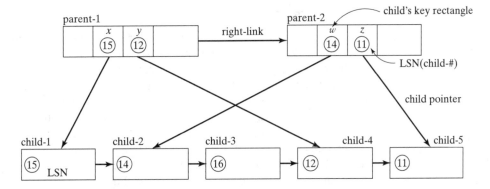

FIGURE 4.20. A subsection of an R-link tree [Kornacker and Banks, 1995].

Entries on internal nodes contain a key rectangle k, a pointer p, and an expected LSN l. There are two cases for an expected LSN:

1. *Normal case: child-level I structure is consistent with parent level $I + 1$.* In the normal case, the pointer p points to a child node N. The right-link of child N points to NULL or to another node R, which is also pointed to by some entry in parent level $I + 1$. In Figure 4.20, entry x points to node child-1; both $x's$ LSN and child-1's LSN are matching, and child-1's right-link points to child-2, which is also pointed to by entry w in parent-2.

2. *Other Case: Child level I structure is newer than parent-level $I + 1$.* In this case, pointer p points to a child node N, where $LSN(N) > l$. Child level I has a node N' whose LSN is l. Child node N' can be reached via the right-link of N in the linked-list at level I. Consider the entry w in parent-2 from Figure 4.20. The $LSN(w)$ is smaller than the $LSN(child-2)$ and is equal to the $LSN(child-3)$. Child-3 can be reached from child-2 via the right-link. Child-3 does not yet have an entry in the parent level. This case is due to a split of node child-2, which will be reflected at the parent level to complete the split.

4.3.3 Spatial Join Index

A spatial join index is a data structure that optimizes the spatial join query processing. Join indexes improve the performance of recurring join queries over tables that have low update rates. Join indexes are interesting for new applications such as data warehousing due to the large volume of data and restricted updates.

The join-index is typically represented as a bipartite graph between the pages of encumbent relations or their surrogates. When the number of buffer pages is fixed, the join-computation problem is transformed into determining a page-access sequence such that the join can be computed with the minimum number of redundant page accesses. This problem is NP-hard, so it is unlikely that a polynomial time solution exists for this problem. Solutions in the literature use a clustering method that groups pages in one or both tables involved in the join to reduce total page accesses. Simpler heuristics either group the pages of a single table via sorting or use incremental clustering methods.

Join Index: Basic Concepts

Consider a database with two relations, facility and forest stand. Facility has a point attribute representing its location, and Forest Stand has a rectangle attribute that represents its extent by a bounding box. The polygon representing its extent may be stored separately. A point is represented by the x and y coordinates on the map. A rectangle is represented by points that represent the bottom left and top right corners.

In Figure 4.21(a), points $a1, a2, a3, b1, b2$ represent facility locations, and polygons $A1, A2, B1, B2, C1, C2$ are the bounding boxes that represent the limits of the forest stands. The circle around each location shows the area within distance D from a facility. The rectangle around each forest boundary represents the minimal orthogonal bounding rectangle (MOBR) for each forest stand. Figure 4.21(b) shows two relations, R and S, for this data set. Relation R represents facilities via the attributes of a unique identifier, $R.ID$, the location (x,y coordinates), and other nonspatial attributes. Relation S represents the forest stands via a unique identifier, $S.ID$, the MOBR, and nonspatial attributes. MOBR ($X_{LL}, Y_{LL}, X_{UR}, Y_{UR}$) is represented via the coordinates of the lower-left corner point (X_{LL}, Y_{LL}) and the upper right corner point (X_{UR}, Y_{UR}). Now, consider the following query: **Q**: "Find all forest stands which are within a distance D from each facility." This query will require a join on the facility and forest stand relations, based on their spatial attributes. A spatial join is more complex than an equi-join and is a special case of a Θ-join, where Θ is a spatial predicate, for example, touch, overlap, and cross. The query **Q** is an example of a spatial join.

A spatial join algorithm may be used to find the pairs (facility, forest stand) that satisfy query **Q**. Alternatively, a join-index may be used to materialize a subset of the result to speed up processing for the future occurrence of **Q**, if there are few updates to the spatial data. Figure 4.21(b) shows a join-index with two columns. Each tuple in the join-index represents a tuple in the table $JOIN(R, S, distance(R.Location, S.MOBR) < D)$. In general, the tuples in a join-index may also contain pointers to the pages of R and S, where the relevant tuples of R and S reside. We omit the pointer information in this chapter to simplify the diagrams.

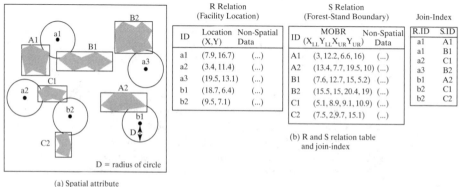

(a) Spatial attribute of R and S

(b) R and S relation table and join-index

FIGURE 4.21. Constructing a join-index from two relations.

A join-index describes a relationship between the objects of two relations. Assume that each tuple of a relation has a surrogate (a system-defined identifier for tuples, pages, etc.) that uniquely identifies that tuple. A join-index is a sequence of pairs of surrogates in which each pair of surrogates identifies the result-tuple of a join. The tuples participating in the join result are given by their surrogates. Formally, let R and S be two relations. Then consider the join of R and S on attributes A of R and B of S. The join-index is thus an abstraction of the join of the relations. If F defines the join predicate, then the join-index is given by the set $JI = \{(r_i, s_j) | F(r_i.A, s_j.B)$ is true for $r_i \in R$ and $s_j \in S\}$, where r_i and s_j are surrogates of the ith tuple in R and the jth tuple in S, respectively. For example, consider the facility and forest stand relational tables shown in Figure 4.21. The facility relation is joined with the forest stand relation on the spatial attributes of each relation. The join-index for this join contains the tuple IDs which match the spatial join predicate.

A join-index can be described by a bipartite graph $G = (V_1, V_2, E)$, where V_1 contains the tuple IDs of relation R, and V_2 contains the tuple IDs of relation S. Edge set E contains an edge (v_r, v_s) for $v_r \in R$ and $v_s \in S$, if there is a tuple corresponding to (v_r, v_s) in the join-index. The bipartite graph models all of the related tuples as connected vertices in the graph. In a graph, the edges connected to a node are called the incident edges of that node, and the number of edges incident on a node is called the degree of that node.

We use Figure 4.22 to illustrate one of the major differences between tuple-level adjacency matrices of linear-key equi-join and spatial join. Figure 4.22(a) shows the adjacency matrix for an equi-join. The horizontal-coordinate shows distinct values of tuple-ids from one relation; the vertical-coordinate shows distinct values of tuple-ids from the other relation. Shaded areas are collections of dots representing tuple-pairs satisfying the equi-join predicate from the set of all tuple-pairs in the cross-product of two relations. White space designates the tuple-pairs which do not satisfy the equi-join predicate. Figure 4.22(b) presents the same information as Figure 4.22(a), where tuples in each relation are sorted by the join attribute. Note that the shaded areas come close to the diagonal for linearly ordered join attributes. Join-processing algorithms (e.g., sort-merge) can take advantage of this property. Figure 4.22(c) shows the adjacency matrix for a Θ-join, e.g., a spatial join. Note that the join attribute (e.g., spatial location) may not be linear in general and may not have a natural sort order. However, one may reorder the rows and columns of the adjacency matrix to bring in as many

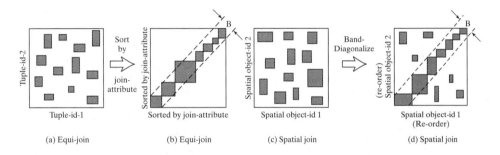

(a) Equi-join   (b) Equi-join   (c) Spatial join   (d) Spatial join

FIGURE 4.22. Comparison of tuple-level adjacency matrices for equi-join and spatial join.

dots (object-id pairs satisfying the spatial-join predicate) near the diagonal as possible. The result of such efforts often yields an adjacency matrix similar to the one shown in Figure 4.22(d), where a substantial number of shaded areas remain away from the diagonal. Join-processing algorithms for spatial-join need to account for the off-diagonal shaded areas.

Page-Connectivity Graph (PGC), Page-Access Sequence

When the join relationship between two relations is described at the page level, we get a PCG. A PCG [Merrett et al., 1981] $B_G = (V_1, V_2, E)$ is a bipartite graph in which vertex set V_1 represents the pages from the first relation, and vertex set V_2 represents the pages from the second relation. The set of edges is constructed as follows: an edge is added between page (node) v_1^i in V_1 and page (node) v_2^j in V_2, if and only if there is at least one pair of objects (r_i, s_j) in the join-index such that $r_i \in v_1^i$ and $s_j \in v_2^j$. Figure 4.23 shows a page-connectivity graph for the join-index from Figure 4.21(b). Nodes (a, b) represent the pages of relation R, and nodes (A, B, C) represent the pages of relation S. A *min-cut* node partition [Hagen and Kahng, 1991; Kernighan and Lin, 1970] of graph $B_G = (V_1, V_2, E)$ partitions the nodes in V into disjoint subsets while minimizing the number of edges whose incident nodes are in two different partitions. The cut-set of a min-cut partition is the set of edges whose incident nodes are in two different partitions. Fast and efficient heuristic algorithms [Karypis et al., 1998; Karypis and Kumar, 1998] for this problem have become available in recent years. They can be used to cluster pages in a PCG.

A join-index helps speed up join processing, because it keeps track of all the pairs of tuples that satisfy the join predicate. Given a join-index JI, one can use the derived PCG to schedule an efficient page-access sequence to fetch the data pages. The CPU cost is fixed because there is a fixed cost associated with joining each pair of tuples, and the number of tuples to be joined is fixed. I/O cost, on the other hand, depends on the sequence of pages accessed. When there is limited buffer space in the memory, some of the pages may have to be read multiple times from the disk. The page-access sequence (and in turn the join-index clustering and the clustering of the base relation) determines the I/O cost.

Example: We illustrate the dependency between the I/O cost of a join and the order in which the data pages are accessed with the help of an example using the page-connectivity graph shown in Figure 4.23. Assume that the buffer space is limited to allow at most two pages of the relations in memory, after caching the whole

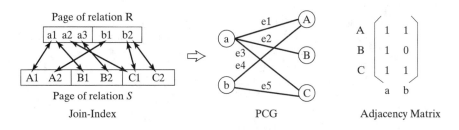

FIGURE 4.23. Construction of a PCG from a join-index.

page-connectivity graph in memory. Consider the two-page access sequences: (i) (a, A, b, B, a, C, b) and (ii) (a, A, b, C, a, B). Each sequence allows the computation of join results using a limited buffer of two pages. However, in the first case, there are a total of seven page accesses, and in the second case there are a total of six page accesses. Note that the lower bound on the number of page accesses is five, as there are five distinct pages in the PCG. However, with two buffer spaces, there is no page-access sequence that will result in five-page accesses. This is because the cycle (a, A, b, C, a) requires that at least three pages be in memory to avoid redundant page accesses. With three buffer spaces, (a, B, A, C, b) is a page-access sequence that results in five-page accesses.

4.4   SUMMARY

Classical storage and access methods face many challenges in managing spatial datasets. Classical methods were designed for keys with total ordering, which is not naturally defined on spatial keys embedded in a multidimensional space. Many spatial objects (e.g., polygons) are extended objects that are often not supported by classical methods. Finally, spatial selection predicates (e.g., overlap, crosses, nearest neighbor) are much richer than those supported by classical methods.

A space filling curve (e.g., Z-curve, Hilbert) imposes a total order on points in a multidimensional space. Using this total order, spatial point objects are to be indexed using a classical index structure such as a B+ tree. Spatial queries can be transformed to range queries on an underlying B+ tree using the space filling curve.

A grid file is a spatial index structure for spatial points. Each dimension is partitioned independently. The partition points are stored in dimension vectors, which imposes a grid structure on the space. A grid directory stores pointers to physical pages storing relevant records.

R-trees are balanced search trees with rectangular search keys. Leaves contain the identifiers and minimum bounding rectangles of spatial objects. Intermediate nodes contain addresses and minimum bounding rectangle for data in children nodes. The R+ tree and R* tree provide performance optimization on the R-tree.

An R-link tree provides an efficient locking protocol for concurrent access to an R-tree index structure. A join-index can be used to speed up spatial joins. TR* trees are used to index edges and nodes within an extended spatial object (e.g., polygons).

BIBLIOGRAPHIC NOTES

4.1.5 For further discussion on the clustering property of the Hilbert Space-Filling Curve, see [Leutenegger and Lopez, 2000]. For spatial clustering, see [Brinkhoff and Kriegel, 1994; Faloutsos and Roseman, 1989].

4.2 A detailed study of spatial indexing is available in [Samet, 1990]. An overview is provided in [Gaede and Gunther, 1998]. [den Bercken et al., 1997] discuss the bulk loading operation, which creates an initial multidimensional index structure for a presumably very large data set. For the implementation of an index type to support medium-dimensionality data in a commercial product, see [Kanth et al., 1999].

4.2.2 The Z-order and the R-tree indexing methods have diffused into commercial products. The R-tree was introduced in [Guttman, 1984]. The Z-order was rediscovered in the database community by [Orenstein and Manola, 1988].

4.2.3 Analytical cost models for R-trees can be found in [Faloutsos and Sellis, 1987; Kamel and Faloutsos, 1993; Pagel et al., 1993b]. Effects of buffering on the performance of R-trees were introduced in [Leutenegger and Lopez, 2000; Theodoridis et al., 2000a].

4.3.2 Concurrency control in the context of spatial databases is still an open area. Our discussion follows [Kornacker and Banks, 1995]. [Chakrabarti and Mehrotra, 1999] discuss the concurrency control problem in multidimensional access methods.

4.3.3 The join-index has wide applicability in the rapidly emerging area of data warehousing. Our discussion is derived from the work of [Shekhar et al., 1999b].

EXERCISES

1. For the set of leaf and intermediate nodes in Figure 4.24, draw the corresponding R-tree structure, and list the nodes searched by the dashed query rectangle. First level nodes are 1 and 2. Second level nodes are A, B, C, D and E. Leaves include a, b, ..., k.
2. Find the z-value and Hilbert curve for the pixels (01, 10) and (11, 11) in Figure 4.9.
3. Large spatial objects (e.g., large polygons or LineStrings) pose a challenge for many spatial indices. One needs to either duplicate pointers to these objects across multiple nodes of an index or decompose the large objects into smaller fragments across many index-nodes. The former leads to a search down multiple paths in the index and duplicate elimination postprocessing, whereas the latter leads to additional postprocessing to merge fragments to reconstruct the object.
   (a) How do R-trees and grid files deal with large objects?
   (b) A recent approach groups extended spatial objects by their sizes, and indexes each group independently. What are the strengths and weaknesses of this scheme?
4. Compare and contrast the following terms:
   (a) Clustering versus indexing
   (b) R-trees versus Grid File
   (c) Hilbert curve versus Z-order
   (d) Primary index versus secondary index
5. Which of the following properties are true for R-trees, grid files, and B-trees with Z-order?
   (a) *Balance* (i.e., distance(root/directory, data-page pointer) is the same for all data-page pointers).
   (b) *Fixed depth* (i.e., distance(root/directory, data-page pointer) is a constant that is predefined).

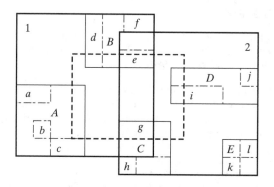

FIGURE 4.24. Exercise 1.

(c) *Nonoverlapping:* different nodes at a given level in an index are mutually disjoint.

(d) *50 percent utilization per node:* no node in an index is half empty.

6. (a) Draw a final grid file structure generated by inserting the following sequence of points. Assume each disk page can hold at most three records.

$$(0, 0), (0, 1), (1, 1), (1, 0), (0, 2), (1, 2), (2, 2), (2, 1), (2, 0)$$

Clearly show the dimension vector, directory grids, and data page.

(b) Repeat Exercise 6 with the R-tree. Assume an interval index node can hold at most three pointers to other index nodes. A leaf index node can hold pointers to three data records.

7. Draw a final grid file structures generated by inserting records with the following sequence of point-keys: (0,0) (1,1) (2,2) (3,3) (4,4) (5,5) (5,1) (5,2) (5,3) (5,4) (5,0). Assume each disk page can hold at most two records. Clearly show the dimension vectors, directory grids, and data pages. Multiple solutions are possible. You are expected to show a valid solution.

8. Repeat the above question with B-tree with Z-order. Assume an index node can hold at most three pointers to other index nodes. A leaf index node can hold pointers to at most two data records.

9. Repeat the above question with R-tree. Assume an index node can hold at most three pointers to other index nodes. A leaf index node can hold pointers to at most two data records.

10. Consider a set of rectangles whose left-bottom corners are located at the set of points given in the previous question. Assume that each rectangle has a length of three units and width of two units. Draw two possible R-trees. Assume an index node can hold at most three pointers to other index nodes. A leaf index node can hold pointers to at most two data records.

11. Compute the Hilbert function for a 4×4 grid shown in Figure 4.9 with the origin changed to bottom-left corner.

12. What is a R-link tree? What is it used for in spatial databases.

13. Draw an R-link tree for the data set shown in Figure 4.15.

14. What is a join-index? List a few applications where join-index may be useful.

15. What is TR* tree? Compare and contrast it with R-trees.

16. Review the grid file in Figure 4.14. Which directory entries are accessed for
    (a) a point query for (30,30),
    (b) a range query for x [10,30] and y [10,30].
    (c) a query to retrieve nearest neighbor of point (30,30).

17. Review the R-tree in Figure 4.16. Which nodes are accessed for
    (a) a point query for a point inside rectangle 5.
    (b) a range query for minimal orthogonal rectangle including rectangles 3 and 12.

18. Review the R+ tree in Figure 4.17. Which nodes are accessed for the queries listed in Exercise 4.17?

19. Compute the Z-order for the pixels contained in object B in Figure 4.7. Compare the computational cost of range searches for objects B and C in Figure 4.7 using Z-ordered storage.

20. Compute Hilbert values for pixels in object A, B, and C in Figure 4.7. Compare the computational cost of range searches for objects B and C using Hilbert curve ordered storage.

C H A P T E R   5

Query Processing and Optimization

Queries to a database are expressed in a high-level, declarative language such as SQL. It is the responsibility of the database software to map the query into a sequence of operations supported by spatial indexes and storage structures. The main goal is to process a query accurately and in the minimum amount of time possible. In this chapter, we focus on techniques that are used to process and optimize queries in the context of spatial databases. In relational databases, most queries are composed from a fixed set of basic operations. These basic relational operations form the building blocks for the composition of all complex queries. Query processing and optimization are thus divided into two steps: (1) design and fine-tune algorithms for each of the basic relational operators, and (2) map high-level queries into a composition of these basic relational operators and optimize, using information from the first step. The same paradigm can be applied in the spatial database context, with a few important differences. First, the application domain of spatial databases is diverse, and there is no consensus set of building blocks (i.e. spatial operations) which can cover all cases. What we have agreed upon are classes of spatial operations. Second, algorithms for spatial operations are both CPU and I/O intensive. This makes the design process more complex than in traditional databases, where common assumptions are that the I/O cost will dominate CPU cost and that a good algorithm is one which minimizes the number of disk accesses.

The chapter is organized as follows. In Section 5.1 we describe design and fine-tuning algorithms for important spatial operators. In Section 5.2 we consider the general problem of query optimization and show how queries composed of both spatial and non-spatial predicates can be optimized. In Section 5.3 we look into some of the quantitative analysis techniques for spatial index structures. In Sections 5.4 and 5.5, we look into distributed and parallel spatial database systems, respectively.

5.1   EVALUATION OF SPATIAL OPERATIONS

5.1.1   Overview

From a query-processing perspective, at least three major issues characterize the differ-ences between spatial and relational databases [Brinkhoff et al., 1993]:

1. Unlike relational databases, spatial databases have no fixed set of operators that serve as building blocks for query evaluation.
2. Spatial databases deal with extremely large volumes of complex objects. These objects have spatial extensions and cannot be naturally sorted in a one-dimensional array.
3. Computationally expensive algorithms are required to test for spatial predicates, and the assumption that I/O costs dominate processing costs in the CPU is no longer valid.

5.1.2   Spatial Operations

Spatial operations can be classified into four groups [Gaede and Gunther, 1998]:

1. *Update operations:* Standard database operations such as modify, create, and so on.
2. *Selection operations:* These can be of two kinds/types:

   (a) *Point query* (PQ): Given a query point P, find all spatial objects O that contain it:
   $$PQ(p) = \{O | p \in O.G \neq \emptyset\}$$
   where $O.G$ is the geometry of object O.

   For example, consider the following query: "Find all river flood-plains which contain the `SHRINE`." `SHRINE` is a constant of the point type.

   (b) *Range or regional query* (RQ): Given a query polygon P, find all spatial objects O which intersect P. When the query polygon is a rectangle, this query is called a window query. These queries are sometimes also referred to as range queries.

   $$RQ(P) = \{O | O.G \cap P.G \neq \emptyset\}$$

   An example query could be, "Retrieve all forest-stands which overlap the flood-plain of `Nile`."

3. *Spatial join*: Like the join operator in relational databases, the spatial join is one of the more important operators. When two tables R and S are joined on a spatial predicate θ, the join is called a spatial join. A variant of the spatial join and an important operator in GIS is the *map overlay*. This operation combines two sets of spatial objects to form a new set. The "boundaries" of a set of these new objects are determined by the nonspatial attributes assigned by the overlay operation. For example, if the operation assigns the same value of a nonspatial attribute to two neighboring objects, then the objects are "merged."

   $$R \bowtie_\theta S = \{(o, o' | o \in R, o' \in S, \theta(o.G, o'.G)\}$$

Some examples of the predicate θ follow:

- `intersect`
- `contains`
- `is_enclosed_by`
- `distance`
- `northwest`
- `adjacent`
- `meets`
- `overlap`

An example of a spatial join is, "Find all forest-stands and river flood-plains which overlap." In SQL, this query will be represented as follows:

```
SELECT   FS.name, FP.name
FROM     Forest_Stand FS, Floodi_Plain FP
WHERE    overlap(FS.G, FP.G)
```

4. *Spatial aggregate*: An example of a spatial aggregate is, "Find the river closest to a campground." Spatial aggregates are usually variants of the *nearest neighbor* search problem: Given an object O', find all objects o having a minimum distance from o'.

$$NNQ(o') = \{o | \forall o'' : dist(o'.G, o.G) \leq dist(o'.G, o''.G)\}$$

5.1.3 Two-Step Query Processing of Object Operations

Spatial query processing involves complex data types, for example, a lake boundary might need a thousand vertices for exact representation. Spatial operations typically follow a two-step algorithm as shown in Figure 5.1 to efficiently process these large objects:

1. `Filter step`: In this step, the spatial objects are represented by simpler approximations such as the MBR. For example, consider the following point query: "Find all rivers whose flood-plains overlap the `SHRINE`." In SQL this will be

```
SELECT   River.Name
FROM     River
WHERE    overlap(River.Flood-plain, :SHRINE)
```

We denote user defined parameters by prepending them with a :, for example, :SHRINE. Now if we approximate the floodplains of all rivers with MBRs, then determining whether the point is in an MBR is less expensive than to check if a point is in an irregular polygon, that is, the exact shape of the floodplain. The answer from this approximate test is a superset of the real answer set. This superset is sometimes called the `candidate` set. Even the spatial predicate may be replaced by an approximation to simplify a query optimizer. For example, `touch(River.Flood-plain, :SHRINE)` may be replaced by `overlap(MBR(River.Flood-plain, :SHRINE), MBR(:SHRINE))` in the filter step. Many spatial operators, for example, `inside`,

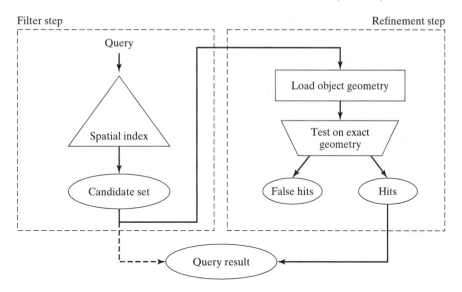

FIGURE 5.1. Multistep processing [Brinkhoff et al., 1994].

north-of, buffer can be approximated using the overlap relationship among corresponding MBRs. Such a transformation guarantees that the no tuple from the final answer using exact geometry is eliminated in the filter step.

2. Refinement step: Here, the exact geometry of each element from the candidate set and the exact spatial predicate are examined. This usually requires the use of a CPU-intensive algorithm. This step may sometimes be processed outside the spatial database in an application program such as GIS, using the candidate set produced by the spatial database in the filter step.

5.1.4   Techniques for Spatial Selection

We now describe the algorithms used for spatial selection. As shown earlier, there are two broad categories of spatial selection: point and range. Consider this selection query:

```
SELECT   F.Name
FROM     Forest-Stand F
WHERE    intersects(F.Geometry, :WINDOW)
```

In this query, we want to identify the names of all forest stands that intersect a given window. This is an example of a range (regional) query.

Here is an example of a point query:

```
SELECT   F.Name
FROM     Forest-Stand F
WHERE    within(:POINT, F.Geometry)
```

This query searches for the forest stand in which :POINT resides. What are the alternative ways of processing these queries? The answer depends on how the file containing the relation(s) being queried is organized. Three alternatives are described below.

Unsorted Data and No Index

In this situation, the only option is to use brute force to scan the whole file and test each record for the predicate. Depending on the size of the relation it might be useful to have a two-step (*filter* and *refine*) process to evaluate the predicate *intersects*. If the forest stand is approximated by its MBR, then the approximation step for the range query would correspond to checking for a rectangle-rectangle intersection. This process is inexpensive compared with the cost of processing the entire object without filtering. The cost of the scan is $O(n)$, where n is the number of pages contained in the relation Forest-Stand. For the point query, the filter step will involve a point-in-rectangle operation. If there is at most one forest stand containing the :POINT, on the average, only half the number of pages will need to be accessed.

Spatial Indexing

We can use spatial indexing methods to access geometric data. A popular choice is the R-tree family of methods to index the MBRs of the spatial attributes of a relation. Thus, for a small overhead, scanning the whole file can be avoided (see Section 4.2.2). Point search can often be processed in $O(\log n)$ time using a search tree. The cost of a query that uses an index tree depends on many factors, including the distribution of the data rectangles, the size of the query window, the height of the tree, and the packing algorithm used to construct the nodes of the index tree. One drawback with R-tree is that the MBRs of branches are allowed to overlap, which can lead to searches along different branches of the index tree. The R+ tree, a variant of the R-tree, avoids overlapping of the internal nodes. The main problem with the R+ tree is the possibility that the data rectangles will be replicated across internal nodes. This might lead to an increase in both search time and node overflow.

Hashing with Space-Filling Curves

Though there is no natural order in multidimensional spaces, there exist one-to-one continuous mappings that map points of multidimensional space into one-dimensional space. This way we can indirectly impose order on higher-dimensional spaces. Common examples of space-filling curves are row-order Peano and Hilbert curves, but none of these has the property that *all* records that are "locationally close" in the multidimensional space are close in the range space of the mapping. Once the data has been "ordered" by a space-filling curve, a B-tree [Orenstein, 1986] index can be imposed on the ordered entries to enhance the search (see Section 4.1). This scenario is the most natural in the case of point data, and the cost of a point query will be $O(log_B(n))$, where B is the blocking factor. For a range query, the cost is on the order of $O(log_B(n)) + \dfrac{\text{query-size}}{\text{clustering-efficiency}}$. Though the Z-order is not as efficient as other spatial access methods such as R-tree, it is one of the few spatial data structures that has found its way into commercial database systems.

5.1.5   General Spatial Selection

In the most general case, a selection condition can be a combination of several "primitive" selection conditions. In traditional databases, general conditions are first expressed in *conjunctive normal form (CNF)*, and then a combination of hashing and index trees is used to accelerate query processing. For general spatial selections, the order in which the individual conditions in CNF is processed is important because different spatial conditions can have very different processing costs. This is not the case in traditional databases, where the standard assumption is that, on average, the cost of processing all nonspatial condition is the same. Hellerstein [Hellerstein and Stonebraker, 1993] has proposed a new measure, *rank*, that takes into account both the selectivity and cost of the spatial functions to order the predicates:

$$\text{Rank} = \frac{\text{selectivity} - 1}{\text{differential cost}},$$

where

$$\text{selectivity}(p) = \frac{\text{cardinality}(\text{output}(p))}{\text{cardinality}(\text{input}(p))}$$

and the differential cost is the per-tuple cost of a predicate. Though the notion of differential cost might seem unnatural for predicates, because they take relations as inputs, it is more natural for user-defined methods. Furthermore, the key property of the differential cost is that it remains constant throughout the life of the function and can be, along with selectivity, stored in the system catalog. The main result is that predicates should be applied in ascending order of rank.

5.1.6   Algorithms for Spatial-Join Operations

The join operation is the principal method of combining two relations. Conceptually a join is defined as a cross-product followed by a selection condition. In practice, this viewpoint can be very expensive because it involves computing the cross-product before applying the selection criterion. This is especially true for spatial databases. Many ingenious algorithms have been proposed to preempt the need to perform the cross-product. We only concentrate on the filter step of the two-step *filter-refine* paradigm. In this way, the spatial overlap operation will be reduced to a rectangle-rectangle intersection, the cost of which is relatively modest compared with the I/O cost of retrieving pages from secondary memory for processing. Consider the following join query in SQL:

```
SELECT  *
FROM    Forest-Stand F, River R
WHERE   overlap(F.Geometry, R.Flood-plain)
```

Assume that the Forest-Stand relation, F, occupies M pages with p_F tuples in each page, and that the River relation, R, occupies N pages with p_R tuples in each page. Furthermore, assume that the average time taken to perform the overlap function is T for a pair of objects.

Nested Loop

In this algorithm, all possible pairs of the tuples of F and R are enumerated and tested against each other with the overlap function.

```
forall tuple f ∈ F
        forall tuple r ∈ R
```

```
            if overlap(F.Geom, R.Flood-Plain)
            then add < f, r > to result
```

Here we scan the outer relation F, and for each tuple in F, we scan the entire relation R. Thus the I/O cost is $M + M = N$, assuming 3 memory buffers and ignoring the cost of writing the results. This cost can be prohibitive, and thus the nested loop algorithm, as outlined earlier, is rarely used. One modification is to make efficient use of the available buffer pages: If B buffer pages are available, then first transfer $B - 2$ pages of the outer relation F, followed by a scan of the inner relation into one of the two remaining buffers. We use the last buffer page to write tuples $< f, r >$, where f belongs to $\{F_1, \ldots, F_{B-2}\}$ and $r \in$ R-page. The cost of the I/O after using the buffer goes down dramatically: $M + N * \lceil \frac{M}{B-2} \rceil$.

Nested Loop with Index
If an index is available on one of the relations, then we can take advantage of that by using the indexed relation in the inner loop. Then we do not have to scan the inner relation completely in each iteration. Instead a range query can be performed, using the index on the inner relation to retrieve the candidate tuple which many match the main memory resident tuples of the outer relation.

Tree Matching [Brinkhoff et al., 1993]

If spatial indices (e.g., R-trees) are available on both relations, the tree-matching strategy becomes applicable. Let us review the R-tree index, and use it to illustrate this strategy. The nodes of the tree contain entries in the form $(ref, rect)$, where ref is the pointer to the child node. The entry $rect$ is the MBR of the entries of a child node or the MBR of the spatial object, depending on whether the node is nonleaf or leaf, respectively. The pages in secondary memory that correspond to the nonleaf nodes are called directory pages, and the pages corresponding to the actual data are called data pages.

Now consider two sets of rectangles, R_1 and R_2, which represent two spatial relations whose spatial objects have been indexed using an R-tree. We want to use the R-tree structure to design an algorithm for the spatial-join operation. The spatial predicate is the intersection of the two rectangles: (r_1, r_2) belong to the join relation if

$$rect(r_1) \cap rect(r_2) \neq \emptyset.$$

If I_{R_1} and I_{R_2} are the numbers of pages occupied by the nodes of the index tree for relations R and S, then a lower bound on the I/O cost is $I_{R_1} + I_{R_2}$.

The algorithm is based on the observation that the rectangles of the nonleaf nodes contain the MBRs of all the rectangles appearing in the child nodes. Thus, if two directory entries, $Er1$ and $Er2$, are disjoint, then so must be all the data rectangles in the subsequent subtrees. If the directory entries do intersect, then data rectangles may intersect somewhere down the subtree.

The basic algorithm follows:

```
SJ(R1, R2:R_NODE);
01      BEGIN
02              FOR (all Er2 in R2) DO
```

```
03                   FOR (all Er1 in R1) DO
04                       IF (overlap(Er1.rect, Er2.rect)) THEN
05                           IF (R1 and R2 are leaf pages) THEN
06                               output(Er1.oid, Er2.oid)
07                           ELSE IF (R1 is a leaf page) THEN
08                               ReadPage(Er2.ptr);
09                               SJ(Er1.ptr, Er2.ptr)
10                           ELSE IF (R2 is a leaf page) THEN
11                               ReadPage(Er1.ptr);
12                               SJ(Er1.ptr, Er2.ptr)
13                           ELSE
14                               ReadPage(Er1.ptr), ReadPage(Er2.ptr);
15                               SJ(Er1.ptr,Er2.ptr)
16                           END-IF
17                       END-IF
18                   END-FOR
19               END-FOR;
20       END.
```

The cost of the join algorithm can be determined from the cost of the spatial range queries, if we take one relation as the source of the data rectangles and the other relation as the source of the query windows. This idea has been used [Aref and Samet, 1994] to derive analytical formulas for spatial-join queries. An overview of the cost analysis for range and join queries appears in the next section.

Partition-Based Spatial Merge Join

[Patel and Dewitt, 1996] have proposed a new method called the partition-based spatial-merge join. We describe the filter step of the algorithm:

- `Filter Step`: Given two relations F and R, the step can be described as follows:

  1. For each tuple in F and R, form the *key-pointer* tuple consisting of the unique OID of the tuple and the MBR of the spatial attribute. Call the new relations F^{kp} and R^{kp}.
  2. If both relations F^{kp} and R^{kp} fit in main memory, then the join relation can be processed using a plane-sweep algorithm.
  3. If the relations are too large to fit in main memory, we partition both the relations into P parts. $F_1^{kp}, \ldots, F_p^{kp}$ and $R_1^{kp}, \ldots, R_p^{kp}$.

- `Partition`: The partition must satisfy two constraints:

  1. For each F_i^{kp}, the overlapping element in R^{kp} lies in R_i^{kp}.
  2. Both F_i^{kp} and R_i^{kp} lie in main memory.

Other strategies (e.g., external plane-sweep or join-index based) for spatial join are available. In fact, design and comparison of strategies for spatial join continue to be an active area of research. We have presented a few representative strategies and refer the interested reader to the technical literature for more details.

5.1.7 Strategies for Spatial Aggregate Operation: Nearest Neighbor

Nearest neighbor queries are common in many applications. For example, a book-order placed on an e-commerce Web site may be assigned to the nearest distribution center. A two-pass algorithm for this problem was discussed at the end of Section 4.1. The first pass retrieves the data page D containing query object QO to determine d, minimum distance between any object in D to QO. The second pass is a range query to retrieve objects within distance d of QO for determination of the nearest neighbor. This approach reuses algorithms for spatial selection, e.g., point query and range query. Processing the nearest neighbor query using a single pass requires different algorithms than those for spatial selection. We present a representative branch and bound algorithm originally proposed in [Roussopoulos et al., 1995]. This approach uses a couple of distance measures, search pruning criteria, and a search algorithm.

Distance measures include min-distance (Point P, Rectangle R) and min-max-distance (P, R). Min-distance (P, R) is zero if P is inside R or on boundary of R. If P is outside R, then min-distance (P, R) is the Euclidean distance between P and any edge of R. It represents the lower bound on the distance of any object inside R from P. Min-max-distance (P, R) is the distance of P from the farthest point on any face of the R containing vertex V, where V is the nearest vertex of R from point P. The construction of an R-tree guarantees that there is an object O inside rectangle R in the R-tree such that distance $(O, P) \leq$ Min-max-distance (P, R). Min-distance (P, R) provides an optimistic ordering of subtrees in nearest neighbor search, while min-max-distance (P, R) provides a somewhat pessimistic ordering.

Search pruning strategies can be based on these measures, as well. For example, an MBR M can be eliminated if there is another MBR M' such that with min-distance $(P, M) >$ min-max-distance (P, M'). An MBR M can also be eliminated if there is an object O such that distance $(P, O) <$ min-distance (P, M). Finally an object O can be eliminated if there is an MBR M such that distance $(P, O) >$ min-max-distance (P, M).

The search algorithm for nearest neighbor starts with the root node of the R-tree and traverses the tree. For example, a breadth first traversal of the R-tree will visit MBRs of the children of the interior nodes of current node for pruning using the above rules. The remaining children will be expanded in the next iteration. The final iteration will have a set of leaf nodes (database object level) from the MBRs that survive level-wise pruning. The algorithm will need to compute the distance of each leaf from query point P to determine the nearest neighbor. Alternatively a depth-first traversal or other traversal of the R-tree may be used. This algorithm can be extended to find K-nearest neighbors by slight modification of the pruning rules to retain the K best candidates. Lastly, pruning criteria is applicable to their rectangle based indexing methods such as Grid Files, Quad-tree, and so forth.

5.2 QUERY OPTIMIZATION

As noted in Chapter 3, queries are usually expressed in a high-level declarative language such as SQL. This means that only the answer set is specified and that the strategy to retrieve the result is left to the database. The metric for the strategy, or the evaluation plan, is the time required to execute the query. In traditional databases, the metric is largely a function of the I/O cost because the datatypes available and the functions that operate on these datatypes are relatively simple to compute. The situation is different for spatial databases, which involve complex data types and CPU-intensive functions. Thus the task of selecting an optimal strategy is more involved for spatial databases than for traditional databases.

The *query optimizer*, a module in the database software, generates different evaluation plans and determines the appropriate execution strategy. The query optimizer draws information from the systems catalog and combines it with certain heuristics and techniques from dynamic programming to arrive at a suitable strategy (see Figure 5.2). The query optimizer rarely, if ever, executes the very best plan. This is due to the computational complexity of the overhead for optimization [Selinger et al., 1979]. The idea is to avoid the worst plans and to select a good one. The procedures undertaken by the query optimizer can be divided into two distinct parts: *logical transformation* and *dynamic programming* [Adam and Gangopadhyay, 1997].

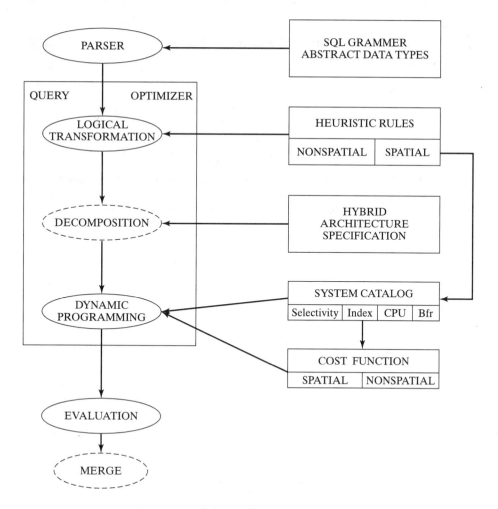

FIGURE 5.2. Schema for a query optimizer.

5.2.1 Logical Transformation

Parsing

Before the query optimizer can operate on the query, the high-level declarative statement must be scanned through a parser. The parser checks the syntax and transforms the statement into a query tree. In traditional databases, the datatypes and functions are fixed, and the parser is relatively simple. Spatial databases are extensible database systems and have provisions for user-defined types and methods. Therefore, compared with traditional databases, the parser for spatial databases has to be considerably more sophisticated to identify and manage user-defined datatypes and map them into syntactically correct query trees. In the query tree, the leaf nodes correspond to the relations involved and the internal nodes to the basic operations that constitute the query. Recall that the basic operations include SELECT, PROJECT, JOIN and other set operations. Query processing starts at the leaf nodes and proceeds up the tree until the operation at the root node has been performed. Consider the following query from Chapter 3:

"Find all lakes which have an area greater than 20 sq. km. and are within 50 km. from the campground."

```
SELECT   L.Name
FROM     Lake L, Facilities Fa
WHERE    Area(L.Geometry) > 20 AND
         Fa.Name = 'campground' AND
         Distance(Fa.Geometry, L.Geometry) < 50
```

Here we are assuming that the area is not precomputed and that it is not stored in the relation. The area is a spatial function whose value is computed every time it is invoked. The query tree generated by the above query is shown in Figure 5.3.

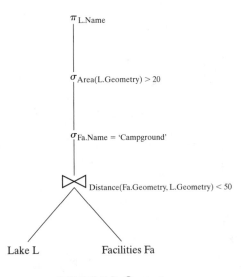

FIGURE 5.3. Query tree.

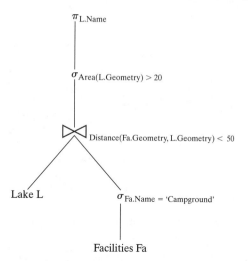

FIGURE 5.4. Pushing down: select operation.

Logical Transformation

If the query tree of Figure 5.3 is used as a basis for generating an execution plan, then the strategy may be poor. The join operation is expensive, and its cost is bounded by the product of the size of the relations involved. We want to reduce the size of the relations involved in the join operation. One option (Figure 5.4) is to push down the nonspatial select operation

```
Fa.Name = 'Campground'.
```

In the *logical transformation* step, the query tree generated by the parser is mapped onto equivalent query trees. This equivalence is the result of a formal set of rules inherited from relational algebra. After the equivalent trees are enumerated, we can apply certain heuristics to filter out obvious noncandidates for the final execution strategy. We just illustrated an example of one heuristic when we pushed down the nonspatial select operation toward the leaves of the tree. The logical transformation is analogous to the filter step in query processing. It is a fast way of eliminating query trees that are usually not optimal. Though certain clear-cut heuristics apply for traditional databases, the rules for spatial databases can be ambiguous. For example, consider what would happen if we pushed the other spatial select operation down the tree (see Figure 5.5):

```
Area(L.Geometry) > 20
```

It would appear that a spatial join should be executed after the spatial predicate. But now there are two user-defined functions, `Area` and `Distance`, whose execution costs must be ranked relative to each other. If the `Area` function is orders of magnitude more CPU-intensive than the `Distance` function, then it might not be advisable to perform the spatial selection before the join. Thus the main heuristic rule for relational databases follows: "Apply select and project before the join and binary operations" are no longer unconditional. All we can say is that the nonspatial select and project operators should be

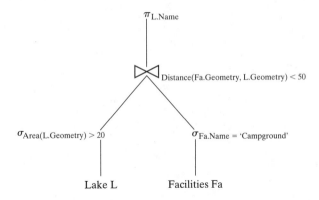

FIGURE 5.5. Pushing down selections is not always helpful.

pushed down toward the leaves of the query tree. Are there any other heuristics that might apply to expensive spatial functions? [Hellerstein and Stonebraker, 1993] has introduced the notion of the *rank* of predicate p to grade different predicates:

$$\text{Rank} = \frac{\text{selectivity} - 1}{\text{differential cost}},$$

where

$$\text{selectivity}(p) = \frac{\text{cardinality(output}(p))}{\text{cardinality(input}(p))}$$

The differential cost is the per-tuple cost of a predicate. Though the notion of differential cost might seem unnatural for predicates, because they take relations as inputs, it is more natural for user-defined methods. Furthermore, the key property of the differential cost is that it remains constant throughout the life of the function and can be, along with selectivity, stored in the system catalog. The main result is that predicates should be applied in ascending order of rank.

The space of alternative plans is generated by certain well-defined rules within relational algebra. These rules are defined from the algebraic notions of *commutativity*, *associativity*, and *distributivity*. We now describe the rules for each of the operations select, project, and join [Ramakrishnan, 1998]. Equivalence rules for a combination of these operators are listed later.

Selections

There are two important equivalences for the `Selection` operator:

1. $\sigma_{c_1 \wedge c_2 \wedge \ldots c_n}(R) \equiv \sigma_{c_1}(\sigma_{c_2}(\ldots(\sigma_{c_n}(R))\ldots))$

This rule allows us to combine several selections into one selection. For spatial query processing, where selection conditions could be a combination of spatial and nonspatial predicates, it would be worthwhile to push all of the nonspatial conditions toward the right (i.e., to perform all of the nonspatial selections before the spatial selections).

2. $\sigma_{c_1}(\sigma_{c_2}(R)) \equiv \sigma_{c_2}(\sigma_{c_1}(R))$

Here the rule specifies that selection conditions can be tested in any order. Again, it is best to test for nonspatial conditions before spatial conditions, due to relative cost.

Projections

- If a_i's are a set of attributes such that $a_i \subset a_{i+1}$ for $i = 1 \ldots n - 1$, then

$$\pi_{a_1}(R) \equiv \pi_{a_1}(\pi_{a_2}(\ldots(\pi_{a_n}(R))\ldots))$$

Cross-Products and Joins

- The join operation is commutative.

$$R \bowtie S \equiv S \bowtie R$$

- The join operation is also associative.

$$R \bowtie (S \bowtie T) \equiv (R \bowtie S) \bowtie T$$

- The above equivalences imply that

$$(R \bowtie T) \bowtie S \equiv (T \bowtie R) \bowtie S$$

Selection, Projection, and Join

For two or more operators, some of the equivalence rules follow:

- If the selection condition involves attributes retained by the projection operator, then

$$\pi_a(\sigma_c(R)) \equiv \sigma_c(\pi_a(R))$$

- If a selection condition c involves an attribute that only appears in R and not in S, then

$$\sigma_c(R \bowtie S) \equiv \sigma_c(R) \bowtie R$$

- Projection can be computed with join:

$$\pi_a(R \bowtie S) \equiv \pi_{a_1}(R) \bowtie \pi_{a_2}(S),$$

where a_1 is a subset of a, which appears in R, and a_2 is a subset of a, which appears in S.

5.2.2   Cost-Based Optimization: Dynamic Programming

Dynamic programming is a technique to determine the optimal execution strategy from a set of execution plans. The optimal solution is derived on the basis of a cost function. Each plan is evaluated by its cost function, and whichever plan minimizes it is the optimal plan. In the dynamic programming step, we focus on each node of the query tree and enumerate the different execution strategies available to process the node. The different processing strategies for each node when combined for the whole query tree constitute the plan space. The cardinality of the plan space is usually large, and the performance within it can vary by orders of magnitude. In addition, the underlying assumptions regarding the various parameters needed by the cost function are often simplistic and sometimes even erroneous. Furthermore, the *optimization time*, the time required to select the execution plan, must be kept at a minimum. All this suggests, as we stated earlier, that our aim is to select a good plan but not necessarily the best.

At the heart of dynamic programming lies the use of the cost function to evaluate each execution strategy. The factors that a good cost function must take into account follow [Elmasri and Navathe, 2000]:

1. **Access cost:** The cost of searching for and transferring data from secondary storage
2. **Storage cost:** The cost of storing intermediate temporary relations that are produced by an execution strategy of the query
3. **Computation cost:** The CPU cost of performing in-memory operations
4. **Communication cost:** The cost of transferring information back and forth between the client and the server

Traditionally, it has been assumed that I/O costs dominate all other costs in query processing. This not true in spatial situations, and both access and computation cost must be considered. Furthermore, with the advent of the worldwide Web and Web programming languages such as Java, spatial databases might be distributed over many sites. In this case, communication costs must also be taken into account in the cost function.

Systems Catalog

The information required by the cost function to design an optimal execution strategy is maintained in the systems catalog. This information includes the size of each file, the number of records in a file, and the number of blocks over which the records are spread. There should also be information about the indexes and indexing attributes. Selectivity and the differential cost of predicates must also be included. In some instances it is useful to materialize expensive, user-defined functions and to index their values for fast retrieval. For instance, in the above example the `Area(Geometry)` function can be precomputed and the values indexed. This definitely speeds up query evaluation, and the system catalog could store information for these "eager" functions.

Cost Functions

The cost functions used in relational databases [Stonebraker and Moore, 1997] are a variation of

$$\text{cost} = \text{Exp(records-examined)} + K^*\text{Exp(pages-read)},$$

where Exp (records-examined) is the expected number of records read and thus is a measure of CPU time and Exp (pages-read) is the expected number of pages read from storage and is a measure of I/O time. The K multiplier is a measure of how important CPU resources are relative to I/O resources.

5.3   ANALYSIS OF SPATIAL INDEX STRUCTURES

This section provides a quantitative analysis of spatial index structures, which are an integral part of SDBMS. The main characterization is to calculate the expected number of disk accesses that are required to perform a spatial query. Though our main focus is on the range query, we also derive estimates for the spatial-join (overlap) operation.

Spatial index structures map spatial objects onto pages of secondary memory called *buckets*. The mapping is based on proximity, that is, an attempt is made to map objects that are "locationally close" to the same page. Of course this is not always possible, because the size of the bucket is fixed (e.g., 8KB). Objects are either point type or have a spatial extent. It is conventional to represent a nonpoint object by its MBR. The physical space corresponding to a bucket is called the *bucket region*. Bucket regions of point data typically partition the data space, whereas those of nonpoint data may overlap and not cover the entire space.

We begin by assuming that the space dimension is $d = 2$ and that address space has been normalized to a unit square. Let $B = \{B_1, \ldots, B_m\}$ be the set of buckets and let $R(B) = \{R(B_1), \ldots, R(B_m)\}$ be the corresponding set of disjoint bucket regions. Furthermore for a given query object Q, let the following hold:

- $P_i(Q)$ is the probability that Q intersects $R(B_i)$.

- $P(Q, j)$ is the probability that Q intersects *exactly* j bucket regions.

Then the expected number, $E(Q)$, of buckets that Q will intersect is

$$E(Q) = \sum_{j=0}^{m} j \cdot P(Q, j)$$

It is not difficult to show [Pagel et al., 1993a] that

$$E(Q) = \sum_{j=0}^{m} j \cdot P(Q, j) = \sum_{i=1}^{m} P_i(Q)$$

Point Query

If the point query Q is equally likely to appear at any point in the address space of unit area, then $P_i(Q)$ is equal to the area of $R(B_i)$. If $R(B_i)$ is a rectangle with sides $(n_{i,1}, n_{i,2})$, then

$$E(Q) = \sum_{i=1}^{m} n_{i,1} * n_{i,2}$$

Range Query

Here we begin by considering the case in single dimension, i.e., $d = 1$. That is, we assume, for the moment, that the query object Q is the interval (q_l, q_r) and that the bucket region $R(B_i)$ is the interval $(d_{i,l}, d_{i,r})$. Then we have the following:

LEMMA 1. Given that $(q_r - q_l) + (d_{i,r} - d_{i,l}) < 1$, then

$$P_i(Q) = (q_r - q_l) + (d_{i,r} - d_{i,l})$$

Proof.

$$
\begin{aligned}
P_i(Q) &= \text{Prob}\{q_l \in (d_{i,l}, d_{i,r})\} + \text{Prob}\{(q_l \ni (d_{i,l}, d_{i,r})) \wedge (q_r \in (d_{i,l}, d_{i,r}))\} \\
&= (d_{i,r} - d_{i,l}) + \text{Prob}\{q_l \in (d_{i,l} - (q_r - q_l), d_{i,l}))\} \\
&= (d_{i,r} - d_{i,l}) + d_{i,l} - (d_{i,l} - (q_r - q_l)) \\
&= (q_r - q_l) + (d_{i,r} - d_{i,l})
\end{aligned}
$$

Thus the expected number of disk accesses for a one-dimensional range query is

$$
E(Q) = \sum_{i=1}^{m}(d_{i,r} - d_{i,l}) + m * (q_r - q_l)
$$

From here it is easy to extrapolate to the general case. For a range $Q(q_1 \times q_2)$ on the bucket regions $n_{i,1} \times n_{i,2}$, the number of disk accesses is

$$
E(Q) = \sum_{i=1}^{m}\prod_{j=1}^{2}(q_j + n_{i,j})
$$

The above formula, valid for all spatial data structures, highlights the need to minimize the perimeter of the MBRs along with their area and can be a useful tool for cost estimation and query optimization. The only missing ingredient is information about the size of the MBRs, the $n'_{i,j}$s in the above formula. We now show how this information can be extracted for the R-tree family of index structures, given a *few* parameters about the data set [Theodoridis and Sellis, 1996].   □

DEFINITION. The density D of a set of m bucket regions with average size $n = (n_1, n_2)$ is the average number of bucket regions that contain a given point of the unit square. $D = D(m, n) = m \cdot n_1 * n_2$

[Theodoridis and Sellis, 1996] have shown that for a range query $Q = (q_1 \times q_2)$,

1.

$$
E(Q) = \sum_{j=1}^{h-1}\left\{ m_j \cdot \prod_{k=1}^{2}(n_{j,k} + q_k) \right\},
$$

where h is the height of the tree (the root at level $j = h$ and the leaf at level $j = 1$), m_j is the expected number of nodes at level j, and $n_{j,k}$ is the average node extent in dimension k.

2. The height of the R-tree is

$$
h = 1 + \left\lceil \log_{ac \cdot mc} \frac{m}{ac \cdot mc} \right\rceil,
$$

where ac is the average node capacity (typically 70 percent), and mc is the maximum number of entries in an R-node.

3. The number of nodes at level j is

$$m_j = \frac{m}{(ac \cdot mc)^j}$$

4. The average node extent at level j is

$$n_{j,k} = \left(\frac{D_j}{m_j}\right)^{0.5}$$

5. and D_j is the density at level j:

$$D_j = \left\{ 1 + \frac{D_{j-1}^{0.5} - 1}{(ac \cdot mc)^{0.5}} \right\}^2, \quad \text{where } D_0 = D$$

Cost Analysis of Spatial Join

Below a cost function is provided [Theodoridis et al., 1998] for the tree-matching join algorithm introduced in the last section.

Given two spatial data sets of cardinality m_{R_1} and m_{R_2} with entries stored in R-tree indexes R_1 and R_2, respectively, our aim is to calculate the expected number of node accesses (NA) needed to perform a join query. In join algorithms, buffer management plays a crucial rule, so there is a difference between node accesses and disk accesses, with the inequality $DA \leq NA$ always being valid. Without getting into the details, the formula for the tree-matching join query is

$$NA\_total(R_1, R_2) = \sum_{i=1}^{h-1} \{NA(R_1, j) + NA(R_2, j)\},$$

where $NA(R_i, j), i = 1, 2$, is the number of node accesses for R_i at level j. This can be calculated from the formulas shown above for R-trees.

5.3.1 Enumeration of Alternate Plans

After the query has been formulated, the optimizer enumerates a set of plans and executes the plan with the lowest estimated cost. The algebra of relational equivalence combined with the implementation techniques available for each spatial and nonspatial operator are used to enumerate the different plans. A query plan consists of a query tree with additional annotations at each node that specify the access method to be used for the nodal operator. For example, consider the following query:

"Find the name of the forest-stands which intersect a given :WINDOW and which overlap flood-plains of rivers":

```
SELECT   F.Name
FROM     Forest-Stand F, River R
WHERE    Intersect(F.Geometry, :WINDOW) AND
         Overlap(F.Geometry, R.Flood-Plain)
```

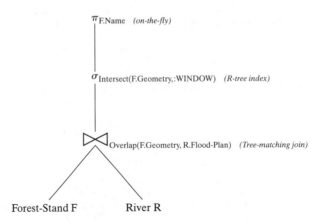

π F.Name   *(on-the-fly)*

σ Intersect(F.Geometry,:WINDOW)   *(R-tree index)*

Overlap(F.Geometry, R.Flood-Plan)   *(Tree-matching join)*

Forest-Stand F   River R

FIGURE 5.6. An execution strategy: query-evaluation plan.

A query-evaluation plan for the above query is shown in Figure 5.6. It specifies that the spatial-join operation is implemented using the tree-matching method followed by a range-query operation using the R-tree index method. The projection operation is applied *on-the-fly*, that is, without the result on the previous intermediate result being materialized. We have other choices available for the query-evaluation plan. For example, instead of the tree-matching algorithm, a block-nested loop could be used for the join operation. We could also have chosen a different, but algebraically equivalent, query tree as the basis of a query-evaluation plan. In fact, the choice of R-tree index for selection predicate is more meaningful when the selection is evaluated before the join.

5.3.2   Decomposition and Merge in Hybrid Architecture

A query in spatial database management systems based on a hybrid architecture is *decomposed* into a spatial and a nonspatial part. The subqueries are optimized in separate modules dedicated to spatial and nonspatial optimization and finally *merged* to provide the desired result. The decomposition is based on three criteria: a subquery is created for each spatial predicate, for each nonspatial predicate connected by conjunction to a spatial predicate, and finally for all nonspatial predicates.

Consider the query tree shown in Figure 5.7. There are many ways of decomposing this query tree into spatial and nonspatial parts. In Figure 5.8, we show two methods of decomposition. Each of these decompositions may give a very different performance, and another layer of software to determine an optimal decomposition has to be incorporated into the query optimizer. Following decomposition, issues regarding the scheduling of the subqueries must be addressed. For example, subqueries can be processed in sequence or in parallel, depending upon how they are coupled.

5.4   DISTRIBUTED SPATIAL DATABASE SYSTEMS

We now briefly describe a relatively new class of database management systems called distributed database management systems (DDMS). Proliferation of computer networks and increased interconnectivity is one reason for the rapid growth in DDMS. A DDMS

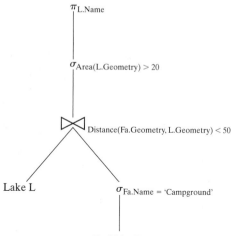

FIGURE 5.7. An execution strategy: query tree.

is a collection of physically distributed databases managed by database management software. SDBs are natural candidates for a DDMS architecture because spatial data is collected by diverse organizations, and it may be difficult to replicate the database at a centralized site.

For example, suppose an insurance company is trying to assess damage from crop diseases for farmers in a county where *all* farms have been affected by various crop diseases. Further suppose the reimbursement depends on the type of disease that has occurred. The insurance company has access to the farm database, which is maintained by the country registrar's office, and also has access to digital maps of disease spread, which are created and maintained by the Department of Agriculture. Instead of obtaining copies of data from two different government agencies, their databases could be part of a distributed database. Then the following queries could be posed in a transparent manner.

```
SELECT  F.id,  D.Name
FROM    Farms F, Disease_Map D
WHERE   Intersects(F.Boundary, D.Boundary)
```

Now how will this query be processed? The query requires that either (1) the Farms relation be shipped to the site of the Disease_Map relation, (2) the Disease_Map relation be transferred to the site of the Farm relation, or (3) the Farm and Disease_Map relations be transferred to the insurance companies database. Though the CPU and the I/O costs will not be affected by the choice of the option invoked, the transmission cost of the data can vary significantly, depending on which of the three strategies is exercised. In distributed databases there is a special join operation called the *semijoin* which can in some instances dramatically reduce the transmission cost of data transfer. Before we give an example of a semijoin operation, we briefly digress to describe the two types of distributed architectures.

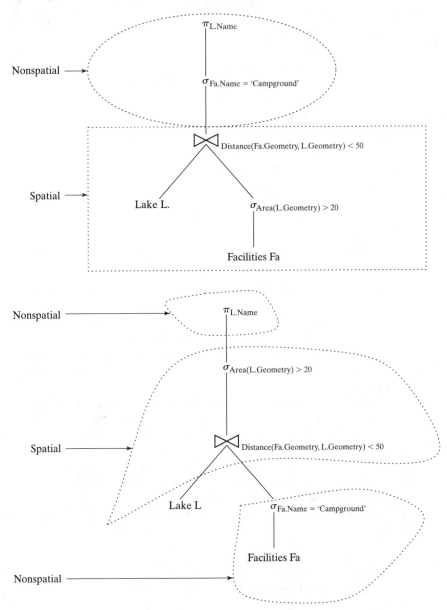

FIGURE 5.8. Two methods of decomposition.

5.4.1 Distributed DBMS Architecture

Depending on how we want to separate functionality across different DBMS-related processes, we can use two types of architecture: a client-server system or a collaborating server system.

In a client-server system, there are one or more client processes and one or more server processes, and a client process can send a query to any server process. Clients are responsible for the user interface, and servers manage the data and execute the transactions. Thus a client process could run on a personal computer and send a query to a server running on a main-frame.

A collaborating server system includes a collection of database servers, each capable of running transactions against local data, which cooperatively execute transactions spanning multiple servers.

The client-server system is more popular than the collaborating server system because of its easy implementation, full utilization of an expensive server, and historic reasons. But when a single query must span multiple servers, it requires more complex and capable clients to some degree such that its functionality could overlap with the server. The collaborating server system comes into play by eliminating the distinction between client and server.

The client-server system provides the possibility of optimizing each module and reducing the volume of transferred data, so this is becoming the most interesting system for the independent implementation of GIS applications and processing large volumes of data. The Internet, defined as a global connection among computers, provides the infrastructure on which applications reside, and the majority of current applications are client-server based.

5.4.2 The Semijoin Operation

In the semijoin operation, the transmission cost data is reduced by (1) shipping only the joining attribute and the primary key from Site 1 to Site 2 and (2) shipping only the relevant tuples from Site 2 and Site 1. For example, consider the FARM and DISEASE_MAP relations shown in Figure 5.9. Now consider the following strategy.

1. Project the FID and FARM_MBR out of relation FARM and ship it to the site of DISEASE_MAP. The number of bytes transferred is $(10 + 16)*1000 = 26,000$ bytes.

2. Join the arrival relation with the DISEASE_MAP relation on the attribute FARM_MBR and D_MBR. Assume that ten tuples of DISEASE_MAP are selected by the spatial join operation. For these ten tuples ship all the attributes to the FARM relation

FARM

FID (10 bytes)	OWNER_NAME (10 bytes)	FARM_BOUNDARY (2000 bytes)	FARM_MBR (16 bytes)

DISEASE_MAP

MAP-ID (10 bytes)	DISEASE_NAME (20 bytes)	DISEASE_BOUNDARY (2000 bytes)	D_MBR (16 bytes)

FIGURE 5.9. Two distributed relations: The FARM relation has 1,000 tuples, and the DISEASE_MAP has 100 tuples.

site. The number of bytes transferred is $(10 + 20 + 2000 + 16)*10 = 20,460$ bytes.

3. On the FARM relation site, join the DISEASE_MAP tuples with the FARM relation. Now our assumption is that *all* the farms are affected by some disease. Now ship the FID, OWNER_NAME, and DISEASE_NAME to the insurance company site. In this instance a total of $(10 + 10 + 20)*1000 = 40,000$ bytes are transferred. Readers can verify that the number of bytes transformed by semi-join are fewer than the size of each relations using Exercise 5.18.

5.4.3 Web-Based Spatial Database Systems

Until recently spatial data products including thematic (forest, urban, wetlands, snow cover, etc.) maps, remote sensing images have been confined to a few research labs and government departments. Limited public access to these data products is provided through paper maps. Ever-increasing demand and easy availability of the Internet have prompted the development of Web-based Geographic Information Systems (WGIS) for easy sharing of spatial data products over the Internet. Initial developments are focused around developing Common Gateway Interface (CGI) wrappers around stand-alone GIS software. Recent advancements in Web technologies and programming environments (e.g., Java applets, ActiveX controls) have prompted the developement of more sophisticated WGISs and applications. Figure 5.10 shows a WGIS architecture (called MapServer) developed at the University of Minnesota. This system was designed and implemented using a standard 3-tier architecture. Core system components are briefly explained below.

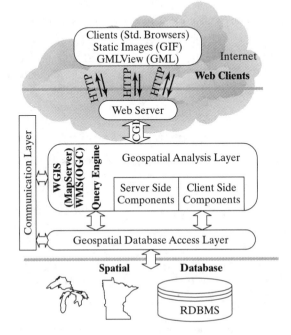

FIGURE 5.10. Web GIS architecture.

Tier 1: The Client

In general, the client is any standard Web browser. The front-end system consists of several Hyper Text Markup Language (HTML) documents which provide a description of the graphical environment for user interaction with the server. These documents consist of standard HTML tags and JavaScript elements. The browser constructs the Universal Resource Locator (URL) from user input, opens an Hyper Text Transfer Protocol (HTTP) connection with the server, and renders the results retrieved from the server.

Tier 2: The Application Server

The application server is the core component of WGIS. It consists of several layers.

Layer 1: The CGI Module

The Common Gateway Interface (CGI) module is the component of the application server that responds to HTTP requests submitted by the clients and decodes the URL into tokens (i.e., CGI variables). The parsed tokens are analyzed to identify whether the client request is for visualization of a set of spatial layers (vector, raster), or query (spatial, nonspatial), or geospatial analysis (filtering, spectral profile analysis, etc.). Based on the task to perform, the request is transferred to the appropriate subsystem. The results retrieved from the subsystem are provided to the client in a form understood by the Web browser.

Layer 2: The GeoSpatial Analysis System

Core geographic analysis functionality is implemented in this layer. It parses the input from the CGI module and sends the request for input data to the communication layer. WGIS is a distributed system, which means that the spatial data may not necessarily reside on the same server as the application server. Furthermore, the data may not even reside on any single server, but instead may be distributed across several servers.

Layer 3: The Communication System

The communication system is responsible for talking to the geospatial database servers available in the communication group. It identifies and accesses the required datasets through the geospatial database system and returns the results to the geospatial analysis system.

Tier 3: The GeoSpatial Database Access System (GSDAS)

GSDAS is based on an open architecture that is not tied down to a particular RDBMS or file format. This layer consists of custom-developed interfaces such as the generic binary band interleaved by the pixel (BIP) access module, public domain libraries to access standard image formats such as GeoTIFF, and vendor-provided libraries for accessing proprietary formats (e.g., the shapelib library for Arc/Info shape files and the "eimg" library for ERDAS IMAGINE files). For nonspatial information, also known as attribute data, the present library consists of native access to the MySQL and ORACLE RDBMS. The GSDAS recognizes known formats and invokes appropriate modules to seamlessly access these varying data sources in a single application.

Web applications are developed using a simple configuration file. This configuration file defines the relationship between CGI variables and the spatial data layers, and is used to control virtually all aspects of an application such as what layers are to be drawn, how they are rendered, and how they are queried. This generic architecture allows easy extendability and sophisticated Web application development environment. This system is natively extended to support recent standards such as the Web map server (WMS) and geographic markup language (GML).

The WMS specification standardizes the way in which maps are requested by clients and the way servers describe their data holdings. Any standard browser (or client system) can ask a WMS compliant server for one or more of the following services: map images (GetMap), service-level metadata (GetCapabilities), and optionally information about particular features (GetFeatureInfo). These requests are submitted to the server in the form of URLs. URLs are formed using a set of standard parameters (see [OGIS, 2000], e.g., width, height, bbox, srs, etc.), based on the user interaction with client system. The WMS complaint system (e.g., WGIS described earlier) will generate the appropriate data set and return it to the client for visualization/processing. In general the data sets are converted into standard image formats such GIF, TIFF, and JPEG. The GIF, TIFF, and JPEG are industry standard image file formats, whose description can be found in [Murray and van Ryper, 1999]. This static representation poses several limitations on client side processing and querying. Recently OGC proposed GML standard to alleviate these problems and promote interoperability among diverse WGISs.

GML is an eXtensible Markup Language (XML) encoding for the transport and storage of geographic information, which includes both the geometry and properties of geographic features. The initial release of GML conforms to OGC's "Simple Features" specification. GML provides support for the geometry elements corresponding to the Point, Linestring, LinearRing, Polygon, MultiPoint, MultiLineString, MultiPolygon, and GeometryCollection. It also provides the coordinate element for encoding coordinates and the box element for defining spatial extents. The major advantage of GML representation is that we can build truly interoperable distributed GISs.

5.5   PARALLEL SPATIAL DATABASE SYSTEMS

Parallelism is an important trend in DBMSs. With the rapid growth of data and the increasing use of Web browsers to access databases, a fast response time to a query is now paramount. The earlier argument about the exorbitant price and fragility of parallel systems is no longer relevant. The prices of conventional memories, processors, and disks are falling rapidly, and now dedicated personal computers (PCs) are being hooked together to simulate parallel environments. Implementing parallelism is not the same as concurrency, because in concurrency a parallel environment is simulated on a sequential machine in order to allow multiple users to access the system simultaneously.

There are two important measures to evaluate parallel systems: linear speed-up and linear scale-up. Linear speed-up implies that by doubling the hardware (from x to $2x$ processors, disks, etc.), the time to complete the tasks will be halved. Linear scale-up means that by doubling the hardware size, a job of size $2x$ can be completed in the same time required for a job of size x on a smaller system. Though the initial impression may be that linear speed-up and scale-up are obvious implications of moving from sequential to parallel systems, there are certain factors that degrade performance. Some of them follow:

- `Startup`: If a parallel operation is subdivided into thousands of small tasks, then the time to start each processor may dominate the total processing time.

- `Interference`: A slowdown can result when different processors are trying to access shared resources.

- `Skew`: When workload on the processor is unequally distributed, the efficiency of a parallel system can be effectively degraded because the processing time is related to the time of the slowest job. Later on we discuss strategies to balance the workload, and thus reduce the skew for a certain class of parallel architectures.

As in the sequential case, the requirements of parallel spatial database systems are different from those of traditional relational systems. The fundamental difference is that spatial operations are both CPU and I/O intensive. Furthermore, SDBs are accessed using a high-level, spatially enabled declarative language, such as OGC SQL, which has more basic operations than traditional SQL. Before we describe how spatial range-query and join-query operations can be implemented in parallel, we briefly digress to outline the different architectural options available for parallel database systems.

5.5.1   Hardware Architectures

In a parallel database system, there are three major types of resources: processors, main memory modules, and secondary storage (usually disks). The different architectures for parallel DBMSs are categorized by the way these resources interact. The three main architectures are shared-memory (SM), shared-disk (SD), and shared-nothing (SN), and they are shown in Figure 5.11.

The SN architecture is shown in Figure 5.11(a). Here each processor is associated with a memory and some disk units that are exclusively accessed by that processor. Together each set is called a *node*, and a network connecting these nodes is responsible for the exchange of information among them. Because it minimizes resource sharing, this architecture tends to minimize the interferences among different processors, which is the basic problem with SM and SD. As a result, its scalability is much better than for the other two architectures. Its capability of linear speed-up and scale-up has been demonstrated. But how to balance the workload among different nodes becomes a difficult task, especially with highly skewed data. Data availability could be a serious problem, because the data on the corresponding disk is unavailable when a processor fails. More intensive reorganization of the DBMS code is also required for this architecture.

The SN architecture is popular, and many commercial and prototype parallel database systems are based on this architecture. However, in SDBs, communication cost and dynamic load balancing in the design and implementation of the parallel algorithm are very important issues with large or more complex objects, or with often-skewed data distribution. Currently, the major concern is minimizing I/O cost, so much research done in this field has been based on the SD architecture, even on the simpler, single-processor, multidisk system, in order to reduce the communication cost. For example, the Paradise

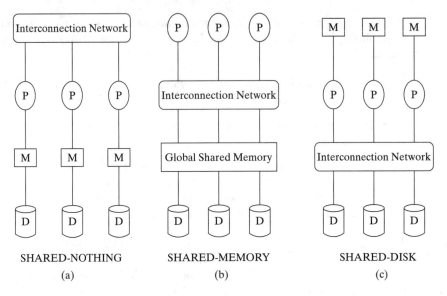

FIGURE 5.11. Parallel architecture options.

object-relational database system, which is a parallel, geospatial DBMS, uses the shared-disk architecture. Parallelizing range queries requires run-time work transfers to achieve a good load balance when spatial data objects have varying sizes and complex shapes. A disadvantage of SN architecture is replication of data across processors for *dynamic load balancing* during run-time. This replication reduces the total memory available for storing spatial data. An SM architecture facilitates these run-time work transfers, as all the data is equally accessible to all the processors.

In SM architecture, multiple CPUs are attached to an interaction network and can access a common, systemwide memory, as well as all disks in the system. Using SM reduces communication overheads and easily achieves synchronization of processors. The equal access to any portion of data for every processor makes this architecture very suitable for load balancing. However, frequent access to the SM and disks by different processors causes the network to form a bottleneck as the number of processors increases. This, together with the fact that database applications are usually data intensive, results in the poor scalability of this architecture.

In SD architecture, each processor has a private memory that can be directly accessed only by that processor, but all processors can directly access all the disks in the system. Reducing resource sharing reduces the major problem associated with the SM architecture: contention for network bandwidth. This architecture thus becomes more scalable; at the same time, it loses some of the advantages of the SM architecture memory. Data-load balancing is relatively easy, for the same reason as in the SM architecture.

5.5.2 Parallel Query Evaluation

Parallel query evaluation may be processed at different levels for database applications. At the system level, concurrent queries can be processed by different processors in parallel to increase the throughput of the system, which is called interquery parallelism.

At the next level, different operations in the same query may be processed by different processors in parallel. This procedure is called *interoperation parallelism.* At the next lower level, the same operation may be processed by different processors in parallel, and this is called *intraoperation parallelism.* Here we only discuss intraoperation parallelism.

Intraoperation parallelism can be achieved either by function partitioning or by data partitioning. Function partitioning uses specialized data structures (e.g., distributed data structures) and algorithms that may be different from their sequential counterparts. Data-partitioning techniques divide the data among different processors and independently execute the sequential algorithm on each processor. Data partitioning in turn is achieved by "declustering" the data.

Spatial Declustering

The basic problem of declustering can be stated as follows: Given a set of atomic data items, N disks, and a set of queries, divide the set of data items among the N disks, respecting the disk capacity constraints, to minimize the response time for the given set of queries. Ideally the response time should be the sequential response time divided by number of processors. Some declustering problems, for example, for the family of all range queries, are known to have no solutions to ideal response time except for a few special cases. Furthermore, declustering problems of many kind are NP-hard, and heuristic solutions are commonly used. Different declustering techniques may be effective for different query types and different query sets. For spatial data, the type of data—point, line, or polygon—being accessed can also affect the choice of the declustering method. Typically the MBR is used as a proxy for extended spatial objects.

Several heuristic methods are available for solving the declustering problem. Depending on when we choose to divide and allocate the data, the declustering methods can be classified into two types: static load balancing, which partitions and allocates the data prior to the computation process; and dynamic load balancing, which works at run time. If the data load balance is bad after static declustering, dynamic load balancing can improve it by transferring spatial objects between processors. Often both static declustering and dynamic load balancing are needed to achieve good speed-ups, due to the highly nonuniform data distribution, as well as the great variation in the size and extent of spatial data. Data replication (duplicating copies of data across multiple disks) is also often needed for dynamic load balancing, as the cost of local processing is usually less than the cost of data transfer for extended objects. We now review a common static declustering method using space-partitioning functions.

Static Declustering via Space Partitioning

Static load balancing is usually implemented via a space-partitioning function which methodically distributes data across different disks. For example, assume that two-dimensional point data is distributed in the upper right quadrant of the coordinate system. Furthermore, a grid imposed on the quadrant divides the two-dimensional space into cells. We can identify cells with a pair of numbers (x, y). We number the first coordinates in the cell identifier (x, y) from left to right, beginning with 0. We number the second coordinates in cell identifier (x, y) from bottom to top. For example, $(0, 0)$ identifies the leftmost cell on the lowest row.

```
3 4 5 6 7 0 1 2    7 0 1 2 3 4 5 6    42 43 46 47 58 59 62 63     2 3 6 7 2 3 6 7    63 62 49 48 47 44 43 42    7 6 1 0 7 4 3 2
6 7 0 1 2 3 4 5    6 7 0 1 2 3 4 5    40 41 44 45 56 57 60 61     0 1 4 5 0 1 4 5    60 61 50 51 46 45 40 41    4 5 2 3 6 5 0 1
1 2 3 4 5 6 7 0    5 6 7 0 1 2 3 4    34 35 38 39 50 51 54 55     2 3 6 7 2 3 6 7    59 56 55 52 33 34 39 38    3 0 7 4 1 2 6 5
4 5 6 7 0 1 2 3    4 5 6 7 0 1 2 3    32 33 36 37 48 49 52 53 ->  0 1 4 5 0 1 4 5    58 57 54 53 32 35 36 37    2 1 6 5 0 3 1 2
7 0 1 2 3 4 5 6    3 4 5 6 7 0 1 2    10 11 14 15 26 27 30 31     2 3 6 7 2 3 6 7    5 6 9 10 31 28 27 26 ->    5 6 1 2 7 4 3 2
2 3 4 5 6 7 0 1    2 3 4 5 6 7 0 1    8 9 12 13 24 25 28 29       0 1 4 5 0 1 4 5    4 7 8 11 30 29 24 25       4 7 0 3 6 5 0 1
5 6 7 0 1 2 3 4    1 2 3 4 5 6 7 0    2 3 6 7 18 19 22 23         2 3 6 7 2 3 6 7    3 2 13 12 17 18 23 22      3 2 5 4 1 2 7 6
0 1 2 3 4 5 6 7    0 1 2 3 4 5 6 7    0 1 4 5 16 17 20 21         0 1 4 5 0 1 4 5    0 1 14 15 16 19 20 21      0 1 6 7 0 3 4 5

  Linear Method        CMD Method
    disk-id =            disk-id =      Z-Curve Method -> disk-id = Z(x, y) mod 8    Hilbert Method -> disk-id = H(x, y) mod 8
   (x + 5y) mod 8      (x + y) mod 8
```

FIGURE 5.12. Example of allocations by different methods.

A space-partitioning function assigns a disk-id to each cell. The disk-ids for a set of N disks can be chosen from the range of integers 0 to $N - 1$. For a two-dimensional space, the function f can be defined as

$$f : Z^+ \times Z^+ \to [0, 1, \ldots, N - 1],$$

where Z^+ is the space of positive integers, and there are N disks, starting from 0. Figure 5.12 shows four examples of an 8×8 positive quadrant that can be mapped onto eight disks numbered from 0 to 7. The Z-curve and Hilbert curve are described in Chapter 4. We now describe a practical application of a parallel SDBMS.

5.5.3 Application: Real-Time Terrain Visualization

A real-time terrain-visualization system (e.g., a distributed, interactive simulation system) is a virtual environment that lets users navigate and interact with a three-dimensional, computer-generated, geographic environment in real time, like other virtual environments, visualization systems, and distributed interactive simulation systems. This type of system has three major components: interaction, 3-D graphics, and an SDBMS. Figure 5.13 shows the different components of a terrain-visualization system for a typical flight simulator. The SDBMS component of the system contains a secondary storage unit for storing the entire geographic database, and a main memory for storing the data related to the current location of the simulator. The graphics engine receives the spatial data from the SDBMS component and transforms this data into 3-D objects, which are then sent to the display unit.

As the user moves over the terrain, the part of the map that is visible changes over time, and the graphics engine has to be fed with the visible subset of spatial objects for a given location and user's viewpoint. The graphics engine transforms the user's viewpoint into a range query and sends it to the SDBMS unit. The SDBMS unit retrieves the geographic description of an 8 km $\times$ 8 km (km = kilometer) area around the current location of the user and sends it back to the graphic engine. For example, Figure 5.14 shows a polygonal map and a range query. The polygons in the map are shown with dotted lines. The range query is represented by the rectangle, and the result of the range query is shown in solid lines. The SDBMS unit retrieves the spatial data from the main memory and computes its geometric intersection with the current viewport of the user, and sends the results back to the graphics engine. The frequency of this operation depends on the speed at which the user is moving over the terrain. For example, in the terrain visualization of a flight simulator, a new range query may be generated twice a second,

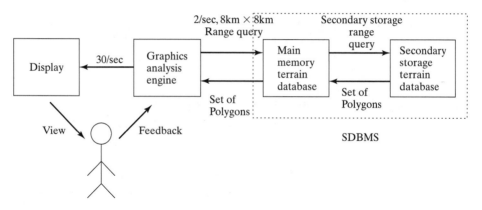

FIGURE 5.13. Components of the terrain-visualization system.

which leaves less than half a second for intersection computation. A typical map used in this application contains tens of thousands of polygons (i.e., millions of edges), and the range-query size can be 20 to 30 percent of the total map. This requires millions of intersection-point computations in less than half a second. In order to meet such

FIGURE 5.14. A sample polygonal map and a range query.

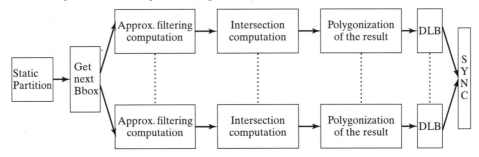

FIGURE 5.15. Different modules of the parallel formulations.

response-time constraints, SDBMS often caches a subset of spatial data in main memory. The main-memory database may in turn query the secondary-storage database to get a subset of data to be cached. The frequency of this operation should be very low for the caching to be effective.

The existing sequential solutions for the range-query problem cannot always be directly used as a solution to the spatial range-query problem, due to the high performance requirements of many applications. For example, the limit on response time (i.e., half a second, as shown in Figure 5.13) for solving the range-query problem necessitates the use of parallel processing to deliver the required performance.

Data-partitioning with declustering and load balancing for parallelizing a sequential algorithm to the GIS range-query problem can be used to meet the high-performance needs of the range query. Figure 5.15 describes the steps in this scheme. The bounding box is initially broadcast to all processors. Each processor then executes the sequential GIS range-query algorithm on the local set of polygons. Dynamic Load Balancing (DLB) techniques can be used to transfer some spatial object to idle processors if static partition fails to equally distribute the load among processors.

Several techniques, such as preprocessing the spatial data, can be used to reduce the sequential cost of the range-query problem. The cost of range-query processing can also be reduced by noting that consecutive range queries may spatially overlap with previous range queries. In this case, the new range query can be considered as an increment of the previous one. Hence, incremental range-query methods can be used to solve this problem. But this incremental range query can be expressed as a combination of one or more smaller range queries.

A range-query problem can also be solved using pre-computation of the results. For this, a fine grid is laid on top of the data, and the intersections of all the spatial objects and the grid cells are computed and stored in the main memory. Because every range query will be some combination of the grid cells, the intersection results for each of the grid cells which make up the range query can be retrieved and sent to the graphics engine. On the other hand, in the case of data-partitioning approaches, large objects may be decomposed into smaller objects to improve the load balance among different processors, thus increasing the efficiency of the solution.

But these two approaches result in increased total work for the graphics engine, as it has to process more objects in the same amount of time. The cost of rendering at the graphics engine also increases with the increased number of polygons. In addition, the decomposition of objects requires more memory to store the objects. On the other hand,

Options for Dividing the Polygon Data

		No Division	Subsets of polygons	Subsets of small polygons	Subsets of edges
Options for Dividing Bounding Box	No Division	I	II	III	IV
	Divide into small boxes	III	III	III	IV
	Divide into edges	IV	IV	IV	IV

FIGURE 5.16. Alternatives for polygon/bounding-box division among processors.

if the smaller pieces are to be merged again into a single object after the range query operation, the merging will result in increased total work for the SDBMS component, as merging of the smaller objects increases the total work.

For example, Figure 5.16 shows different combinations for partitioning polygonal data into smaller sets. These combinations can be grouped into four types: Type I has no division of data. Type II divides the set of polygons into subsets of polygons; however, each polygon is treated as an atomic unit, and subdivision at the polygon level is not allowed. In contrast, Type III divides the areas of individual polygons/bounding boxes among different processors. Type IV schemes divide both the areas and the edges of the individual polygons and the bounding box. The potential advantage of Type III and IV schemes over a Type II scheme is the possibility of better load balance and less processor idling, resulting in reduced parallel computation time. However, note that Type III and IV schemes result either in increased total work or in increased work for the polygonization of the result.

5.6   SUMMARY

Queries in a DBMS are expressed in declarative form. The DBMS software typically has several components that are responsible for executing the queries in an efficient manner.

Spatial query operations can be classified into four groups: *point, range, spatial join*, and *spatial aggregate*. The spatial component of a complex SQL is typically built using elements in these four groups.

The distinguishing feature of query processing for spatial database management is that spatial queries are both CPU and I/O intensive. For spatial query processing, the *filter-refine* paradigm is used to minimize both the CPU and I/O cost.

For a given query there are several typical strategies to execute the query. The *query optimizer* is a component in the DBMS that generates several plans for query execution and then selects an optimal or an almost optimal plan. There are two well-known techniques for query optimization: *logical transformation* and *cost-based optimization*.

Parallelism and distributivity are an important trend in DBMSs to address the rapid growth of data and widespread usage of the worldwide Web. Widespread demand and use of the Internet for spatial data distribution and processing have prompted OGIS to define standards such as WMS and GML. Compliance of WGISs to these standards facilitates interoperability and promotes collaborative systems. Parallel spatial query processing has evoked considerable interest in cutting-edge technologies such as real-time terrain visualization.

BIBLIOGRAPHIC NOTES

5.1 For the two-step filter-refine paradigm and the algebra of spatial operators, see [Brinkhoff and Kriegel, 1994; Guting, 1994a].

5.1.6 Many algorithms for the important spatial-join operation have appeared in the literature. For instance, see [Brinkhoff et al., 1993; Patel and DeWitt, 1996], and [Lo and Ravishankar, 1996; Mamoulis and Papadias, 1999; Patel and DeWitt, 2000; Song et al., 1999]. For the case where neither of the inputs are indexed [Arge et al., 1998], consider the filter step of the spatial-join problem. [Faloutsos et al., 2000] discuss a law governing the spatial join selectivity across two sets of points. For spatial distance join processing, see [Shin et al., 2000].

5.1.7 For further discussion on Nearest Neighbor Search, see [Seidl and Kriegel, 1998] and [Goldstein and Ramakrishnan, 2000]. For "K Closest Pairs Query," which combines join and nearest neighbor queries and discovers the K pairs of smallest distance objects from two data sets, see [Corral et al., 2000]. [Korn and Muthukrishnan, 2000] discusses the concept of reverse nearest neighbors, which are the points that have the query point as their nearest neighbor.

5.2 Query optimization is another open area in the context of SDBs. Some important progress is noted in [Hellerstein and Stonebraker, 1993], and [Chaudhuri and Shim, 1996]. [Theodoridis et al., 2000b] discuss the analytical models that estimate the cost of selection and join queries using R-tree based structure. For selectivity estimation in spatial databases, see [Acharya et al., 1999]. [Leutenegger and Lopez, 2000] discuss the effect of buffering on the performance of R-trees.

5.3 For a more detailed analysis of spatial index structures, consult [Faloutsos and Kamel, 1994; Pagel et al., 1993a; Theodoridis et al., 1998].

5.4.3 More details on WGIS can be found in [Vatsavai et al., 2000]. This paper presents a novel load balancing client/server architecture, which gives better performance than the typical server-centric or client-centric systems.

5.5 More details on parallel GIS can be found in [Shekhar et al., 1998].

EXERCISES

1. For the given data space consisting of nine octahedrons (see Figure), calculate the cost of processing a range query:
   (a) Directly
   (b) Using the filter-refine strategy
   Assume there is no index on the space and the cost of processing each polygon is equal to the number of edges. For the filter step, assume each polygon is represented by its MBR.
2. How will the result change if the octahedrons are replaced by hexagons?
3. What is special about query optimization in SDBs relative to traditional relational databases?

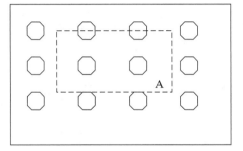

4. Consider the following strategies for spatial-join tree matching, nested loop with index, choose applicable strategies for a spatial join under the following scenarios:
   (a) Overlap join: neither data-set has available R-tree indices
   (b) Overlap join: one data-set has available R-tree indices
   (c) Overlap join: both data-sets have available R-tree indices
5. Which join strategies can be used for spatial join, with join predicates other than overlap?
6. Tree transformation: draw query trees for the following queries:
   (a) Which city in city table is closest to a river in the river table (Section 3.5)? Put SQL equivalent.
   (b) List countries where GDP is greater than that of Canada
   (c) List countries that have at least as many (lakes/neighbors?) as France.
7. Apply the tree transform rules to generate a few equivalent query trees for each query tree generated above.
8. Consider a composite query with a spatial join and two spatial selections. However, this strategy does not allow the spatial join. Take advantage of the original indexes on lakes and facilities. In addition, does writing and reading of file 1 and file 2 add into costs? Devise an alternate strategy to simultaneously process join and the two selections underneath.
9. We focused on strategies for point-selection, range-query selection, and spatial join for overlap predicates in this chapter. Are these adequate to support processing of spatial queries in SQL3/OGIS? (See Chapter 3.)
10. How can we process various topological predicates (e.g., inside, outside, touch, cross) in terms of the overlap predicate as a filter, followed by an exact geometric operation?
11. Design an efficient single-pass algorithm for nearest neighbor query using one of the following storage methods: Grid file, B+ tree with Z-order.
12. Study evolution of XML in the context of internet and web commerce. Redraw the Figure 1.5 to incorporate recent trends in XML data management.
13. Compare the computational cost of the two-pass and one-pass algorithms for nearest neighbor queries. When is one-pass algorithm preferred?
14. Compare and contrast the concepts in the following pairs:
    (i)   parallel vs. distributed databases
    (ii) declustering vs. dynamic load balancing
    (iii) shared nothing vs. shared disk architectures
    (iv) client server vs. collaborative systems
15. What is GML? Why is it interesting to spatial databases and GIS?
16. Extend the one-pass algorithm for nearest neighbor query to answer K-nearest neighbor query.

17. Consider the spatial join query between Farms and Disease-map presented in Section 5.4 using table definition of Figure 5.9. Compute the communication cost (number of bytes transferred) of 3 strategies listed below:

   (i) Semi-join

   (ii) Transfer Farm relation to other site

   (iii) Transfer Disease-map to other site

Is semi-join strategy always cheaper than the other two strategies?

18. Study the static declustering techniques based on space partitioning functions in Figure 5.12. Evaluate the I/O speed-up achieved by each method for the following queries assuming each cell (x, y) resides in an independent disk block:

   (i) row query, e.g., cells in lowest row

   (ii) Column query, e.g., cells in leftmost column

   (iii) range query, e.g., cells in bottom 4 rows of 2 leftmost columns.

C H A P T E R   6

Spatial Networks

6.1 EXAMPLE NETWORK DATABASES

6.2 CONCEPTUAL, LOGICAL, AND PHYSICAL DATA MODELS

6.3 QUERY LANGUAGE FOR GRAPHS

6.4 GRAPH ALGORITHMS

6.5 ACCESS METHODS FOR SPATIAL NETWORKS

Spatial network databases (SNDB) are an important component of SDBs. SNDBs form the kernel of many important applications, including transportation planning, air traffic control, water, electric and gas utilities, telephone networks, urban management, river transportation and irrigation canal management. Until now we have focused on spatial objects and their interrelationships, which are based on the notion of proximity. Clearly spatial proximity influences the behavior of nearby objects, but in SNDB a fundamental role is played by relationships based on connectivity.

This shift in viewpoint from proximity to connectivity necessitates that SNDB be treated separately. In this chapter we focus on how the different database techniques that we have introduced—data modeling, query language, and indexing—have to be modified to address the special needs of spatial network applications.

In Section 1 we introduce two network applications to guide and motivate the different concepts that are introduced in this chapter. Section 2 provides a basic introduction of graph concepts and graph operations. In Section 3 we see why standard query languages fall short of adequately answering common graph queries. We also introduce two extensions to augment these shortcomings. Section 4 is a brief survey of graph algorithms with an emphasis on minimizing the I/O cost. Finally, in Section 5 we focus on ways of optimizing standard graph operations.

6.1 EXAMPLE NETWORK DATABASES

We introduce two examples to motivate and guide us through the material presented in this chapter. The two examples, a train network and a pair of river drainage systems, are examples of well-known spatial networks. Starting with some typical queries associated with the two networks, we address all relevant database management issues: data modeling, query language, and indexing.

Train Network

The Bay Area Rapid Transit (BART) train system serves San Francisco and its neighboring area in northern California. The five lines and ten routes (one for each direction) crisscross

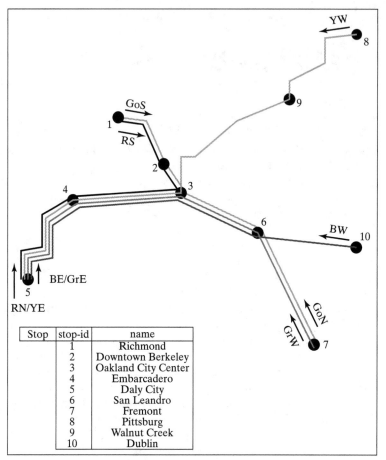

Stop	stop-id	name
	1	Richmond
	2	Downtown Berkeley
	3	Oakland City Center
	4	Embarcadero
	5	Daly City
	6	San Leandro
	7	Fremont
	8	Pittsburg
	9	Walnut Creek
	10	Dublin

(a) BART

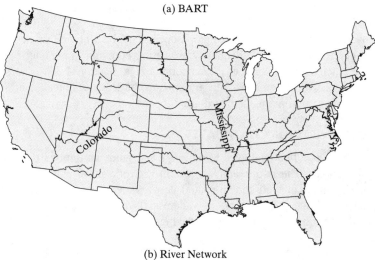

(b) River Network

FIGURE 6.1. Two examples of spatial networks.

through many urban and suburban townships. All the lines converge in downtown San Francisco and then spread out in opposite directions. A map (simplified) of the BART system is shown in Figure 6.1(a). We list some typical queries associated with the transit system.

1. Find the number of stops on the Yellow West (YW) route.
2. List all stops which can be reached from Downtown Berkeley, without changing trains.
3. List the route numbers that connect Downtown Berkeley and Daly City.
4. Find the last stop on the Blue West (BW) route.

River Network

The second example concerns two of the major river systems in the United States. The Mississippi and the Colorado river systems consist of the Mississippi and the Colorado rivers and many of their important tributaries. A map of the two systems is shown in Figure 6.1(b). Again, we list a few relevant queries on the river networks.

1. List the names of all direct and indirect tributaries of the Mississippi river within the state of Minnesota.
2. List the direct tributaries of the Colorado.
3. Which rivers could be affected if there is a spill in river P1?

6.2 CONCEPTUAL, LOGICAL, AND PHYSICAL DATA MODELS

We will first step through the database design process that was introduced in Chapter 2. The spatial network application is first modeled at the conceptual level and then subsequently mapped into a logical model.

We focus on the ubiquitous *graph* abstract datatype to model spatial network applications. The most important notion for spatial networks, namely, the connectivity between objects, can be neatly expressed in a graph-theoretic framework. The graph abstract data types can be embedded into logical modes, for example, object-relational, SQL3, and so on. Graph pictograms can be used in conceptual data models, for example, ER model, UML, to simplify diagrams via making graph-based relationships implicit. We leave choice of pictograms to the reader as Exercise 9.

6.2.1 A Logical Data Model

Basic Graph Concepts

A *graph*, $G = (V, E)$ consists of a finite set of *vertices* V and a set of edges E, between the vertices in V. Thus the edge set E is a binary relationship on V. The graph is *directed* if the pair of vertices that constitute the edge set are ordered; otherwise the graph is *undirected*. Vertices and edges are sometimes called nodes and links respectively. The first element of an ordered pair of vertices is sometimes referred to as the *predecessor* or *source*, and the second element is referred to as the *successor* or *destination* or *sink*.

In the BART example, the nodes are the stations in the train system, and links represent direct connections between the stations. The nodes do not have to be points. In the River Network example, the nodes of a possible graph are rivers (and not their endpoints), and if one river falls into another, this relationship is represented by a link. Different graph representations of the River Network may be suitable for other applications. The BART system can be modeled as a *directed* or an *undirected* graph, depending on the application, but the River Network is most naturally represented as a *directed* graph.

Sometimes *labels* and *weights* are attached to the nodes and links of a graph to encode additional information. For example, a name, geographic coordinates, or both can be attached to the nodes of the train system, and distances between the station can be captured as weights on the edges.

Two edges are *adjacent* if they share a common node. A sequence of adjacent edges constitutes a *path*. For example, the sequence $(v_0, v_1), (v_1, v_2), \ldots, (v_{n-2}, v_{n-1}), (v_{n-1}, v_n)$ represents a path because each edge has a common node with the previous or successor edge. If the endpoints v_0 and v_n are equal, then the path is called a *cycle*. There are no cycles in the river network, but a round trip journey on the train system constitutes a cycle.

Basic Graph Operations

Applications that are modeled as graphs have many common operations. We list some of these operations in a high-level object-oriented notation extending the graph model presented in [Bailey, 1998]. We assume that the reader is familiar with rudimentary, object-oriented terminology and Java syntax. More detailed description of Java interfaces for important graph classes can be found in [Bailey, 1998]. We want to emphasize that each of these operations can be implemented in different ways, depending on the application and the storage structure of the graph.

There are three fundamental classes (or entities) in graphs: Graph, Vertex, and Edge. For each class we list a series of common operations, or *methods*, that are associated with the class.

```
public class Graph
{
        public   void   add(Object label);
        // label represents the vertex to be added

        public   void   addEdge(Object v1, Object v2, Object label);
        // an edge is inserted between the two vertices v1 and v2

        public Object delete(Object label);
        // removes a vertex

        public Object deleteEdge(Object v1, Object v2);
        // the edge spanned by vertices v1 and v2 is removed

        public Object get(Object label);
        // the label of the vertex is returned

        public Edge getEdge(Object v1, Object v2);
        // the edge spanned by vertices v1 and v2 is returned

        public Object get-a-Successor(Object label);
        // an adjacent node of the vertex is returned
```

```
public Iterator getSuccessors(Object label);
// all the adjacent neighbors are returned

public Iterator getPredecessors(Object label);
// all the parents are returned

public boolean isDirected();
// returns true if the graph is directed
```

}

Vertex and Edge are the other two important classes. Most *graph* algorithms keep track of the Vertices and Edges they have visited by marking them. It is thus useful to provide direct support for these operations. The Vertex is visible from the *graph* interface, the class is declared public.

```
public class Vertex
{
        public Vertex(Object label)
        // the constructor for the class. A node with the appropriate
        label is created.

        public Object label()
        // returns a label associated with the vertex

        public boolean visit()
        // marks the vertex as being visited.

        public boolean isVisited()
        // returns true if and only if the vertex has been visited.
```

}

Similar to the Vertex class, the Edge class is declared public because it is visible from the *graph* interface due to the *getEdge* method used in the *graph* class. We only list a few of the basic Edge methods. The readers are invited to provide more methods that they deem important.

```
public class Edge
{
        public Edge(Object v1, Object v2, Object label, boolean directed)
        // the constructor for the class. The edge is ''directed''
        // if set true.

        public Object start()
        // returns the first node of the edge

        public Object end()
        // returns the second node of the edge
```

}

Some systems include additional data types, e.g., route or path [Guting, 1994b; Shekhar and Liu, 1997]. Informally, a path is a sequence starting with a node and ending at another node. It contains other nodes and edges in traversal order. Routes in Bart example represent paths. The rewrite operation on a path takes a set of transforms on subsets of the nodes and edges to produce another path. For example, rewrite (edge $\rightarrow$, path P) will drop all edges from P. The path evaluation operation aggregates a property (e.g., edge length) of nodes and edges in the path to return a scalar (e.g., number).

6.2.2 Physical Data Models

The classes Graph, Node, and Edge are not exhaustive, but are common primitives that are needed by many graph algorithms such as connectivity, shortest path, and so on. Consensus sets of the abstract datatype to model spatial networks are in discussion, and we hope to see standards soon. The Adjacency-matrix and the Adjacency-list are two well-known main-memory data structures for implementing graphs. In the Adjacency-matrix the rows and the columns of a graph represent the vertices of the graph. A matrix entry can be either 1 or 0, depending on whether there is an edge between the two vertices, as shown in Figure 6.2(b). If the graph is undirected, then the resulting matrix is symmetric. The Adjacency-matrix structure is efficient for answering edge queries: Is edge (u, v) in G?

The Adjacency-list structure is efficient for queries that involve enumerating the vertices of a graph, e.g. find all neighbors of v. The Adjacency-list data structure is an array of pointers. Each element of the array corresponds to a vertex of the graph, and the pointer points to a list of immediate successors of the vertex as shown in Figure 6.2(c).

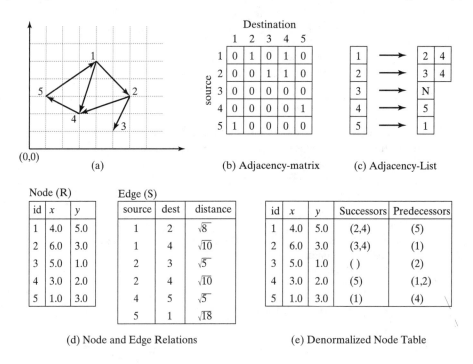

(a)   (b) Adjacency-matrix   (c) Adjacency-List

(d) Node and Edge Relations   (e) Denormalized Node Table

FIGURE 6.2. Three different representations of a graph.

As we have remarked before, main-memory data structures are not suitable for database applications because the database is usually too big to fit in main memory at one time. Thus graph algorithms have to guarantee efficient I/O processing before they can be deployed in a DBMS.

Directed graphs can be implemented in a relational model using a pair of relations R and S for the nodes and edges of the graph. The Node relation R and the Edge relation S are shown in Figure 6.2(d). Notice that the edges in the relation S may be physically clustered according to the value of the first attribute. We have also included the coordinate points of the nodes in the R relation and the distance between the nodes (weights) in the S relation.

A denormalized representation is shown in Figure 6.2(e) is often used to speed-up the shortest path computation. This representation of node table contains coordinates, list of successors, and list of predecessors. Other tabular representations for graphs are possible. For example, one may use a node table, and a route table to capture the relationships between nodes and routes arising in the application domain of public transportation.

We now revisit the example spatial networks: BART and River Network. Information related to BART is collected in three relations. The first relation, Stop, has two attributes, stopid and name. These two attributes correspond to the identification number and name of the stop. The two attributes of the second relation, DirectedRoute, are number and name of the routes. The tables related to these two relations are shown in Table 6.1. The RouteStop relation of the BART system is shown in Table 6.2. The three attributes of the relation correspond to the routenumber; the stop identification number, stopid; and the position of the stop in the route, route.

The River Network has two relations: River and FallsInto, shown in Table 6.3. The two attributes of the River, *riverid* and *name*, correspond to the identification number and the name of the river, respectively. The FallsInto relation also has two attributes: source and dest, which are foreign keys to the River relation. The source attribute corresponds to a river that will flow into the river referenced in the dest attribute.

In the BART example, all the paths corresponding to the routes of the different trains have been materialized in the RouteStop relation. In the River Network relation, only the vertices and edges of the network graph are enumerated.

TABLE 6.1: The Stop and DirectedRoute Tables of BART

Stop	stopid	name	DirectedRoute	number	name
	1	Richmond		1	Red South
	2	Downtown Berkeley		2	Red North
	3	Oakland City Center		3	Gold South
	4	Embarcadero		4	Gold North
	5	Daly City		5	Yellow West
	6	San Leandro		6	Yellow East
	7	Fremont		7	Blue West
	8	Pittsburg		8	Blue East
	9	Walnut Creek		9	Green West
	10	Dublin		10	Green East

TABLE 6.2: The RouteStop Table of BART

RouteStop	routenumber	stopid	rank
	1	1	1
	1	2	2
	1	3	3
	1	4	4
	1	5	5
	2	5	1
	2	4	2
	2	3	3
	2	2	4
	2	1	5
	3	1	1
	3	2	2
	3	3	3
	3	6	4
	3	7	5
	4	7	1
	4	6	2
	4	3	3
	4	2	4
	4	1	5
	5	8	1
	5	9	2
	5	3	3
	5	4	4
	5	5	5
	6	5	1
	6	4	2
	6	3	3
	6	9	4
	6	8	5
	7	10	1
	7	6	2
	7	3	3
	7	4	4
	7	5	5
	8	5	1
	8	4	2
	8	3	3
	8	6	4
	8	10	5
	9	7	1
	9	6	2
	9	4	3
	9	5	4
	10	5	1
	10	6	2
	10	10	3
	10	7	4

TABLE 6.3: The `River` and `FallsInto` Relations of `River Network`

River	riverid	name
	1	Mississippi
	2	Ohio
	3	Missouri
	4	Red
	5	Arkansas
	6	Platte
	7	Yellowstone
	8	P1
	9	P2
	10	Y1
	11	Y2
	12	Colorado
	13	Green
	14	Gila
	15	G1
	16	G2
	17	GI1
	18	GI2

FallsInto	source	dest
	2	1
	3	1
	4	1
	5	1
	6	3
	7	3
	8	6
	9	6
	10	7
	11	7
	13	12
	14	12
	15	13
	16	13
	17	14
	18	14

6.3 QUERY LANGUAGE FOR GRAPHS

In Chapter 3 we discovered that the functionality of common query languages, such as RA and SQL92, had to be extended in order to query spatial data. In this section we will see that many important graph operations cannot be expressed in RA and SQL92. One of the important operations in graphs is to determine all the nodes in a graph from which a given node is accessible. Query languages based on relational algebra are unable to express certain important graph queries without making certain assumptions about the graphs.

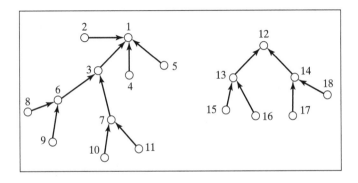

FIGURE 6.3. A graph model for River Network example.

6.3.1 Shortcomings of RA

An important graph operation is to determine the *transitive closure* of a graph. The transitive closure G^* of a graph $G(V, E)$ is a graph that has the same vertex set V as G but whose edge set consists of all paths in G. Consider the example shown in Figure 6.4. The transitive closure of G (Figure 6.4[a]) is shown in Figure 6.4(c). The graph G^* has four new edges, each corresponding to a path in G. For example, G^* has the edge $(1, 3)$ because the node 3 is reachable from node 1 in the original graph G.

The relations corresponding to graphs G and G^* are shown in Figure 6.4(c) and 6.4(d), respectively. Using RA operations, it is not possible to derive the relation G^* from G unless additional information about the structure of the graph is available. In particular, the length of the longest path must be known to derive the transitive closure. The following sequence of RA operations derives the transitive closure G^* from G.

1	*Rename*		$G_1 = G \text{ and } G_2 = G.$
2	T_1	$=$	$\Pi_{G_1.source, G_2.dest}(G_1 \bowtie_{G_1.dest=G_2.source} G_2).$
3	T_2	$=$	$G \cup T_1.$
4	T_3	$=$	$G \bowtie_{G.dest=T_2.source} T_2.$
5	T_4	$=$	$\Pi_{T_3.source, T_3.dest} T_3.$
6	G^*	$=$	$T_2 \cup T_4.$

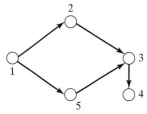

(a) Graph G

R

SOURCE	DEST
1	2
1	5
2	3
3	4
5	3

(b) Relation form

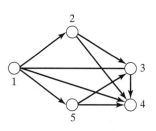

(c) Transitive closure (G) = Graph G*

X

SOURCE	DEST
1	2
1	5
2	3
3	4
5	3
1	3
2	4
5	4
1	4

(d) Transitive closure in relational form

FIGURE 6.4. A relation R and its transitive closure X.

The sequence of steps to derive the transitive closure required two join operations. This is because the longest path in the graph G passes through two intermediate nodes. If this information was not available, then no RA operation could decide when the transitive closure is achieved. Notice that

$$G^* = G^* \cup (G^* \bowtie G)$$

More formally, for a given relation R, the transitive closure X is the least fixed-point solution of the *recursive* equation

$$X = X \cup (R \bowtie X)$$

In the SQL3, a recursion operation RECURSIVE has been proposed to handle the transitive closure operation. Before we introduce the RECURSIVE operation, we discuss a similar operation, CONNECT, which is already available in many implementations of SQL92.

6.3.2 SQL CONNECT **Clause**

The CONNECT clause can be used to traverse a directed acyclic graph (DAG). Graph traversal is controlled by 'START WITH' and 'CONNECT BY' clauses. The root node is specified by the 'START WITH' clause. The relationship between parent rows and child rows is defined with the 'CONNECT BY' clause. The search direction is governed by the use of a 'PRIOR' operator. The River-Network is an example of a DAG where the direction of each edge is determined by the flow of the river. With the help of examples, we show how important queries related to the River-Network can be expressed in SQL using the CONNECT BY clause.

1. List the riverid of all direct and indirect tributaries of the river with riverid equal to 1 (Mississippi).

```
SELECT    source
FROM      FallsInto
CONNECT   BY PRIOR source = dest
START     WITH dest = 1
```

Comments: The intermediate results and final output of this query are shown in Figure 6.5. The query begins with the START WITH clause. It selects all rows in the FallsInto table whose dest is equal to 1. The result is shown in Figure 6.5(b). In the next step, using the source = dest hierarchy in the CONNECT clause, all the rivers that are part of the hierarchy (i.e., flow into the selected rivers) are added to the output. This process is repeated recursively until all the nodes of the hierarchy have been visited. The CONNECT clause traverses the DAG using breadth-first search (BFS). We discuss BFS in greater detail in Section 6.4.

Note: The PRIOR keyword determines the search direction. In this example all the child nodes of the node rooted at 1 will be returned. On the other hand if we modify the above query with 'CONNECT BY source = PRIOR dest', then all the parent nodes of the node rooted at 1 will be returned.

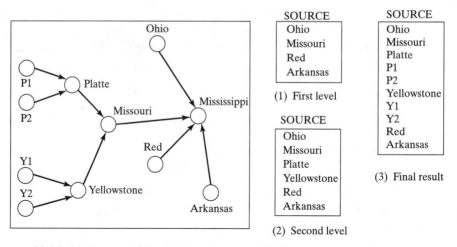

(a) Missisippi network (Y1 = Bighorn river,   (b) The sequence of the CONNECT clause
    Y2 = Powder river, P1 = Sweet water river,
    P2 = Big Thompson river).

FIGURE 6.5. SQL's CONNECT clause operation.

2. List the names of all direct and indirect tributaries of the Mississippi.

```
SELECT    name
FROM      River
WHERE     riverid IN
(
SELECT    source
FROM      FallsInto
CONNECT   BY PRIOR source = dest
START     WITH dest IN
(
SELECT    riverid
FROM      River
WHERE     name = 'Mississippi'
)
)
```

Comments: This is a double-nested query. The added complexity is a consequence of the fact that the CONNECT clause is processed before the WHERE
clause.

3. List all the direct tributaries of the Colorado River.

```
SELECT    name
FROM      River
WHERE     riverid IN
(
SELECT    source
FROM      FallsInto
```

```
WHERE     Level ≤ 1
CONNECT   BY PRIOR source = dest
START     WITH dest IN
(
SELECT    riverid
FROM      River
WHERE     name = 'Colorado'
)
)
```

Comments: In the previous query we noted that the WHERE clause is processed after the CONNECT clause. We can use this to select the levels of the DAG. This can be done by using Level in the WHERE clause. Because this query only requires the direct tributaries of the Mississippi, we set the Level ≤ 1.

4. How many rivers may be affected if there is a hazardous spill in river P1.

```
SELECT    COUNT(source)
FROM      FallsInto
CONNECT   BY source = PRIOR dest
START     WITH source IN
(
SELECT    riverid
FROM      River
WHERE     name = 'P1'
)
```

Comments: We can go "up" a hierarchy by switching the location of PRIOR within the CONNECT clause.

6.3.3 Example Queries on the BART System

We now give examples of querying the BART system based upon the relations shown in Tables 6.1 and 6.2. In Table 6.2 we have explicitly shown all the routes, their stops, and the rank of the stops within the route.

1. How many stops are there on the Yellow West (YW) route.

```
SELECT   COUNT(R.stopid)
FROM     RouteStop R, DirectedRoute D
WHERE    R.routenumber = D.rnumber AND
         D.name = 'Yellow West'
```

Comments: Because the RouteStop table contains information about the route numbers and not their names, we have to join the RouteStop relation with the DirectedRoute relation to answer this query.

2. List the stops on Red North in alphabetical order.

```
SELECT   S.name
FROM     Stop S, RouteStop R, DirectedRoute D
```

```
WHERE   D.number = R.routenumber AND
        R.stopid = S.stopid AND
        D.name = 'Red North'
ORDER   BY name
```

Comments: Information about the names of the stops and routes is given in the `Stop` and `DirectedRoute` tables, respectively. Information about stops and routes that visit them is given in `RouteStop` table. Thus two joins are required: between `RouteStop` and `DirectedRoute` and between `RouteStop` and `Stop`. The alphabetical order of the stops is furnished by the `ORDER BY` clause.

Answer The output of this query is the following table:

Daly City
Downtown Berkeley
Embarcadero
Oakland City Center
Richmond

3. List the second stop on `Red South`.

```
SELECT   S.name
FROM     Stop S, RouteStop R, DirectedRoute D
WHERE    D.number = R.routenumber AND
         R.stopid = S.stopid AND
         R.rank= 2 AND
         D.name = 'Red South'
```

Comments: This is similar to the above query, except that the `WHERE` clause includes an additional constraint: R.rank=2.

4. List the last stop on `Blue West`.

```
SELECT   S.name
FROM     Stop S, RouteStop R, DirectedRoute D
WHERE    S.stopid = R.stopid AND
         R.routenumber = D.rnumber AND
         D.name = 'Blue West' AND
         R.rank =
(
SELECT   Max(R1.rank)
FROM     RouteStop R1, DirectedRoute D1
WHERE    D1.rnumber = R1.routenumber AND
         D1.name = 'Blue West'
)
```

Comments: This is a nested query.

5. List the route numbers which connect `Downtown Berkeley` and `Daly City`.

```
SELECT    R1.routenumber
FROM      RouteStop R1, RouteStop R2, Stop S1, Stop S2
WHERE     R1.routenumber = R2.routenumber AND
          R1.stopid = S1.stopid AND
          R2.stopid = S2.stopid AND
          S1.name = 'Downtown Berkeley' AND
          S2.name = 'Daly City'
```

Comments: First we join the relation `RouteStop` with itself. This is called a self-join. Then we join the `Stop` relations on both sides of the self-joined relation. The final step is to project the `routenumber` attribute of those rows in which both Downtown Berkeley and Daly City appear.

6. List all stops that can be reached from Downtown Berkeley without transferring to a different line.

```
SELECT    Distinct(S2.name)
FROM      RouteStop R1, RouteStop R2, Stop S1, Stop S2
WHERE     R1.routenumber = R2.routenumber AND
          R1.stopid = S1.stopid AND
          R2.stopid = S2.stopid AND
          S1.name = 'Downtown Berkeley' AND
          R1.stopid <> R2.stopid
```

Comments: The SQL expression for this query is similar to the previous one. The `RouteStop` tables are self-joined on the attribute `routenumber`. The `Stop` tables are joined on both ends to the self-joined route table.

Answer The output from this query is:

Daly City
Embarcadero
Fremont
Oakland City Center
Richmond
San Leandaro

6.3.4 Trends: SQL3 Recursion

The SQL3 provides constructs for computing the *transitive closure* of a relation. For example, the transitive closure X of the relation R, which is shown in Figure 6.4, can be derived as follows:

```
1)   WITH  RECURSIVE  X(source, dest) AS
2)                    (SELECT source, dest FROM R)
3)                    UNION
4)                    ( SELECT R.source, X.dest
```

```
5)                          FROM R, X
6)                          WHERE R.dest = X.source);
7)    SELECT   * FROM X
```

Comments: Recursive relations or relations whose value will be computed in a recursive fashion are defined using the keyword phrase `WITH RECURSIVE` followed by the schema of the recursive relation. Formally,

`WITH RECURSIVE` ⟨Relation-Schema⟩   ⟨ Query involving recursive relation ⟩

On Line (1) the recursive relation X is defined. Line (2) essentially initializes X with the relation R because the relation X contains the relation R. Lines (4) to (6) are where the recursion actually takes place. Essentially the following transitive rule is being materialized in Lines (4) to (6):

$$X(a, b) \text{ and } X(b, c) \rightarrow X(a, c)$$

Line (7) lists all the tuples of relation X.

6.3.5   Trends: SQL3 ADTs for Networks

We now discuss how to construct the basic ADT's encountered in spatial networks. Using the object-relational features of Oracle8, one may create ADTs corresponding to *Vertex, Edge,* and *Graph.*

To begin with one may create a new type `vertexType`. The `vertexType` has three attributes: *vid, x,* and *y. Vid* is a unique identification for the vertex; *x* and *y* correspond to the spatial location of the vertex.

The edgeset E of a graph $G(V, E)$ is a binary relation on the vertex set V. Therefore the two attributes of `edgeType`, namely, *source* and *dest*, may be declared as references to `vertexType`. This is essential if we want to keep the relations normalized. The *weight* attribute in `edgeType` corresponds to the weight of an edge.

We can create tables corresponding to `vertexType` and `edgeType`. After the two tables have been created, we can populate them by using the `INSERT` clause in SQL. For example, the following statements will insert two tuples into the `Vertex` table.

```
INSERT INTO Vertex VALUES(1,3.0,4.0)
INSERT INTO Vertex VALUES(2,0.0,1.0)
```

Inserting data into the `Edge` table is slightly more involved because the *source* and *dest* attributes are references to `vertexType`. The following SQL statement will insert an edge whose *weight* is 10 and whose *source* and *dest* ids are 1 and 2, respectively.

```
INSERT   INTO Edge
SELECT   10, ref(v), ref(w)
FROM     Vertex v, Vertex w
```

Having populated two tables corresponding to the vertices and edges of a graph, we can combine them to create a graph ADT. Given a graph $G = (V, E)$, the two attributes *vset* and *eset* correspond to V and E, respectively. In `graphType` we also have a member function getsuccessor. This function admits an instance of vertexType as parameter, called *node*, and returns the adjacency list of *node*. The return type of this function is a set of vertices. We invite the reader to create a new ADT vsubset and complete the definition of the member function. The PRAGMA clause is necessary if the getSuccessor function will be used in queries. It specifies that the function will not change the state of the database. As with Vertex and Edge, a table corresponding to graphType can be created using the CREATE TABLE clause in SQL.

We now can insert data into the Graph table as follows:

```
INSERT  INTO Graph
SELECT  ref(v), ref(e)
FROM    Vertex v, Edge e
```

Querying the Graph table is quite natural if we use the dot notation and keep track of the references. For example, the query "Find the weight of the edge whose source id is 1 and dest id is 2," can be expressed as

```
SELECT  distinct(g.eset.weight)
FROM    Graph g
WHERE   g.eset.source.vid = 1 AND
        g.eset.dest.vid = 2
```

6.4 GRAPH ALGORITHMS

In Section 6.3 we explored ways of extending SQL to query graphs. In particular we described the SQL CONNECT operation and the SQL3 RECURSIVE operation. In this section we elaborate on a variety of algorithms that are deployed to implement these operations.

Frequent queries on spatial networks can be divided into three categories, single scan queries, join queries and network analysis queries. Single scan queries include point and range queries, for example, get, getEdge, get-a-successor, getSuccessors, and path evaluation operations. Join queries on graph represent map overlay of multiple spatial networks, for example, identify non-intersecting pairs of highways and city-roads which are within 50 meters of each other. Network analysis queries represent a set of graph queries based on transitive closure. These queries include shortest path, determination of connectivity, shortest tours, location and allocation etc. For example, ESRI's network engine supports network analysis operations like allocate (which assigns parts of network to resources based on impedance and demand), tour (orders a series of stops and creates a minimized path that visits each stop once), directions (generates a list of directions that describe a route). Many single scan and join queries can be processed using the techniques discussed in chapter 5, but network analysis queries can not be. We focus on algorithms for processing network analysis queries in this section. In particular, we focus on algorithms for shortest path and graph traversal problems since these are used in processing of many network analysis queries as well some single scan and join queries. We first provide the basic algorithms suitable for main memory resident spatial networks and then describe hierarchical algorithms suitable for large spatial networks which may not fit inside main memory.

6.4.1 Path-Query Processing

Path-query processing is an important ingredient in spatial network applications. Support for navigation, route planning, and traffic management essentially reduces to providing *path options* based on some application-dependent criterion. For example, a well-known graph operation is determining the "shortest" path between two points A and B on a road network where the "shortest" criterion could be based on distance, travel time, or some other user-specified constraint.

Path computations can be classified into three classes: single pair, single source, and all pairs.

- **Single Pair** Given a graph $G = (V, E)$ and vertices u and v in N, find an optimal path between u and v. A special case is the well-known shortest-path problem.

- **Single Source** Given a source node u, find optimal paths from u to all *reachable* nodes in G. This is also known as the *partial transitive closure* problem.

- **All Pairs** Find the optimal path in G between all pairs of nodes u and v in N. This is related to the *transitive closure* problem.

Underlying the computation of all path queries are *graph traversal* algorithms which search for paths by traversing from one node to another along the edges of a graph. As we have seen before, searching for paths is a recursive operation, and therefore the adjacency lists of nodes have to be repeatedly transferred from secondary storage to the main memory buffer. Specific steps must be taken to design graph algorithms that minimize the I/O cost in order to make query processing of graph operations efficient and effective.

6.4.2 Graph Traversal Algorithms

Graph traversal algorithms form the backbone of all path computation algorithms. Examples of well-known graph traversal algorithms are the *breadth-first*, *depth-first*, and *Dijkstra's*. We now briefly describe each of these algorithms; more details can be found in [Jiang, 1991].

Breadth-First Search (BFS)

Given a graph G and a source node v in G, the BFS algorithm visits all nodes that are reachable from v. The algorithm first visits all the immediate neighbors of the source node v. The immediate neighbors of a node are exactly the elements in the adjacency list of the node. It then recursively visits the adjacency lists of the immediate neighbors and so on. If the tuples of the edge relation are physically clustered according to the value of their source nodes, then the majority of the members in the adjacency list are likely to be found on the same disk page. This can greatly alleviate the I/O cost and improve the overall efficiency of the algorithm. The pseudocode of the BFS algorithm is shown below. An example run for a sample graph is shown in Figure 6.6 starting with node 1. It visits nodes (2,4) in first iteration and nodes (3,5) in next iteration.

```
procedure BFS(G, v)
{          var  u, w: integer;
           visited := {v };
```

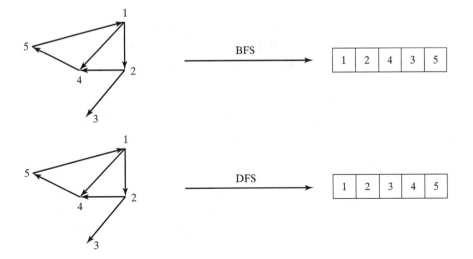

FIGURE 6.6. The result of BFS and DFS on a graph with source node 1.

if *nonsink*[*v*] **then** *queue* := *v* ;

foreach *w* **in** *queue*   **do**
        foreach *u* **in** *adj* − *list*$_w$ **do**
        if u ∋ visited **then**
            {   visited := visited ∪ { u };
                if *nonsink*[*u*] **then**
                    queue := queue • u;
            }

}

v denotes the source node from where the graph traversal begins. The *nonsink* array is to make sure that the algorithm does not loop through nodes which have no immediate neighbors, that is, nodes that are *sinks*. The "•" symbol stands for the insert-in-queue operation.

Depth-First Search

In contrast with BFS, the depth-first search (DFS) algorithm visits an immediate neighbor of a source node and its successive neighbors recursively before visiting other immediate neighbors. Thus DFS first exhausts the "depths" of each link before returning to the top level to exhaust other "depths." The pseudocode of DFS is shown below.

procedure *DFS*(*G*, *v*)
        visited := {v };
        if *nonsink*[*v*] **then** *VISIT*(*v*) ;

}

procedure *Visit*(*w*)
{   **var** u, : **integer**;
        foreach *u* **in** *adj* − *list*$_w$ **do**

```
                    if u ∋ visited then
                        {   visited := visited ∪ { u };
                            if nonsink[u] then VISIT(u)
                        }

}
```

An example run for a sample graph is shown in Figure 6.6 starting with node 1. It may visit node 2, 3, 4, and 5 in that order. Alternative orders of visit in DFS are (1,4,5,2,3), and (1,2,4,5,3).

Dijkstra's Algorithm

Dijkstra's algorithm can be used to solve the single-source (partial transitive closure) problem. The pseudocode is shown below.

```
procedure Dijkstra(G(V, E), v);
{
            var: integer;
            foreach u in  V do {C(v, u) = inf; C(v, v) = 0; path(v, u) := null}
            frontierSet := [v ]; exploredSet := emptySet;
            while not_empty(frontierSet) do
            {   select w from frontierSet with minimum C(v, w);
                frontierSet := frontierSet- [w]; exploredSet := exploredSet + [w];
                if (u = d) then   terminate
                else { fetch( w.adjacencyList);
                        foreach < u, C(w, u) > in w.adjacencyList
                        if C(v, u) > C(v, w) + C(w, u) then
                        {
                          C(v, u) := C(v, w) + C(w, u);
                          path(v, u) := path(v, w) + (w, u) ;
                                    if u ∋ frontierSet ∪ exploredSet then
                                    frontierSet := frontierSet + [u];
                        }
                    }
            }
}
```

The input v in the procedure is the source node. The Dijkstra's algorithm will compute the shortest path from the source node to all other reachable nodes. We enumerate the steps of the algorithm.

1. The cost $C(v, v)$ is set equal to zero. All other costs are set to infinity: $C(v, u) =$ inf. The $path(u, v)$ is set to null.
2. The frontierSet is set equal to the source node v. The exploredSet is initialized to the empty set.
3. As long as the $frontierSet$ is not empty, the following computations are carried out.
4. A node w is selected from the frontierSet, which has the shortest path from the source node v. In the first iteration the source node is selected because the cost $C(v, v)$ is zero while all other costs are infinity.

5. The selected node w is removed from the `frontierSet` and added to the `exploredSet`.

6. The adjacency list of w is retrieved from secondary storage if it is not already in the main memory buffer.

7. For each element $< u, C(w, u) >$ in the adjacency list satisfying the condition: $C(v, u) > C(v, w) + C(w, u)$ (i.e., there exists a shorter path from v to u via w), the updates are performed.

8. The cost of the path from the source node v to u is updated to $C(v, u) = C(v, w) + C(w, u)$ and the $path(v, u) = path(v, w) + path(w, u)$.

9. u is added to the $frontierSet$ if it is not in the $frontierSet$ or the $exploredSet$.

Consider the graph in Figure 6.2(a) with edge costs representing the distance shown in Edge(s) table in Figure 6.2(d). Consider the problem of determining shortest path from node 1 to node 5. Dijktra's algorithm will examine edges (1,2) and (1,4) in iteration 1 to set c(1,2) = distance(1,2) and c(1,4) = distance(1,4).

It selects node 2 for next iteration since distance(1,2) < distance(1,4). It examines edges (2,3) and (2,4) in iteration 2 to revise c(1,3) = distance(1,2) + distance(1,3). c(1,4) is not revised since cost of path (1,2), (2,4) is higher than c(1,4). It picks node 4 for exploration in iteration 3 since c(1,4) < c(1,3). Iteration 3 updates c(1,5) to be distance (1,4) + distance(4,5) = length of path (1,4), (4,5).

6.4.3   Best-First Algorithm for Single Pair (v, d) Shortest Path

The Best-first search has been a framework for heuristics which speed up algorithms by using semantic information about a domain. A* is a special case of best-first search algorithms. It uses an estimator function $f(v, d)$ to underestimate the cost of the shortest path between node v and d. Best-first search without estimator functions is not very different from Dijkstra's algorithm. The pseudocode is shown below.

```
procedure Dijkstra(G(V, E), v, d, f);
{
                var: integer;
                foreach u in  V do {C(v, u) = inf; C(v, v) = 0; path(v, u) := null}
                frontierSet := [v]; exploredSet := emptySet;
                while not_empty(frontierSet) do
                {    select w from frontierSet with minimum (C(v, w)+ f(w, d));
                     frontierSet := frontierSet- [w]; exploredSet := exploredSet + [w];
                     if (u = d) then  terminate
                     else { fetch( w.adjacencyList);
                            foreach < u, C(w, u) > in w.adjacencyList
                            if C(v, u) > C(v, w) + C(w, u) then
                            {
                              C(v, u) := C(v, w) + C(w, u);
                              path(v, u) := path(v, w) + (w, u) ;
                                      if u ∌ frontierSet ∪ exploredSet then
                                      frontierSet := frontierSet + [u];
                            }
                     }
                }
}
```

The procedure terminates after the iteration which selects destination node d as the best node in the *frontierSet*. The procedure can terminate quickly if the shortest path from s to d has fewer edges, if $f(v, d)$ is an underestimate of actual cost of shortest path from v to d. It does not have to examine all nodes to discover the shortest path in many cases. Furthermore, the estimator can provide extra information to focus the search on the shortest path to the destination, reducing the number of nodes to be examined. Consider the problem of determining shortest path from node 1 to node 5 in Figure 6.2(a). Best first A* picks node 4 to be explored further in iteration 1 instead of node 2 using euclidean distance as an estimator function. It finds a path to node 5 in next iteration.

6.4.4   Trends: Hierarchical Strategies

Hierarchical algorithms decompose a large spatial graph into a boundary graph and a collection of fragment graphs, each of which is much smaller than the original graph. Hierarchical graphs are particularly useful in reducing I/O costs and main-memory buffer requirements for processing queries on graphs that are too large to fit inside the main-memory buffers.

The basic idea of a hierarchical algorithm for computing a shortest path is to decompose the original graph into a set of smaller fragment graphs and a summary graph called a *boundary* graph. Proper construction of the boundary graph allows an optimality preserving decomposition of the shortest path query on the original graph into a set of shortest path queries on the smaller graphs.

The hierarchical graph has a two-level representation of the original graph. The lower level is composed of a set of fragments of the original graph. The higher-level graph is comprised of the boundary nodes (BN) and is called the boundary graph (BG). Boundary nodes are defined as the set of nodes that have a neighbor in more than one fragment, i.e. $N_i \in BN \iff \exists E_{i,j}, E_{i,k} | FRAG(k) \neq FRAG(j)$. Edges in the boundary graph are called boundary edges, and the boundary nodes of a fragment form a clique in boundary graph, that is, are completely connected. The cost associated with the boundary edge is the shortest-path cost through the fragment between the boundary nodes. A boundary edge is associated with a fragment identifier. A *boundary path* is the shortest path through the boundary graph.

THEOREM 1. $BG.SP(s, d)rewrite[Edge \rightarrow] = G.SP(s, d)rewrite^1$
$[BoundaryNode \rightarrow BoundaryNode, InteriorNode \rightarrow, Edge \rightarrow]$ *if* $s, d \in BG$

Proof. Consider an optimal path G.SP(s,d) from s to d in G. From this path, rewrite operation drops all the edges and interior (i.e., non-boundary) nodes. The resulting path p_g is a path consisting only of boundary nodes. Now, consider any pair of adjacent boundary nodes, both the boundary nodes share a common fragment and its interior nodes; also the path between them is optimal in that fragment because the path G.SP (s,d) from s to d is optimal in G. Hence, there will exist a boundary edge in the boundary graph between these boundary nodes corresponding to the shortest path in that fragment; thus p_g exists in the boundary graph. Also, because all the edges

---

[1] Rewrite [Guting, 1994b] in this case drops all the interior nodes and edges in the path and keeps just the boundary nodes.

in the boundary graph correspond to a shortest path in their individual fragments, there does not exist any path shorter than p_g in the boundary graph between s and d; therefore p_g is the shortest directed path BG.SP (s,d) from s to d in BG. This can be proved by induction on the number of boundary edges in the shortest path through the boundary graph.   □

THEOREM 2. $p_g = (G.SP(s,d)rewrite[BoundaryNode \rightarrow BoundaryNode, InteriorNode \rightarrow, Edge \rightarrow]) \in P_{set}.$ where $P_{set} = \{p_{ij}rewrite[Edge \rightarrow] \mid p_{ij} = BG.SP(b_i, b_j), b_i \in BoundaryNodes(Fragment(s))$ $b_j \in BoundaryNodes$ $(Fragment(d))\}$

Proof. Consider an optimal path from s to d in G. The subpath between the first boundary node b_i and the last boundary node b_j in the path is optimal in G; hence from *Theorem 1*, we have $p_g \in P_{set}$.   □

Hierarchical Routing Algorithm

The following algorithm gives a template for finding a path in a hierarchical graph.

```
//BG = boundary graph
//CASE 1: Both Source s and Destination d are boundary nodes
boundaryPath = BG.GetPath(s,d);
path = ExpandBoundaryPath(boundaryPath);
//CASE 2: Source s is a local node and destination d is a boundary node
c = INFINITY;
for each bN in BoundaryNodes(Fragment(s)) do
      if ((cpc = Fragment(s).SPC(s, bN) + BG.(bN,d)) < c) {
            c = cpc;
            minB = i;
      }
path = Fragment(s).SP(s, minB) + ExpandBoundaryPath(BG.SP(minB, d);
//CASE 3: Destination is a local node and source is a boundary node
//Similar to CASE 2, but with source and destination reversed
//CASE 4: Both source and destination are local nodes
c = INFINITY;
for each sBN in BoundaryNodes(Fragment(s)) do
            for each dBN in BoundaryNodes(Fragment(d)) do
                  if ((cpc=Fragment(s).SPC(s,sBN) + BG.SPC(sBN,dBN)
                  + Fragment(d).SPC(dBN,d))< c) {
                        c = cpc;
                        minSB = sBN;
                        minDB = dBN;
                  }
if (Fragment(s) == Fragment(d) && c > Fragment(s).SPC(s,d))
      path = Fragment(s).SP(s,d);
else
      path = Fragment(s).SP(s, minSB) + ExpandBoundaryPath(BG.SP(minSB, minDB))
      + Fragment(d).SP(minDB, d);
```

The following queries are sent to the database to compute the optimal path:

- `SP(s,d)`: This query returns the shortest path between node s and d in given graph, for example, G, BG or a fragment.

- `SPC(s,d)`: Query to find the cost of the shortest path from a source s to a destination d in a given graph.

- `BoundaryNodes(f)`: Query that returns the set of boundary nodes for fragment f.

- `Fragment(n)`: This query returns the fragment identifier for interior node n.

- `ExpandBoundaryPath(boundaryPath)`: Query that expands the path through the boundary graph and returns the corresponding path in *G* by using the `ExpandBoundaryEdge(boundaryEdge)` query for each edge in the boundary path.

- `ExpandBoundaryEdge(boundaryEdge)`: This query expands a boundary edge and returns a corresponding path in *G* by computing the shortest path between the endpoints of the edge in the fragment.

The hierarchical algorithm is composed of three steps: finding the relevant boundary-node pair in the boundary graph, computing the boundary path, and expanding the boundary path. The first step in determining the shortest path is to compute the boundary node through which the shortest path leaves the source's fragment and enters the destination's fragment. If both the source and destination are boundary nodes, then it is trivial. If the source is an internal node and the destination is a boundary node, the boundary node through which the shortest path leaves the source's fragment is found by querying the fragment graph for the cost of the path from the source to all boundary nodes of that fragment, and by querying the boundary graph for the cost of the shortest path from all boundary nodes of the source's fragment to the destination. The source-boundary-destination triple with the lowest aggregate cost determines the appropriate boundary node. The case where the source is a boundary node and the destination is an internal node is similar, but the roles of the source and destination are reversed. When both the source and destination are internal nodes, the appropriate boundary node pair is found by querying the fragment graphs to determine the cost of the shortest path from the internal nodes to all boundary nodes of the fragment, as shown in Figure 6.7(a). Next, the boundary graph is queried to compute the shortest path cost between all selected pairs of boundary nodes, as illustrated in Figure 6.7(b). The path with the lowest aggregate cost determines the boundary-node pair. Once the appropriate boundary-node pair has been determined, the boundary graph is queried to determine the shortest path between those boundary nodes, as Figure 6.8(a) shows. The final step is to expand the boundary path by querying the fragments for the shortest path through them. Adjacent nodes in the boundary path form source/destination pairs on which the shortest-path query can be run on in a fragment as shown in Figure 6.8(b).

LEMMA 1. The hierarchical routing algorithm finds an optimal path from *s* to *d* [Jing et al., 1998].

Proof. The shortest path (s,d) is either interior to a fragment or has at least one boundary node. The former case is covered by calling frag[i].GetPath(s,d). It is important to note that even if the source and destination are in the same fragment,

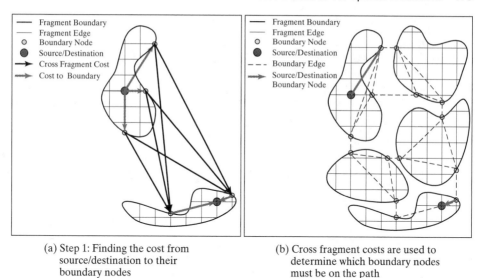

(a) Step 1: Finding the cost from
source/destination to their
boundary nodes

(b) Cross fragment costs are used to
determine which boundary nodes
must be on the path

FIGURE 6.7. Routing example.

the shortest path between those two points may leave the fragment. In the latter case, the shortest path (s,d) can be broken into three components: The path is from s to the first boundary node b_1, then the path from b_1 to the last boundary node b_l, and finally the path from b_l to d. From *Theorem 2*, the path from b_1 to b_l is in P_{set}. □

6.5 TRENDS: ACCESS METHODS FOR SPATIAL NETWORKS

SQL92 supports recursive queries using the CONNECT clause on a network which can be modeled as a *Directed Acyclic Graph*. A RECURSIVE clause is included in the SQL3

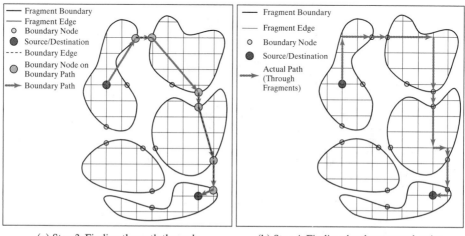

(a) Step 3: Finding the path through
the boundary graph

(b) Step 4: Finding the shortest path using
boundary path information

FIGURE 6.8. Routing example.

to support transitive closure operations. The query optimizer will optimize the transitive closure operation in queries by selecting a suitable algorithm. The optimizer will consider different sets of algorithms for different kinds of path computations. The ability to match a path computation algorithm with the application query is of great importance in object-relational and object-oriented databases.

In Section 6.2 we defined an interface for the `Graph` class which included many important graph operations. An efficient implementation of these operations, or *access methods*, is a prerequisite for the fast evaluation of any graph algorithm.

Both path computation queries and general management of network databases require that the following operations be efficiently supported:

1. `Create: <list of node records> → Network`

2. `get: <node-id, Network> → node properties`

3. `add: <node-id, node-properties, Network> → Network`
   `addEdge: <edge, edge-properties, Network> → Network`

4. `delete: <node-id, Network> → Network`
   `deleteEdge: <edge, edge-properties, Network> → Network`

5. `get-Successors: <node-id, Network> → list of <node-id, node-properties> of successors`

6. `get-a-Successor: <node-id, successor-id, Network> → node-properties of the successor`

The first four operations are common to many data structures and not just graphs. The `Get-Successors` and `get-a-successor` operations are unique to graph applications because such applications access data by connectivity and traversal order. The proximity relation plays a secondary role in network operations.

`Get-a-Successor` retrieves a specified successor of a given node, and `get-Successors` retrieves the records for all successor nodes of a given node. `Get-a-Successor` is used in route evaluation queries, whereas get-Successors() is used in graph search algorithms such as Dijkstra's. Though `get-Successors` and `get-a-Successor` can be implemented as a sequence of *Find* on relevant successors, more efficient implementations are possible by defining that operation as distinct. The `get-Successors` and `get-a-Successor` operations represent the dominant I/O cost of many path queries on networks, including route evaluation and path computations.

Common tabular representation for a graph data-structure for efficient implementation of a graph algorithm is the denormalized node table (Figure 6.9). We will base the rest of the discussion in this section on this representation.

6.5.1   A Measure of I/O Cost for Network Operations

In Chapter 5 we showed how the expected cost of point and range queries can be calculated. We derived a data-structure-independent measure for computing the I/O cost. Such a measure can be used to compare and contrast different indexes and clustering methods such as the R-tree and Z-order.

The measure for computing the I/O for point and range queries is clearly not adequate in the context of spatial networks. This is, again, due to the fact that relationships on networks are largely governed by the connectivity rather than the proximity relations.

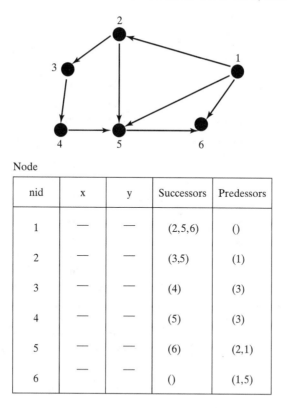

Node

nid	x	y	Successors	Predessors
1	—	—	(2,5,6)	()
2	—	—	(3,5)	(1)
3	—	—	(4)	(3)
4	—	—	(5)	(3)
5	—	—	(6)	(2,1)
6	—	—	()	(1,5)

FIGURE 6.9. Graph with its denormalized table representation.

For example, in the `River Network` example, the Yellowstone is closer to the Colorado but flows into and thus is connected to the Missouri.

One simple and intuitive measure to compute the I/O for network operations is related to the number of *unsplit* edges. An edge is *unsplit* if its two endpoints reside on the same disk page. Similarly an edge is *split* if its two endpoints reside on different disk pages.

Consider the graph and its node and edge relation shown in Figure 6.9. The attributes of the node relation are the node-id and x and y coordinates (not shown). The attributes of the edge relation are source, destination, and weight. The weight attribute could potentially encode spatial, temporal, and statistical information about the edge, like the distance, travel time, and the frequency of edge usage. For example, a route evaluation algorithm in traffic management is more likely to access a major highway rather than an adjoining service road.

Assume that the node relation is physically clustered (as shown in Figure 6.9) according to the value of the node-id and the disk page size is two tuples for the node relation. In other words, node 1 and 2 share a page. There are two other pages, one with nodes (3,4) and other with nodes (5,6). Then the operation `get-Successors(1)`, which retrieves the adjacency-list of node 1, will have to traverse 1 unsplit edge, (1,2), and two split edges (1,5) and (1,6). If we can cluster the nodes which minimize the number of unsplit edges, then that will reduce the I/O cost of network operations.

Formally, we define the *Connectivity Residue Ratio (CRR)* as

$$CRR = \frac{Total\ number\ of\ unsplit\ edges}{Total\ number\ of\ edges}$$

It can be shown that maximizing the CRR will minimize the average I/O cost of network operations like `get-a-Successors()`, and it usually reduces the cost of `get-successors()` as well. As an example, consider the CRR for above discussed paging scheme. For pages ((1,2), (3,4), (5,6)) of the graph shown in Figure 6.9, the CRR is $3/8 = 0.375$. If each page accomodate 3 nodes then higher CRR can be achieved. For example, CRR ((1,2,3), (4,5,6)) is $4/8 = 0.5$ and CRR ((1,5,6), (2,3,4)) is $5/8 = 0.625$.

6.5.2 A Graph-Partitioning Approach to Reduce Disk I/O

Graph partitioning was introduced in Chapter 4 in the context of computing the spatial-join of two relations in the presence of a join-index. The `graph-partitioning` problem is to partition the nodes of a graph with costs (weights) on its edges into subsets of given sizes, so as to minimize the sum of costs on all the cut edges. A *cut edge* is an edge that straddles two nodes in different partitions. In our case, the size of the subsets is bounded by the disk page size.

Thus, one approach to maximize the *CRR* is to partition the weighted graph using a graph-partitioning algorithm. Many public domain packages are now available which can rapidly partition graphs of extremely large sizes: up to a *million* nodes. Figure 6.10

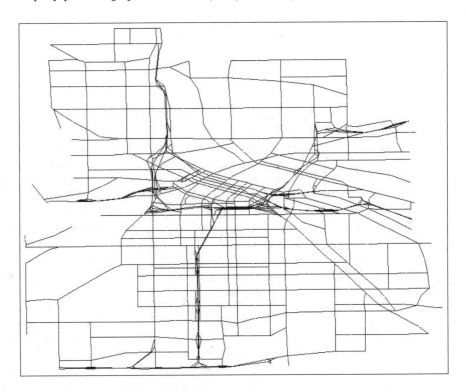

FIGURE 6.10. Major roads in the city of Minneapolis.

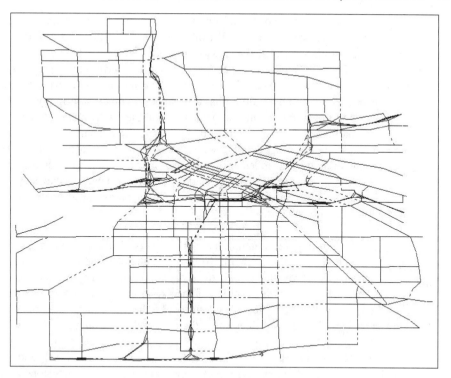

FIGURE 6.11. Cut-edges in CCAM paging of Minneapolis major roads.

shows the map of the major highways and streets in the city of Minneapolis, Minnesota, in the United States. Figure 6.11 shows the cut edge (dashed) and the unsplit edges (solid line) inside individual data pages of CCAM representation for the road map of Minneapolis. CCAM is described in next subsection. It uses min-cut graph partitioning.

6.5.3   CCAM: A Connectivity Clustered Access Method for Spatial Network

CCAM clusters the nodes of the network via graph partition. In addition, an auxiliary secondary index is used to support the Find(), get-a-Successor(), and get-Successors() operations. The choice of a secondary index can be tailored to the application. Some use the B+ tree with Z-order. Other access methods, such as the R-tree and Grid File, can alternatively be created as secondary indexes in CCAM to suit the application. In this section, we describe the file-structure and procedures used to implement the various operations on networks.

Connectivity-Clustered Data File

For each node, a record stores the node data, coordinates, successor list, and predecessor list. A successor list (predecessor list) contains a set of outgoing (incoming) edges, each represented by the node-id of its end (start) node and the associated edge cost. The successor list is also called the adjacency list, and is used in network computations. The predecessor list is used in updating the successor list during the Insert() and Delete() operations.

We will refer to the neighbor list of a node x as the set of nodes whose node-id appears in the successor list or predecessor list of x. We note that the records do not have fixed formats because the size of the successor list and predecessor list varies across nodes.

CCAM assigns nodes to the data page by a graph partitioning approach, which tries to maximize the CRR. Each data page is kept at least half full whenever possible. Records of the data file are not physically ordered by node-id values. A primary index cannot be created without renaming the nodes to encode disk-page information in the node-id, and it requires additional overhead during update operations. Therefore, a secondary index can be created on top of the data file with an index entry for each record in the data file.

If networks are embedded in geographic space, (x, y) coordinates for each node are also stored in the record. Then a spatial indexing scheme on the (x, y) coordinates can be used as the secondary index. This secondary index can support point and range queries on spatial databases.

Example: In Figure 6.12, a sample network and its CCAM is shown. The left half of Figure 6.12 shows a spatial network. Nodes are annotated with the node-id (an integer) and geographical coordinates (a pair of integers). To simplify the example, the node-id is an integer representing the Z-order of the (x, y) coordinates. For example, the node with the coordinates (1, 1) gets a node-id of 3. The solid lines that connect the nodes represent edges. The dashed lines show the cuts and partitioning of the spatial network into data pages. There exists a cut on edge e(u, v) if node u and node v fall into different partitions. The partitions are (0, 1, 4, 5), (2, 3, 8, 9), (6, 7, 12, 13), and (10, 11, 14, 15). The right half of Figure 6.12 shows the data pages and the secondary index. We note that the nodes are clustered into data pages by CCAM, using a graph-partitioning

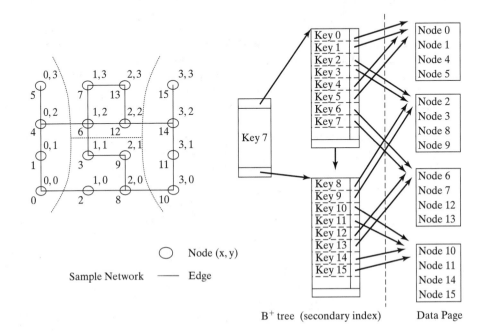

FIGURE 6.12. Clustering and storing a sample network (key represents spatial order).

approach. Nodes in the same partition set are stored on the same data page. They are not physically ordered by their node-id values. A secondary index ordered by node-id is used to facilitate the Find() operation. The secondary index in this example is a B+ tree on the Z-order of (x,y) coordinates of each node.

6.5.4   Summary

Spatial networks, for example, road maps, represent one of the fastest growing applications of SDBs. Spatial network data is often modeled as graphs, where nodes are points embedded in space. Spatial networks are accessed via get-a-Successor(), and get-successors() operations for path evaluation and shortest path computation. Efficient implementation of these operations are often based on connectivity among nodes rather than Euclidean distances.

Relational databases may represent graphs via a node table and an edge table. Simple operations, for example, get-Successor() can be performed. However, RA-based query languages (e.g., SQL2) are not capable of many graph operations (e.g., shortest path) which require a transitive closure operation. Database query languages have recently added the transitive closure operation. Specialized GIS products (e.g., ESRI Network Engine) also supported spatial network data and computations.

Many database components (e.g., query processing strategies, storage and access methods) are impacted from the addition of a graph operation in a query language. The transitive closure can be processed using a BFS or a DFS strategy. Dijktra's algorithm is a popular choice for computing partial transitive closures. Shortest path computation has specialized strategies (A*, hierarchical) as well. Storage and access methods maximizing CRR, a data-structure independent measure, tend to be most I/O efficient for graph operations (e.g., get-a-Successor()). Special clustering methods, CCAM, cluster node records using min-cut graph-partitioning algorithms to maximize CRR.

BIBLIOGRAPHIC NOTES

6.1 See [Guting, 1994b] for an extensive discussion on graph data models. The network model implemented in the NETWORK extension of Arc/Info is widely disseminated [ESRI, 1991]. A detailed description of Java interfaces for important graph classes is given in [Bailey, 1998].

6.2 For further discussion on extending query languages for networks see [Mannino and Shapiro, 1990] and [Biskup et al., 1990]. Consult [van der Lans, 1992] for a detailed discussion on the CONNECT clause. [Ullman and Widom, 1999], present a comprehensive description on the RECURSIVE clause in SQL3.

6.3 See [Jing et al., 1998], and [Jiang, 1991] for graph algorithms that focus on I/O cost.

6.4 The CCAM access method, specifically designed for spatial network databases, is described in [Shekhar and Liu, 1997].

EXERCISES

1. A unique aspect of spatial graphs is the Euclidean space in which they are embedded, which provides directional and metric properties. Thus nodes and edges have relationships such as left-of, right-of, north-of, and so on. An example is the restriction "no left turn" on an intersection in the downtown area.

    Consider the problem of modeling road maps using the conventional graph model consisting of nodes and edges. A possible model may designate the road intersections to be the nodes, with road segments joining the intersections to the edges. Unfortunately, the turn restrictions (e.g., No Left Turn) are hard to model in this context. A routing algorithm (e.g., A^*, Dijkstra) will consider all neighbors of a node and would not be able to observe the turn restriction. One way to solve this problem is to add attributes to nodes and edges and modify routing algorithms to pay attention to those attributes. Another way to solve the problem is to redefine the nodes and edges so that the turn restrictions modeled within the graph semantics and routing algorithms are not modified.

Propose alternative definitions of nodes and edges so that the routing algorithm need not be changed.

2. Study internet sites (e.g. mapquest.com) providing geographic services (e.g. routing). List spatial data types and operations needed to implement these geographic information services.

3. Express the following queries in SQL based on the table in Figure 6.1 and 6.2.
   (a) Find the last stop on the Red North route.
   (b) Which routes connect Richmond with San Leandro?
   (c) Find the number of stops between Downtown Berkeley and Dublin.

4. What is special about spatial networks relative to spatial databases with polygonal/linear objects?

5. We learned about graph operators (e.g., transitive closure, in the context of spatial networks). Is this operator relevant to spatial databases with point, linear or polygonal objects? Consider the GIS operation of `reclassify`, for example, given an elevation map, produce a map of mountainous regions (elevation > 600m). Note that adjacent polygons within mountains should be merged to remove common boundaries.

6. Given a polygonal map of the political boundaries of the countries of the world, do the following:
   (a) Classify the following queries into classes of transitive closure, shortest path, or other.
      (1) Find the minimum number of countries to be traveled through in going from Greece to China.
      (2) Find all countries with a land-based route to the United States.
   (b) Write SQL3/recursive queries for the above queries.

7. Most of the discussion in this chapter focused on graph operations (e.g., transitive closure, shortest path) on spatial networks. Are OGIS topological and metric operations relevant to spatial networks? List a few point and OGIS topological and metric operations.

8. Propose a suitable graph representation of the River Network to precisely answer the following query: Which rivers can be polluted if there is a spill in a specific tributary.

9. Extend the set of pictograms discussed in Chapter 2 for conceptual modeling of spatial networks.

10. Produce denormalize node table similar to Figure 6.2(e) for the River Network example.

11. Extend the logical data model for spatial network by adding a sub-class "Path" for the class "Graph." List a few useful operations and application domains. List a few other interesting sub-class of "Graph."

12. Turn-restrictions are often attached to road networks, for example, left-turn from a residential road onto an intersecting highway is often not allowed. Propose a graph model for road networks to model turn restrictions. Identify nodes and edges in the graph. How will one compute the shortest path honoring turn restrictions?

13. Compare and contrast the CCAM with the R-trees. For each basic graph operation, identify the efficient storage method between the two. Briefly explain your answer.

14. Compare and contrast the Dijktra's algorithm with the Best-first algorithm for computing the shortest path.

15. What is a hierarchical algorithm for shortest path problem? When should it be used?

16. Compare and contrast adjacency-list and adjacency-matrix representation for graphs. Create adjacency-list and adjacency-matrix representation for following graphs:
    (i)   Graph G in Fig 6.4
    (ii) Graph G* in Fig 6.4
    (iii) River network in Figure 6.3

17. What is the transitive closure of a graph? Construct transitive closure of the graph in Figure 6.2(a).

18. What is CRR? Compute CRR for the CCAM paging scheme for the graph in Figure 6.12. Also compute CRR for the following geometric paging scheme: page 1 contains (0,1,2,3), page 2 contains (4,5,6,7), page 3 contains (8,9,10,11) and page 4 (12,13,14,15).

19. Revisit map-reclassify operation discussed in Section 2.1.5. Discuss if SQL3 Recursion and OGIS operations may be used to implement it.

20. Compare breadth first search, Dijktra's algorithm and best first search. When does Dijktra's algorithm reduce to breadth first search? When does best first search reduce to breadth first search?

21. Consider a spatial network representing road maps with road-intersections as nodes and road-segments between adjacent intersections as edges. Coordinates of center points of road-segments are provided. In addition, stores and customer tables provide names, addresses and location of retail-stores and customers. Explain how shortest path algorithm may be used for the following network analysis problems:
    (i)   For a given customer, find the nearest store using driving distance along road network.
    (ii)   For a given store S and a set of customers, find cheapest path to visit all customers starting from S and returning to S.
    (iii) For each store determine the set of customers it should serve minimizing the total cost of serving all customers by using nearest stores.
    (iv)   Determine appropriate location for a new store to serve customers farthest from current stores.

CHAPTER 7

Introduction to Spatial Data Mining

In this chapter we present an overview of some important concepts related to the relatively new and rapidly developing field of *data mining*. Our focus, of course, is on the *mining* of spatial data, but the set of techniques that we discuss applies to many different types of data sets, including temporal, multimedia, and text databases.

Data mining is the process of discovering interesting and potentially useful *patterns* of information embedded in large databases. The mining metaphor is meant to convey an impression that *patterns* are *nuggets* of precious information hidden within large databases waiting to be discovered. Data mining has been quickly embraced by the commercial world as a way of harnessing information from the large amounts of data that corporations have collected and meticulously stored over the years.

If data mining is about extracting patterns from large databases, then the largest databases have a strong spatial component. For example, the Earth Observation Satellites, which are systematically *mapping* the entire surface of the earth, collect about one terabyte of data every day. Other large spatial databases include the U.S. census, and the weather and climate databases. The requirements of mining spatial databases are different from those of mining classical relational databases. In particular, the notion of *spatial autocorrelation* that similar objects tend to cluster in geographic space is unique to spatial data mining.

The complete data-mining process is a combination of many subprocesses that are worthy of study in their own right. Some important subprocesses are data extraction and data cleaning, feature selection, algorithm design and tuning, and the analysis of the output when the algorithm is applied to the data. For spatial data, the issue of scale, that is, the level of aggregation at which the data is being analyzed, is also very important. It is well known in spatial analysis that identical experiments at different levels of scale can sometimes lead to contradictory results. Our focus in this chapter is limited to the design of data-mining algorithms. In particular we describe how classical data-mining algorithms can be extended to model the spatial autocorrelation property. Here it is important to understand the distinction between spatial data mining and spatial data analysis. As the name implies, spatial data analysis covers a broad spectrum of techniques that deals with both the spatial and nonspatial characteristics of the spatial objects. On the other hand, spatial data mining techniques are often derived from spatial statistics, spatial analysis, machine learning, and databases, and are customized to analyze massive data sets. This chapter provides an introduction to the upcoming field of spatial data mining often building on the well-known techniques in spatial analysis and spatial statistics. More rigorous treatment of spatial analysis and spatial statistics can be found in [Bailey and Gatrell, 1995]; [Cressie, 1993]; [Fischer and Getis, 1997]; [Goodchild, 1986]; [Fotheringham and Rogerson, 1994].

In Section 7.1 we introduce the data-mining *process* and enumerate some well-known techniques that are associated with data mining. In Section 7.2 we introduce the important concept of spatial autocorrelation and show how it can be calculated and integrated into *classical* data-mining techniques. In Section 7.3 we discuss classification techniques and introduce the PLUMS model. Section 7.4 deals with association rule discovery techniques, and Section 7.5 deals with various clustering techniques. In Sections 7.6 we discuss spatial outlier detection techniques.

7.1 PATTERN DISCOVERY

Data mining is the process of discovering potentially interesting and useful *patterns* of information embedded in large databases. A pattern can be a summary statistic, like the mean, median, or standard deviation of a dataset, or a simple rule such as "Beach property is, on average, 40 percent more expensive than inland property."

A well-publicized pattern, which has now become part of data mining lore, was discovered in the transaction database of a national retailer: "People who buy diapers in the afternoon also tend to buy beer." This was an unexpected and interesting finding which the company put to profitable use by rearranging the store. Thus data mining encompasses a set of techniques to generate hypotheses, followed by their validation and verification via standard statistical tools. For example, if the store has a modest 1000 items, then finding which two items are correlated, or "go together," will require half a million correlation tests. This can be very expensive computationally given large set of transactions. Association rule algorithms can filter out a large fraction of these correlation tests using much less computation. The promise of data mining is the ability to rapidly and automatically search for *local* and potentially *high-utility* patterns using computer algorithms.

7.1.1 The Data-Mining Process

The entire data-mining process is shown in Figure 7.1. In a typical scenario, a domain expert (DE) consults a data-mining analyst (DMA) to solve a specific problem. For example, a manager in a city law enforcement department may want to explain the unusually high crime rate that the city is witnessing that year. The DE has access to a database that may provide clues to the specific problem that she wants the DMA to solve. An iterative process leads the DE and the DMA to agree upon a *problem statement* whose solution may provide a satisfactory answer to the original problem.

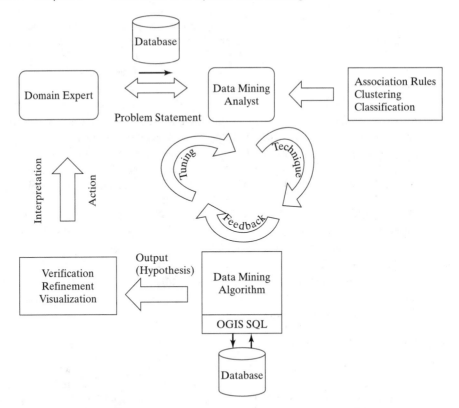

FIGURE 7.1. Data-mining process. The data-mining process involves a close interaction between a domain expert and a data-mining analyst. The output of the process is a set of hypotheses (patterns), which can then be rigorously verified by statistical tools and visualized using a GIS. Finally the analyst can interpret the patterns and make and recommend appropriate action.

Now the DMA must decide which technique or combination of techniques is required to address the problem. For example, the DMA may decide that the problem is best addressed in the framework of *classification*, in which case the goal may be to build a model that predicts the crime rate as a function of other socioeconomic variables. Once an appropriate technique is selected, a suitable data-mining algorithm is chosen to implement the technique. For classification, the DMA may decide to use *linear regression* instead of decision trees because the class attribute is continuous valued.

In an ideal case the data-mining algorithm should be designed to directly access the database using SQL (OGIS SQL for spatial databases) but typically a time-consuming exercise is involved in transforming the database into an algorithm-compatible format. The selection of a technique and the choice of an appropriate algorithm is also a non-deterministic, iterative process. For example, most algorithms require the adjustment of user-defined parameters, and in most cases there is no way to judge beforehand what are the right parameters to set for a specific database.

The output of a data-mining algorithm is typically a *hypothesis* that can be in the form of model parameters (as in regression), rules, or labels. Thus the output is a potential *pattern*. The next step is verification, refinement, and visualization of the pattern. For spatial data this part of the process is typically done with the help of GIS software. The final part of the data-mining process is the interpretation of the pattern, and, where possible, a recommendation for appropriate action. For example, the conclusion might be that the high crime rate is directly attributable to a downturn in the city's economic condition, in which case the law enforcement manager can direct the result to the appropriate authorities in the city government. Or the data-mining results might indicate that the high crime rate is a result of exceptionally high crime activity in a few neighborhoods ("hot spots"). In this case the law enforcement agencies can *saturate* those neighborhoods with police patrols.

7.1.2   Statistics and Data Mining

The entire data-mining process described looks suspiciously like statistics! So where is the difference? One way to view data mining is as a *filter* (exploratory data analysis) step before the application of rigorous statistical tools. The role of the filter step is to literally plow through reams of data and generate some potentially interesting hypotheses which can then be verified using statistics. This is similar to the use of R-trees to retrieve MBRs to answer range queries. The R-tree and MBRs provided a fast filter to search the space for potential candidates which satisfy a range query. The difference is that though R-trees guarantee completeness, i.e., there will be no *false dismissals*. Such a concept exists for a few (e.g., association rules) but not all (e.g., clustering) data mining techniques. A detailed discussion of differences between data mining and statistics is given in [Hand, 1999].

7.1.3   Data Mining as a Search Problem

Data mining is the search for *interesting* and *useful* patterns in large databases. A data-mining algorithm searches a potentially large space of patterns to come up with candidate patterns which can be characterized as interesting or useful or both. For example, consider a 4×4 image where we want to classify each pixel into one of two classes, *black* or *white* in Figure 7.2. Then there are a total of 2^{16} potential combinations. Now if we assert that each 2×2 block can only be assigned to one class, black or white, then the number of combinations reduces to 2^4. This restriction, though severe, is not completely unjustified. As it happens, most neighboring pixels of an image tend to belong to the same class, especially in a high-resolution image, due to spatial auto-correlation as well as large sizes of many features.

7.1.4   Unique Features of Spatial Data Mining

The difference between classical and spatial data mining parallels the difference between classical and spatial statistics. One of the fundamental assumptions that guide statistical analysis is that the data samples are independently generated, as with successive tosses of a coin, or the rolling of a die. When it comes to the analysis of spatial data, the assumption about the independence of samples is generally false. In fact, spatial data tends to be highly self-correlated. For example, people with similar characteristics, occupations, and backgrounds tend to cluster together in the same neighborhoods. The economies of a region tend to be similar. Changes in natural resources, wildlife, and temperature vary gradually over space. In fact, this property of like things to cluster in space is so fundamental that geographers have elevated it to the status of the first law of geography:

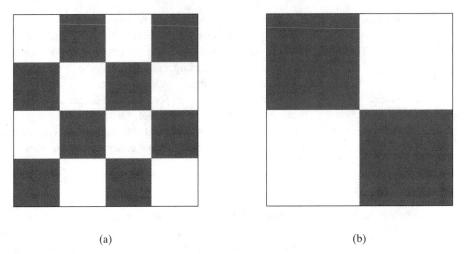

(a)   (b)

FIGURE 7.2. Search results of a data-mining algorithm. (a) One potential pattern out of a total of 2^{16}. (b) If we constrain the patterns to be such that each 4×4 block can only be assigned one class, then the potential number of patterns is reduced to 2^4. Based on other information, a data-mining algorithm can quickly discover the "optimal" pattern.

Everything is related to everything else, but nearby things are more related than distant things [Tobler, 1979]. In spatial statistics, an area within statistics devoted to the analysis of spatial data, this is called `spatial autocorrelation`.

7.1.5 Famous Historical Examples of Spatial Data Exploration

Spatial data mining is a process of automating the search for potentially useful patterns. Some well-known examples of what we now call spatial data mining occurred well before the invention of computers. [Griffith, 1999] provides some examples:

1. In 1855 when the Asiatic cholera was sweeping through London, an epidemiologist marked all locations on a map where the disease had struck and discovered that the locations formed a cluster whose centroid turned out to be a water pump. When the government authorities turned off the water pump, the cholera began to subside. Later scientists confirmed the water-borne nature of the disease.

2. The theory of Gondwanaland that all the continents formed one land mass was postulated after R. Lenz discovered (using maps) that all the continents could be fitted together into one-piece (like one giant jigsaw puzzle). Later fossil studies provided additional evidence supporting the hypothesis.

3. In 1909 a group of dentists discovered that the residents of Colorado Springs had unusually healthy teeth, and they attributed it to high level of natural fluoride in the local drinking water supply. Researchers later confirmed the positive role of fluoride in controlling tooth decay. Now all municipalities in the United States ensure that all drinking water is fortified with fluoride.

The goal of spatial data mining is to automate the discoveries of such correlations, which can then be examined by specialists for further validation and verification.

7.2 MOTIVATING SPATIAL DATA MINING

7.2.1 An Illustrative Application Domain

We now introduce an example that will be used throughout this chapter to illustrate the different concepts in spatial data mining. We are given data about two wetlands on the shores of Lake Erie in Ohio, United States, in order to *predict* the spatial distribution of a marsh-breeding bird, the red-winged blackbird (*Agelaius phoeniceus*). The names of the wetlands are Darr and Stubble, and the data was collected from April to June in two successive years, 1995 and 1996.

A uniform grid was imposed on the two wetlands, and different types of measurements were recorded at each cell or pixel. The size of each pixel was 5×5 meters. The values of seven attributes were recorded at each cell, and they are shown in Table 7.1. Of course domain knowledge is crucial in deciding which attributes are important and which are not. For example, `Vegetation Durability` was chosen over `Vegetation Species` because specialized knowledge about the nesting habits of the red-winged blackbird suggested that the choice of nest location is more dependent on the plant structure and its resistance to wind and wave action than on the plant species.

Our aim is to build a model for predicting the location of bird nests in the wetlands. Typically the model is built using a portion of the data, called the *learning* or *training* data and then tested on the remainder of the data, called the *testing* data. For example, later on we show how to build a model using the 1995 data on the Darr wetland and then test it on either the 1996 Darr or 1995 Stubble wetland data. In the learning data, all the attributes are used to build the model, and in the training data one value is *hidden* (in our case the location of the nests). Using knowledge gained from the 1995 Darr data and the value of the independent attributes in the test data, we want to predict the location of the nests in Darr 1996 or in Stubble 1995.

In this chapter we focus on three independent attributes, namely, *vegetation durability*, *distance to open water*, and *water depth*. The significance of these three variables was established using classical statistical analysis. The spatial distribution of these variables

TABLE 7.1: Habitat Variables Used for Predicting the Locations of the Nests of the Red-Winged Blackbird. *Note*: There are six independent variables and one dependent variable. The type of the dependent variable is binary

Attribute	Type	Role	Description
Vegetation Durability(VD)	Ordinal	Independent	Ordinate scale from 10 to 100
Stem Density (SD)	Numeric	Independent	In number of stems/m^2
Stem Height (SH)	Numeric	Independent	In centimeters above water
Distance to Open Water(DOP)	Numeric	Independent	In meters
Distance to Edge (DTE)	Numeric	Independent	In meters
Water Depth (WD)	Numeric	Independent	In centimeters
Red-winged Blackbird	Binary	Dependent	Record the presence/absence of the nest in the cell

and the actual nest locations for the Darr wetland in 1995 are shown in Figure 7.3. Gray scale is used to depict values of each attributes in Figure 7.3(b),(c) and (d) with darker shade representing higher values. The number of pixels with non-zero (nz) values in each map are shown below the map. For example, there are 85 nest locations and 5372 habitatable locations (pixels). These maps illustrate two important properties which are inherent in spatial data.

1. The values of attributes which are referenced by spatial location tend to vary gradually over space. Though this may seem obvious, classical data-mining techniques, either explicitly or implicitly, assume that the data is *independently* generated. For example, the maps in Figure 7.4 show the spatial distribution of attributes if they were independently generated. This property of "smoothness" across space is called *spatial autocorrelation.*

2. The spatial distribution of attributes sometimes shows distinct local trends which contradict the global trends. This is most vivid in Figure 7.3(b), where the spatial distribution of *vegetation durability* is jagged in the western section of the wetland compared to the overall impression of uniformity across the wetland. Thus spatial data is not only not *independent*, it is also not *identically* distributed.

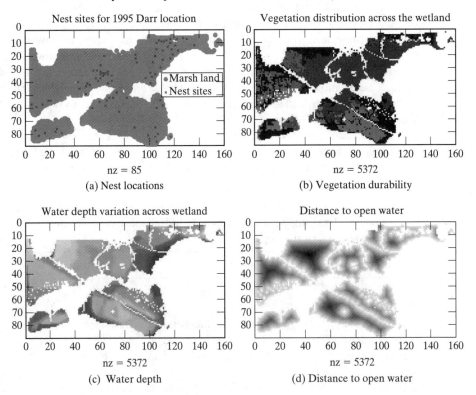

FIGURE 7.3. Darr wetland, 1995. (a) Learning dataset: The geometry of the marshland and the locations of the nests; (b) spatial distribution of *vegetation durability* over the marshland; (c) spatial distribution of *water depth*; and (d) spatial distribution of *distance to open water*.

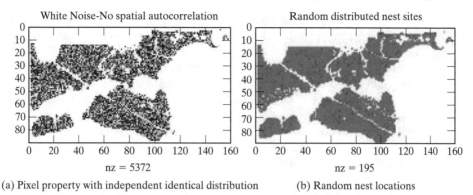

(a) Pixel property with independent identical distribution

(b) Random nest locations

FIGURE 7.4. Spatial distribution satisfying random distribution assumptions of classical regression.

We now show how to quantify the notion of spatial autocorrelation and spatial heterogeneity.

7.2.2 Measures of Spatial Form and Auto-correlation

As discussed in previous chapters, space can be viewed as *continuous* or *discrete*. Spatial continuity is common in most earth science data sets. Often it is difficult to represent data in continuous form, as an infinite number of samples exist in continuous space. On the other hand, only finite number of samples are enumerated in discrete space. In continuous space places are identified by coordinates, and in discrete space places are identified as objects. Spatial statistics are used for exploring geographic information. The term *geostatistics* is normally associated with continuous space and the term *spatial statistics* is associated with discrete space.

Centrality, dispersion and shape are used to characterize spatial form for a collection of points.

Mean center is the average location, computed as the mean of X and mean of Y coordinates. The mean center is also known as the center of gravity of a spatial distribution. Often the *weighted mean center* is the appropriate measure for several spatial applications, example, center of population. The *weighted mean center* is computed as the ratio between the sum of the coordinates of each point multiplied by its weight (e.g., number of people in block) and the sum of the weights. The measure *center* is used in several forms. It can be used to simplify complex objects (e.g., to avoid storage requirements and complexity of digitation of boundaries, a geographic object can be represented by its center), or for identifying the most effective location for a planned activity (e.g., a distribution center should be located at a central point so that travel to it is minimized).

Dispersion is a measure of the spread of a distribution around its center. Often used measures of dispersion and variability are *range, standard deviation, variance*, and *coefficient of variance*. Dispersion measures for geographic distributions are often calculated as the summation over the ratio of the weight of geographic objects and the proximity between them. *Shape* is multidimensional, and there is no single measure to capture all of the dimensions of the shape. Many of shape measures are based on comparison of the shape's perimeter with that of a circle of the same area.

It is a very common observation in many geospatial applications that the events at a location are influenced by the events at neighboring locations. *Spatial dependence* can be defined as "the propensity of a variable to exhibit similar (of different) values as a function of the distance between the spatial locations at which it is measured." Spatial autocorrelation is used to measure spatial dependence.

Spatial autocorrelation is a property that is often exhibited by variables which are sampled over space. For example, the temperature values of two locations near to each other will be similar. Similarly, soil fertility varies gradually over space and so do rainfall and pressure. In statistics there are measures to quantify this interdependence. One such measure is called Moran's I.

Moran's I: A Global Measure of Spatial Autocorrelation

Given a variable $x = \{x1, \ldots, x_n\}$ which is sampled over n locations, Moran's I coefficient is defined as

$$I = \frac{z W z^t}{z z^t},$$

where $z = \{x_1 - \bar{x}, \ldots, x_n - \bar{x}\}$, $\bar{x}$ is the mean of x, W is the $n \times n$ row-normalized contiguity matrix, and z^t is the transpose of z. For example, a spatial lattice, its contiguity matrix, and its row-normalized contiguity matrix are shown in Figure 7.5. The row labelled C in Figure 7.5(b) and Figure 7.5(c) has two non-zero entries for columns B and D to represent that B and D are neighbors of C in Figure 7.5(a).

The key point to note here is that Moran's I coefficient depends not only on the different values of the variable x but also on their arrangement. For example, Moran's I coefficients of the two 3×3 images shown in Figure 7.6 are different even though the sets of values of the pixels are identical. Readers are encouraged to compute the values for Moran's I to confirm this. Moran's I coefficients for the four-neighbor relation and the eight-neighbor relation are shown in Table 7.2.

Local Indicators of Spatial Autocorrelation

With the wide availability of high-resolution image data and the increasing use of GPS devices to mark the locations of samples in fieldwork, the fact that spatial autocorrelation exists is often moot. As a consequence, spatial statisticians often use local measures of spatial autocorrelation to track how spatial dependence varies in different areas within the

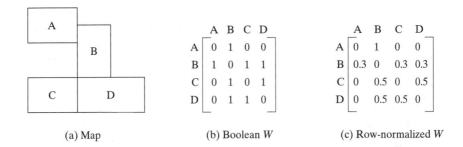

| (a) Map | (b) Boolean W | (c) Row-normalized W |

	A	B	C	D
A	0	1	0	0
B	1	0	1	1
C	0	1	0	1
D	0	1	1	0

	A	B	C	D
A	0	1	0	0
B	0.3	0	0.3	0.3
C	0	0.5	0	0.5
D	0	0.5	0.5	0

FIGURE 7.5. (a) A spatial lattice; (b) its contiguity matrix; (c) its row-normalized contiguity matrix.

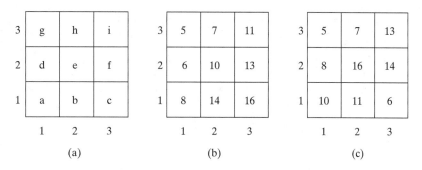

FIGURE 7.6. The Moran's I coefficient. The pixel value sets of the two images (b) and (c) are identical, but they have different Moran's I coefficients.

same spatial layer. A substantial variation in local autocorrelation at different locations indicates the presence of spatial heterogeneity, as is evident in the *vegetation durability* layer in Figure 7.3(b). The *local Moran's I* measure defined at location i is

$$I_i = \frac{z_i}{s^2} \sum_j \frac{W_{ij}}{z_j}, \ i \neq j,$$

where $z_i = x_i - \bar{x}$ and s is the standard deviation of x. For example, in Table 7.3 Moran's I coefficient is

$$I_{75} = \frac{(75 - 55.82)}{675.32}(71 + 85 + 61 + 63 - 4(55.82)) = 1.6109$$

7.2.3 Spatial Statistical Models

Statistical models are often used to represent the observations in terms of random variables. These models then can be used for estimation, description, and prediction based on probability theory.

Point Process

A point process is a model for the spatial distribution of the points in a point pattern. Several natural processes can be modeled as spatial point patterns. The positions of trees

TABLE 7.2: Moran's I Coefficient of Explanatory Variables to Predict Nest Locations for the Red-Winged Blackbird

Explanatory Variable	Four-Neighbor	Eight-Neighbor
Distance to edge	0.7606	0.9032
Distance to open water	0.7342	0.8022
Depth	0.6476	0.7408
Vegetation height	0.7742	0.8149
Stem density	0.6267	0.7653
Vegetation durability	0.3322	0.4851

TABLE 7.3: A 16×16 Gray-Scale Image

40	41	39	44	52	64	74	67	63	63	57	47	48	59	62	50
48	50	51	45	78	82	92	109	115	98	83	74	70	76	95	70
40	40	41	46	86	92	79	97	123	107	115	110	101	83	78	56
40	39	38	47	74	103	82	89	94	91	115	121	113	104	88	56
45	44	46	51	82	98	74	72	59	71	83	83	83	103	106	64
50	43	44	44	67	88	74	59	45	85	107	88	70	97	115	75
48	40	41	41	71	85	98	82	51	86	118	91	66	86	100	78
48	45	40	47	98	95	89	71	52	81	110	71	45	46	54	53
52	48	56	61	103	91	85	75	63	72	94	57	37	35	36	39
48	48	79	78	40	45	51	61	64	58	58	48	53	47	40	43
37	45	47	41	26	25	28	29	31	33	35	37	56	57	46	47
27	28	29	28	27	26	27	29	28	28	29	32	44	45	40	47
29	26	24	27	29	28	27	27	27	28	28	34	41	38	38	47
28	27	25	27	27	27	26	27	27	28	27	38	53	47	36	48
25	27	26	25	28	34	31	27	27	28	28	34	45	48	38	48
25	26	27	28	34	39	32	29	27	29	28	31	37	41	41	47

in a forest, locations of gas stations in a city, are all examples of point patterns. A spatial point process is defined as $Z(t) = 1; \forall t \in T$ or $Z(A) = N(A), A \subset T$, where both $Z(.)$ and T are random. Here T is the index set ($T \subset \Re^d$), and $Z(.)$ is the spatial process. Spatial point processes can be broadly grouped into random or nonrandom processes. Real point patterns are often compared with a random pattern (generated by a Poisson process) using the average distance between a point and its nearest neighbor. For a random pattern, this (average) distance is expected to be $\frac{1}{2*\sqrt{density}}$, where density is the average number of points per unit area. If for a real process, this computed distance falls within a certain limit, then we conclude that the pattern is generated by a random process; otherwise it is nonrandom process. Patterns generated by a nonrandom process can be either clustered (aggregated patterns) or uniformly spaced (regular or declustered patterns).

Lattices

A lattice D is denoted by $Z(s) : s \in D$, where the index set D is a countable set of spatial sites at which data are observed. Here the lattice refers to a countable collection of regular or irregular spatial sites. Census data defined on census blocks is an example. Several spatial analysis functions (example, applied on lattice spatial dependence, spatial autoregression, Markov Random Fields) can be applied on lattice models.

Geostatistics

Geostatistics deals with the analysis of spatial continuity, which is an inherent characteristic of spatial data sets. Geostatistics provides a set of statistical tools for modeling spatial variability and interpolation (prediction) of attributes at unsampled locations. Spatial variability can be analyzed using *variograms*. The amount and form of spatial autocorrelation can be described by a variogram, which summarizes the relationship between differences in pairs of measurements and the distance between corresponding pairs of points. Spatial interpolation (prediction) techniques are used to estimate the values at unsampled locations using the known values at sampled locations assuming the lack of geo-stationarity in the domain, which rules out global models. Kriging is a well-known estimation procedure used in geostatistics. Kriging uses known values (at sampled locations) and a semivariogram (estimated from the data) to determine unknown values. Kriging offers better estimates over conventional interpolation methods (such as weighted average, nearest neighbor) for spatial data sets, because it takes into account the spatial autocorrelation.

7.2.4   The Data-Mining Trinity

Data mining is a truly multidisciplinary area, and there are many novel ways of extracting patterns from data. Still, if one were to *label* data-mining techniques, then the three most noncontroversial labels would be *classification, clustering*, and *association rules*. Before we describe each of these classes in detail, we present some representative examples where these techniques can be applied.

Location Prediction and Thematic Classification

The goal of *classification* is to estimate the value of an attribute of a relation based on the value of the relation's other attributes. Many problems can be expressed as classification problems. For example, determining the locations of nests in a wetland based upon the value of other attributes (*vegetation durability, water depth*) is a classification problem sometimes also called the *location prediction* problem. Similarly, predicting where to *expect* hot spots in crime activity can be cast as a location prediction problem. Retailers essentially solve a location prediction problem when they decide upon a location for a new store. The well-known expression in real-estate, "Location is everything," is a popular manifestation of this problem.

In thematic classification, the goal is to categorize the pixels of satellite images into classes (e.g., water, urban, rural, forest,...) based upon the values of the "spectral signatures" recorded by receivers on board the satellite. The problem of thematic classification has deep spatial connections because in most instances pixels, which are neighbors on the image, belong to the same class. Thus satellite images naturally exhibit high spatial autocorrelation, if pixel sizes are smaller than the size of spatial features.

Determining the Interaction among Attributes

Rapid pattern detection within a large volume of data that is being continuously generated and stored in databases is one of the motivations behind data mining. One of the simplest and probably most well-known data-mining techniques is the discovery of relationships within attributes of a relation. For example, in the context of supermarket data analysis, a pattern of the form $X \rightarrow Y$ means that people who buy the product X also have a high likelihood of buying product Y. In the context of spatial databases, we have rules of the form of $is\_close(house, beach) \rightarrow is\_expensive(house)$, that is, houses which are close to the beach are likely to be expensive. In the context of the bird habitat, examples of the rules obtained were *low vegetation durability* $\rightarrow$ *high stem density*. In Section 7.4.1, we discuss *Apriori*, arguably the most well-known algorithm for discovering association rules.

Due to computational efficiency reasons, associations and association rules are often used to select candidate subsets of features for more rigorous statistical correlation analysis.

Identification of Hot Spots: Clusters and Outliers

As noted in Section 7.1.1, law enforcement agencies use hot spot analysis to determine areas within their jurisdiction that have unusually high levels of crime. They do this by recording the location of each crime and then using outlier detection and clustering techniques to determine areas of high crime density. Outlier detection and clustering can also be used to determine hot spots of nest location and disease clusters for cancer.

Another practical example of using spatial point clustering is to determine the location of service stations. For example, suppose a car company has information about the geographic location of all its customers and would like to open new service centers to cater exclusively to their customers. Clustering methods can be employed to determine the "optimal" location of service centers.

Clustering is an example of unsupervised learning, as no knowledge of the labels or the numbers of labels is known a priori. As a result, clustering algorithms have to work "harder" to determine the likely clusters. We discuss two methods of clustering later. The K-medoid is a deterministic clustering algorithm where each record is placed exclusively in one cluster. Probabilistic clustering on the other hand specifies the probability of each record belonging to any cluster.

The traditional goal of outlier detection is to discover a "small" subset of data points that are often viewed as noise, error, deviations, or exceptions. Outlier have been informally defined as observations that appear to be inconsistent with the remainder of the data set. The identification of outliers can lead to the discovery of unexpected knowledge and has a number of practical applications in areas such as credit card fraud, the performance analysis of athletes, voting irregularities, bankruptcy, weather prediction, and hot spot detection.

In their simplest form, hot spots are regions in the study space that stand out compared with the overall behavior prevalent in the space. Thus, hot spots can be identified by visually inspecting the distribution of the data on the map or by thresholding. For example, all regions where the attribute value (for example, crime rate) is at least two standard deviations away from the mean can be labeled as hot spots. From a spatial autocorrelation perspective, hot spots are locations where high local spatial autocorrelation exists.

In the following three sections, we cover three major approaches in data mining, namely, classification, association rules, as well as clustering and outlier detection.

7.3 CLASSIFICATION TECHNIQUES

Simply stated, the classification is to find a function

$$f : D \to L.$$

Here D, the domain of f, is the space of attribute data, and L is the set of labels. For example, in our illustrative bird-habitat domain, D is the three-dimensional space consisting of *vegetation durability*, *water-depth*, and *distance to open water*. The set L consists of two labels: *nest* and *no-nest*. The goal of the classification problem is to determine the appropriate f, from a given finite subset $Train \subset D \times L$. The success of classification is determined by the accuracy of f when applied to a data set $test$ which is disjoint from the *train* data. The classification problem is known as *predictive modeling* because f is used to predict the labels L when only data from the set D is given.

There are many techniques available to solve the classification problem. For example, in maximum-likelihood classification the goal is to completely specify the joint-probability distribution $P(D, L)$. This is usually accomplished by an application of the Bayes theorem and is the method of choice in remote-sensing classification. In the business community, decision-tree classifiers are the method of choice because they are simple to use. The decision-tree classifiers divide the attribute space (D in our case) into regions and assign a label to each region. Neural networks generalize the decision-tree classifiers by computing regions that have nonlinear boundaries. Another common method is to use regression analysis to model the interaction between D and L, using an equation. For example, the linear equation $y = mx + c$ is used for modeling class boundary in linear regression analysis.

In this chapter our focus is on extending classical data-mining techniques to incorporate spatial autocorrelation, which is the key distinguishing property of spatial data. Using linear regression as a proptype, we will show how classification methods can be extended to model spatial autocorrelation. We have chosen linear regression analysis to expound spatial classification because this method is most widely known, and spatial regression is probably the most well-studied method for spatial classification in the spatial statistics community. Other classification techniques (e.g. neural networks, decision trees, rules) can be extended as well.

7.3.1   Linear Regression

When the class variable is real-valued, it is more appropriate to calculate the conditional expectation rather than the conditional probability. Then the goal of classification is to compute

$$E[C|A_1, \ldots, A_n]$$

Writing in a more familiar notation, with C replaced by Y and the $A_i's$ by $X_i's$, and assuming that all the attributes are *identically* and *independently* generated standard normal random variables, the *linear* regression equation is

$$E[Y|\mathbf{X} = \mathbf{x}] = f(\alpha + \beta \mathbf{x}),$$

where $\mathbf{X} = (X_1, \ldots, X_n)$. This expression is equivalent to the more familiar expression $\mathbf{Y} = \mathbf{X}\beta + \epsilon$. Once again, the training data can be used to calculate the parameter vector β, which in turn can be used to calculate the value of the *class* attribute in the test data set. Function f maps $\alpha + \beta \mathbf{x}$ to a number between 0 and 1 to return probability. Commonly a logistic function (e.g., logit, probit) is used for f.

7.3.2   Spatial Regression

As we have shown before, when variables are spatially referenced, they tend to exhibit spatial autocorrelation. Thus the above assumption of identical independent distribution (i.i.d.) of random variables is not appropriate in the context of spatial data. Spatial statisticians have proposed many methods to extend regression techniques that account for spatial autocorrelation. The simplest and most intuitive is to modify the regression equation with the help of the contiguity matrix W. Thus the spatial autoregressive regression (SAR) equation is

$$\mathbf{Y} = \rho W \mathbf{Y} + \mathbf{X}\beta + \epsilon$$

The solution procedure for the SAR equation is decidedly more complex than that for the classical regression equation because of the presence of the ρWY term on the right side of the equation. Also notice that the W matrix is quadratic in size relative to the size of the data samples. Fortunately very few entries of W are nonzero, and sparse matrix techniques are used, which exploit this fact, to speed up the solution process.

7.3.3 Model Evaluation

We have discussed two general models to solve the classification problem, namely, linear regression and SAR. We now show the standard ways to evaluate the performance of models and explain why the standard ways of evaluation are not adequate in the context of spatial data mining.

In the case of a two-class classification problem, like nest or no-nest, there are four possible outcomes that can occur. For example, a nest can be correctly predicted, in which case it is called a true-positive (TP). A model can predict a *nest* where actually there was a no-nest, in which case it is a false-positive (FP). Similarly a no-nest can be correctly classified, a true-negative (TN), and a no-nest can be predicted where there was actually a nest, which is a false-negative (FN). All the four combinations are shown in Figure 7.7.

In classification the goal is to predict the conditional probability of one attribute on the basis of the values of the other attributes. Thus the outcome of classification techniques are probabilities. The way the probabilities are converted to actual class labels is to choose a cut-off probability b, and label all records whose predicted probability is greater than b by one class label, say *nest* and label the remaining records as *no-nest*. By varying b we can get a good estimate of how two different classifiers are behaving vis-à-vis each other. Thus for a given cut-off b, the True-Positive Rate (TPR(b)) and the False-Positive Rate (FPR(b)) are defined as

$$TPR(b) = \frac{TP(b)}{TP(b) + FN(b)}$$

$$FPR(b) = \frac{FP(b)}{FP(b) + TN(b)}$$

Now if we plot TPR versus FPR for the two classifiers under consideration, then the classifier whose curve is further above the diagonal $TPR = FPR$ is the better model

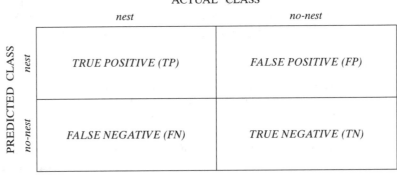

FIGURE 7.7. The four possible outcomes for a two-class prediction.

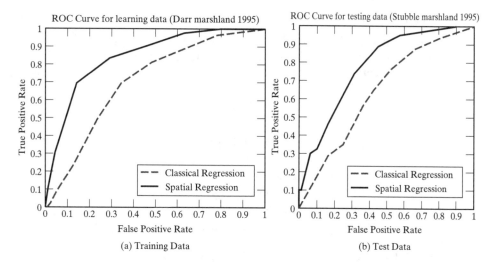

FIGURE 7.8. ROC curves (a). Comparison of the ROC curves for classical and SAR models on the 1995 Darr wetland data. (b) Comparison of the two models on the 1995 Stubble wetland data.

for that specific data set. These curves are called receiver operating characteristics (ROC) curves. We have compared the classical regression and SAR model on the Darr 1995 training set and the Stubble 1995 test set. The results in Figure 7.8 clearly show that including the spatial autocorrelation term ρWY leads to substantial improvement in the learning and predictive power of the regression model.

The model evaluation technique described above is not perfect in the context of spatial data. Consider the example shown in Figure 7.9. Here the goal is to predict the locations marked A. The ROC curves will fail to distinguish between the model that predicts the locations shown in Figure 7.9(c) and another model that predicts locations shown in Figure 7.9(d), even though the predictions in Figure 7.9(d) are closer to the actual locations than those predicted by Figure 7.9(c). One may use this observation to design a new framework to solve the two-class spatial classification problem in the context of the location prediction problem, which is described next.

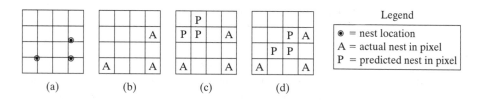

FIGURE 7.9. Problems of ROC curves with spatial data. (a) The actual locations of nests; (b) pixels with actual nests; (c) location predicted by a model; (d) location predicted by another mode. Prediction (d) is spatially more accurate than (c). Classical measures of classification accuracy will not capture this distinction.

7.3.4 Predicting Location Using Map Similarity (PLUMS)

The location prediction problem is a generalization of the nest-location prediction problem. It captures the essential properties of similar problems from other domains, including crime prevention and environmental management. The problem is formally defined as follows:

Given:

1. A spatial framework S consisting of sites $\{s_1, \ldots, s_n\}$ for an underlying geographic space G.
2. A collection of explanatory functions $f_{X_k} : S \to R^k, k = 1, \ldots K$, where R^k is the range of possible values for the explanatory functions.
3. A dependent class variable $f_C : S \to C = c_1, \ldots c_M$
4. An value for parameter α, relative importance of spatial accuracy.

Find: Classification model: $\hat{f}^C : R^1 \times \ldots R^k \to C$.

Objective: Maximize similarity $(map_{s_i \in S}(\hat{f}_C(f_{X_1}, \ldots, f_{X_k})), map(f_C))$
$$= (1 - \alpha)\, \text{classification\_accuracy}(\hat{f}_C, f_C) + (\alpha)\, \text{spatial\_accuracy}((\hat{f}_C, f_C)$$

Constraints:

1. Geographic space S is a multidimensional Euclidean space.[1]
2. The values of the explanatory functions, $f_{X_1}, \ldots, f_{X_k}$, and the dependent class variable, f_C, may not be independent with respect to the corresponding values of nearby spatial sites (that is, spatial autocorrelation exists).
3. The domain R^k of the explanatory functions is the one-dimensional domain of real numbers.
4. The domain of the dependent variable, $C = \{0, 1\}$.

This above formulation highlights two important aspects of location prediction. It explicitly indicates that (i) the data samples may exhibit spatial autocorrelation and (ii) an objective function (i.e., a map similarity measure) is a combination of classification accuracy and spatial accuracy. The *similarity* between the dependent variable f_C and the predicted variable $\hat{f}_C$ is a combination of the "traditional classification" accuracy and representation-dependent "spatial classification" accuracy. The regularization term α controls the degree of importance of **spatial accuracy** and is typically domain dependent. As $\alpha \to 0$, the map similarity measure approaches the traditional classification accuracy measure. Intuitively, α captures the spatial autocorrelation present in spatial data.

7.3.5 Markov Random Fields

Markov random field (MRF) based Bayesian classifiers estimate classification model $\hat{f}_C$ using MRF and Bayes' rule. A set of random variables whose interdependency relationship is represented by an undirected graph (i.e., a symmetric neighborhood matrix) is

---

[1] The entire surface of the earth cannot be modeled as a Euclidean space, but locally the approximation holds true.

called a Markov Random Field (MRF). The Markov property specifies that a variable depends only on its neighbors and is independent of all other variables. The location prediction problem can be modeled in this framework by assuming that the class label, $l_i = f_C(s_i)$, of different locations, s_i, constitute an MRF. In other words, random variable l_i is independent of l_j if $W(s_i, s_j) = 0$.

The Bayesian rule can be used to predict l_i from feature value vector X and neighborhood class label vector L_i as follows:

$$Pr(l_i|X, L_i) = \frac{Pr(X|l_i, L_i)Pr(l_i|L_i)}{Pr(X)} \tag{7.1}$$

$L_i = L \backslash l(s_i)$ denotes the collection of class labels in the neighborhood of site s_i excluding the class label at s_i.

A solution procedure can estimate $Pr(l_i|L_i)$ from the training data, where L_i denotes a set of labels in the neighborhood of s_i excluding the label at s_i, by examining the ratios of the frequencies of class labels to the total number of locations in the spatial framework. $Pr(X|l_i, L_i)$ can be estimated using kernel functions from the observed values in the training data set. For reliable estimates, even larger training data sets are needed relative to those needed for the Bayesian classifiers without spatial context, because we are estimating a more complex distribution. An assumption on $Pr(X|l_i, L_i)$ may be useful if the training data set available is not large enough. A common assumption is the uniformity of influence from all neighbors of a location. For computational efficiency it can be assumed that only local explanatory data $X(s_i)$ and neighborhood label L_i are relevant in predicting class label $l_i = f_C(s_i)$. It is common to assume that all interaction between neighbors is captured via the interaction in the class label variable. Many domains also use specific parametric probability distribution forms, leading to simpler solution procedures. In addition, it is frequently easier to work with a Gibbs distribution specialized by the locally defined MRF, through the Hammersley-Clifford theorem.

Both SAR and MRF Bayesian classifiers model spatial context and have been used by different communities for classification problems related to spatial datasets. Now we compare these two approaches to modeling spatial context, using a probabilistic framework.

Comparison of SAR and MRF Using a Probabilistic Framework

We use a simple probabilistic framework to compare SAR and MRF in this section. We will assume that classes $l_i \in (c_1, c_2, \ldots, c_M)$ are discrete and that the class label estimate $\hat{f}_C(s_i)$ for location s_i is a random variable. We also assume that feature values (X) are constant as there is no specified generative model. Model parameters for SAR are assumed to be constant, (i.e., β is a constant vector and ρ is a constant number). Finally, we assume that the spatial framework is a regular grid.

We first note that the basic SAR model can be rewritten as follows:

$$y = X\beta + \rho Wy + \epsilon$$

$$(I - \rho W)y = X\beta + \epsilon$$

$$y = (I - \rho W)^{-1}X\beta + (I - \rho W)^{-1}\epsilon = (QX)\beta + Q\epsilon \tag{7.2}$$

where $Q = (I - \rho W)^{-1}$ and β, ρ are constants (because we are modeling a particular problem). The effect of transforming feature vector X to QX can be viewed as a spatial smoothing operation. The SAR model is similar to the linear logistic model in terms of the transformed feature space. In other words, the SAR model assumes the linear separability of classes in transformed feature space.

Figure 7.10 shows two data sets with a *salt and pepper* spatial distribution of the feature values. There are two classes, c_1 and c_2, defined on this feature. Feature values close to two map to class c_2, and feature values close to one or three will map to c_1. These classes are not linearly separable in the original feature space. Local spatial smoothing can eliminate the *salt and pepper* spatial pattern in the feature values to transform the distribution of the feature values. In the top part of Figure 7.10, there are few values of three and smoothing revises them close to one since most neighbors have values of one. SAR can perform well with this data set because classes are linearly separable in the transformed space. However, the bottom part of Figure 7.10 shows a different spatial data set, where local smoothing does not make the classes linearly separable. Linear classifiers cannot separate these classes even in the transformed feature space assuming $Q = (I - \rho W)^{-1}$ does not make the classes linearly separable.

Although MRF and SAR classification have different formulations, they share a common goal, estimating the posterior probability distribution: $p(l_i|X)$ where l_i

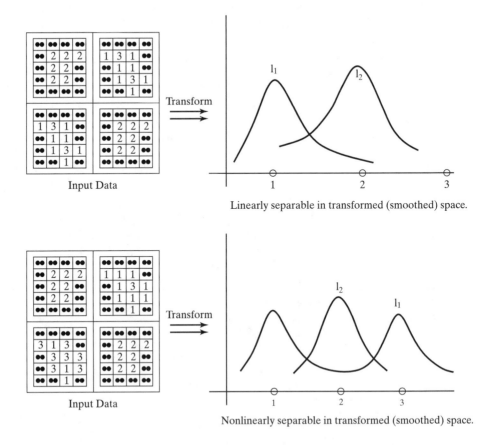

FIGURE 7.10. Spatial data sets with *salt* and *pepper* spatial patterns.

abbreviates $l(s_i)$. However, the posterior for the two models is computed differently with different assumptions. For MRF the posterior is computed using Bayes's rule. On the other hand, in logistic regression, the posterior distribution is directly fit to the data. For logistic regression, the probability of the class-label map $C = \{l(s_i \forall i\}$ is given by:

$$Pr(C|X) = \prod_{i=1}^{N} p(l_i|X) \tag{7.3}$$

One important difference between logistic regression and MRF is that logistic regression assumes no dependence on neighboring classes. Given the logistic model, the probability that the binary label takes its first value c_1 at a location s_i is:

$$Pr(l_i|X) = \frac{1}{1 + \exp(-Q_i X \beta)}, \tag{7.4}$$

where the dependence on the neighboring labels exerts itself through the W matrix, and subscript i (in Q_i) denotes the ith row of the matrix Q. Here we have used the fact that y can be rewritten as in equation 7.2.

To find the local relationship between the MRF formulation and the logistic regression formulation (for the two class case $c_1 = 1$ and $c_2 = 0$), at point s_i for $C = \{0, 1\}$

$$Pr((l_i = 1)|X, L_i)$$

$$= \frac{Pr(X|l_i = 1, L_i) Pr(l_i = 1, L_i)}{Pr(X|l_i = 1, L_i) Pr(l_i = 1, L_i) + Pr(X|l_i = 0, L_i) Pr(l_i = 0, L_i)}$$

$$= \frac{1}{1 + \exp(-Q_i X \beta)}, \tag{7.5}$$

which implies

$$Q_i X \beta = \ln \left(\frac{Pr(X|l_i = 1, L_i) Pr(l_i = 1, L_i)}{Pr(X|l_i = 0, L_i) Pr(l_i = 0, L_i)} \right) \tag{7.6}$$

This last equation shows that the spatial dependence is introduced by the W term through Q_i. More importantly, it also shows that in fitting β we are trying to simultaneously fit the relative importance of the features and the relative frequency $\left(\frac{Pr(l_i=1,L_i)}{Pr(l_i=0,L_i)} \right)$ of the labels. In contrast, in the MRF formulation, we explicitly *model* the relative frequencies in the class prior term. Finally, the relationship shows that we are making distributional assumptions about the class conditional distributions in logistic regression. Logistic regression and logistic SAR models belong to a more general exponential family. The exponential family is given by

$$Pr(u|v) = e^{A(\theta_v) + B(u, \pi) + \theta_v^T u} \tag{7.7}$$

where u, v are location and label respectively. This exponential family includes many of the common distributions such as Gaussian, Binomial, Bernoulli, and Poisson as special cases. The parameters θ_v and π control the form of the distribution. Equation 7.6 implies that the class conditional distributions are from the exponential family. Moreover, the distributions $Pr(X|l_i = 1, L_i)$ and $Pr(X|l_i = 0, L_i)$ are matched in all moments higher than the mean (e.g., covariance, skew, kurtosis, etc.), such that in the difference

$ln(Pr(X|l_i = 1, L_i)) - ln(Pr(X|l_i = 0, L_i))$, the higher order terms cancel out, leaving the linear term $(\theta_v^T u)$ in equation 7.7 on the left-hand side of equation 7.6.

7.4   ASSOCIATION RULE DISCOVERY TECHNIQUES

Association rules are patterns of the form $X \rightarrow Y$. One of the more famous patterns in data mining, *Diapers* → *Beer*, is an example of an association rule. Association rules, as they are currently expressed, are a weaker form of correlation, as they do not discover negative associations. For example, the rule *Tofu* $\overset{neg}{\rightarrow}$ *Beef* (*people who buy tofu are not likely to buy beef*) may hold true but is not considered an association rule. In probabilistic terms an association rule $X \rightarrow Y$ is an expression of conditional probability, $P(Y|X)$.

An association rule is characterized by two parameters: *support* and *confidence*. Formally let $I = \{i_1, i_2, \ldots, i_k\}$ be a set of items, and $T = \{t_1, t_2, \ldots, t_n\}$ be a set of transactions, where each t_i is a *subset* of I. Let C be a subset of I. Then the *support* of C with respect to T is the number of transactions that contain C: $\sigma(C) = \{t | t \in T, C \subset t$. Note that $\sigma(C)$ denotes the cardinality of set C in this context instead of the relational algebra operator. Then $i_i \rightarrow i_2$ if and only if the following two conditions hold:

Support: i_1 and i_2 occur in at least s percent of the transactions: $\frac{\sigma(i_1 \wedge i_2)}{|T|}$.

Confidence: Of all the transactions in which i_1 occurs, at least c percent of them contain i_2: $\frac{\sigma(i_1 \wedge i_2)}{\sigma(i_1)}$.

For example, consider a set $I = \{A, B, C, D, E, F\}$ of letters and a transaction set $T = \{ABC, ABD, BDE, CEF\}$ of words where the intraword ordering is irrelevant (i.e., $ABC = BCA = CAB$). Table 7.4 shows the support and confidence of three rules: $A \Rightarrow B$, $B \Rightarrow C$, $F \Rightarrow E$. For another example, see Figure 7.11, which shows a snapshot of sales at an electronics store. Also shown are examples of item sets which enjoy high support and association rules with high confidence. We now describe *Apriori*, an algorithm to rapidly discover association rules in large databases.

7.4.1   *Apriori: An Algorithm for Calculating Frequent Itemsets*

The *Apriori* algorithm is probably the most well-known algorithm for discovering frequent item sets. Frequent item sets are sets that satisfy the support threshold as defined earlier. The algorithm exploits a simple but fundamental monotonicity property of the support measure: *If an itemset has high support, then so do all its subsets.* An outline of the *Apriori* algorithm is shown below.

FrequentItemSet := $\emptyset$;
$k := 1$;

TABLE 7.4: Support and Confidence of Three Rules

Rule	Support	Confidence
$A \Rightarrow B$	0.50	1.0
$B \Rightarrow C$	0.25	0.33
$F \Rightarrow E$	0.25	1.0

ITEMS

Car CD Player	D
Car Alarm	A
TV	T
VCR	V
Computer	C

FREQUENT ITEMSETS

SUPPORT	ITEMSETS
100%(6)	A
83%(5)	C, AC
67%(4)	C, T, V, DA, DC, AT, AV, DAC
50%(3)	DV, TC, VC, DAV, DVC, ATC, AVC, DAVC

TRANSACTIONS

1	D A V C
2	A T C
3	D A V C
4	D A T C
5	D A T V C
6	A T V

ASSOCIATION RULES WITH CONFIDENCE = 100%

D ⟶ A (4/4)	D ⟶ A (4/4)	VC ⟶ A (3/3)
D ⟶ C (4/4)	D ⟶ A (3/3)	DV ⟶ A (3/3)
D ⟶ AC (4/4)	D ⟶ A (3/3)	VC ⟶ A (3/3)
T ⟶ C (4/4)	D ⟶ A (4/4)	DAV⟶ A (3/3)
V ⟶ A (4/4)	D ⟶ A (3/3)	DVC⟶ A (3/3)
C ⟶ A (5/5)	D ⟶ A (3/3)	AVC⟶ A (3/3)

ASSOCIATION RULES WITH CONFIDENCE >=80%

C ⟶ D (4/5)	A ⟶ C (5/6)	C ⟶ DA (4/5)

FIGURE 7.11. Example transaction database, frequent itemsets, and high-confidence rules.

While $CandidateSet_k \neq \emptyset$ **do**
    Create counter for each itemset in $CandidateSet_k$
    forall transactions in database **do**
        Increment counter of itemset in $CandidateSet_k$
        which occurs in the transaction;
    $Level_k$:= All elements in $CandidateSet_k$ which
        exceed the support threshold
    FrequentItemSet : = FrequentItemSet $\cup Level_k$;
    $CandidateSet_{k+1}$: = All k+1-itemsets whose k-item subsets
        are in $Level_k$.
    $k := k + 1$;
end

Apriori first discovers all the 1-itemsets (singletons) that are *frequent* (i.e., that exceed the support threshold). The second step is to combine all frequent itemsets to form 2-itemsets: $CandidateSet_2$. The algorithm then evaluates this set to search for frequent 2-itemsets. This process goes on: frequent 2-itemsets are combined to form 3-itemsets, until the set $CandidateSet_k$ is empty.

    After all the frequent itemsets have been calculated, the next step is to search for rules that satisfy the minimum confidence requirement. This is done as follows. Given a frequent itemset $\{ABC\}$, all possible rules are checked to see if they satisfy the confidence parameter c. For example, for each of the following rules,

$$\{AB\} \rightarrow \{C\}$$
$$\{BC\} \rightarrow \{A\}$$
$$\{CA\} \rightarrow \{B\}$$

the *confidence* measure is to be checked. Those that cross the threshold c are legitimate *association rules*. Confidence of these rules can be computed from the support of frequent itemsets.

There are two approaches toward generating spatial association rules. In the first approach, the focus is on spatial predicates rather than items. The second approach generalizes the notion of a transaction to include neighborhoods and the notion of association rules to colocation rules.

7.4.2 Spatial Association Rules

Spatial association rules are defined in terms of spatial predicates rather than items. A spatial association rule is a rule of the form

$$P_1 \wedge P_2 \wedge \ldots \wedge P_n \rightarrow Q_1 \wedge \ldots \wedge Q_m,$$

where at least one of the $P_i's$ or $Q_j's$ is a spatial predicate. For example, the rule

$$is\_a(x, country) \wedge touches(x, Mediterranean) \overset{s\%, c\%}{\rightarrow} is_a(x, wine - exporter)$$

(i.e., a country that is adjacent to the Mediterranean Sea is a wine exporter) is an association rule with support s and confidence c. Table 7.5 shows examples of association rules that were discovered in the Darr 1995 wetland data. Association rules were designed for categorical attributes, and therefore their application to datasets which are numeric is limited. This is because the transformation from numeric to categorical data involves a process of discretization which in most instances is somewhat arbitrary. For example, in the Darr wetland example, what is a `high Stem-Height`?

7.4.3 Colocation Rules

Colocation rules attempt to generalize association rules to point collection data sets that are indexed by space. There are several crucial differences between spatial and nonspatial associations including:

TABLE 7.5: Examples of Spatial Association Rules Discovered in the 1995 Darr Wetland Data

Spatial Association Rule	Sup.	Conf.
$Stem\_height(x, high) \wedge Distance\_to\_edge(x, far)$ $\rightarrow Vegetation\_Durability(x, moderate)$	0.1	0.94
$Vegetation\_Durability(x, moderate) \wedge Distance\_to\_water(x, close)$ $\rightarrow Stem\_Height(x, high)$	0.05	0.95
$Distance\_towater(x, far) \wedge Water\_Depth(x, shallow)$ $\rightarrow Stem\_Height(x, high)$	0.05	0.94

1. The notion of a *transaction* is absent in spatial situations, since data is embedded in continuous space. Partitioning space into transactions can lead to overestimate or underestimate of interest measures, for example, support or confidence.

2. Size of itemset in spatial databases in small, that is, there are many fewer *items* in the itemset in a spatial situation than in a nonspatial situation. For example, in a retail setting it is common to deal with distinct items that run into the tens of thousands. This is not the case for spatial data sets where the equivalent of spatial items are almost never more than few dozens. This implies that the cost of candidate generation is no more a dominant factor as in *Apriori* algorithm. Enumeration of neighborhood (e.g., instance of frequent itemsets) dominate the total computational cost.

3. In most instances, spatial *items* are discretized version of continuous variables. For example, in the United States high per-capita income regions may be defined as regions where the mean yearly income is greater than fifty thousand dollars.

In this approach of spatial association rules discovery, the notion of a transaction is replaced by neighborhood. We illustrate this approach with the help of an example. The colocation pattern discovery process finds frequently colocated subsets of spatial event types given a map of their locations (see Figure 7.12). For example, analysis of habitats

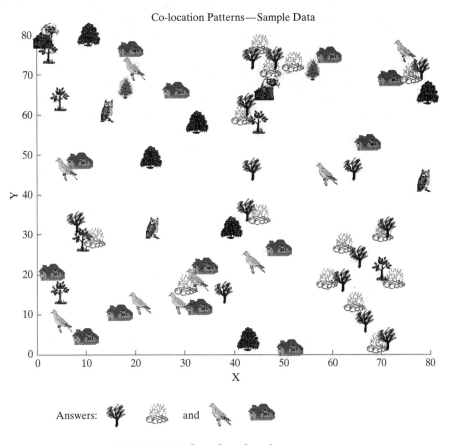

FIGURE 7.12. Sample colocation patterns.

of animals and plants may identify the colocation of predator-prey species, symbiotic species, and fire events with ignition sources. Readers may find it interesting to analyze the map in Figure 7.12 to find colocation patterns. There are two colocation patterns of size two in this map as noted at the bottom of the figure.

7.5 CLUSTERING

Clustering is a process for discovering "groups," or clusters, in a large database. Unlike classification, clustering involves no a priori information either on the number of groups or what the group labels are. Thus there is no concept of training or test data data in clustering. This is the reason that clustering is also referred as *unsupervised learning*.

The clusters are formed on the basis of a "similarity" criterion which is used to determine the relationship between each pair of tuples in the database. Tuples that are similar are usually grouped together, and then the group is labeled. For example, the pixels of satellite images are often clustered on the basis of the spectral signature. This way a remotely sensed image can be quickly segmented with minimal human intervention. Of course, a domain expert does have to examine, verify, and possibly refine the clusters. A famous example of population segmentation occurred in the 1996 U.S. presidential election when political pundits identified "Soccer Moms" as the swing electorate who were then assiduously courted by major political parties. Clustering is another technique to determine the "hot spots" in crime analysis and disease tracking.

Clustering is a very well-known technique in statistics, and the data-mining's role is to scale a clustering algorithm to deal with the large data sets that are now becoming the norm rather than the exception. The size of the database is a function of the number of records in the table and also the number of attributes (the dimensionality) of each record. Besides the volume, the type of data, whether it is numeric, binary, categorical, or ordinal, is an important determinant in the choice of the algorithm employed.

It is convenient to frame the clustering problem in a multidimensional attribute space. Given n data objects described in terms of m variables, each object can be represented as a point in an m-dimensional space. Clustering then reduces to *determining high-density groups of points from a set of nonuniformly distributed points.* The search for potential groups within the multidimensional space is then driven by a suitably chosen similarity criterion.

For example, the counties in the United States census data be clustered on the basis of, say, four attributes: *rate-of-unemployment, population, per-capita-income,* and *life-expectancy.* Counties that have similar values for these attributes will be grouped or clustered together.

When dealing with attribute data that is referenced in physical (e.g., geographic) space the clustering problem can have two interpretations. Consider the plot shown in Figure 7.13, which shows the variation of an attribute value (example, population density) as a function of location shown on the x-axis. Now what are the clusters, and how do we interpret them? For example, if our goal is to identify hot spots, for example, *central* cities and their zones of influence from a set of cities that dominate other cities as measured by the variance of an attribute value across the landscape, then we are looking for spatial clusters marked S1 and S2 in Figure 7.13. On the other hand, if our goal is to identify pockets in the landscape where an attribute (or attributes) are homogeneously expressed, then we are looking for clusters marked A1 and A2. Though the second interpretation is

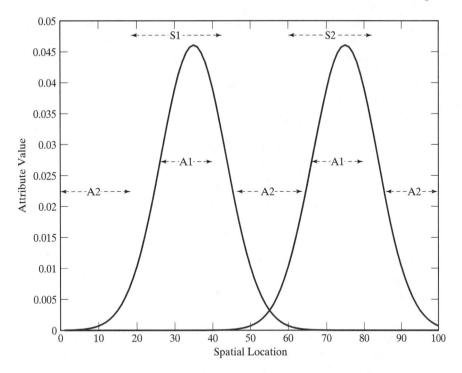

FIGURE 7.13. Two interpretations of spatial clustering. If the goal is to identify locations that dominate the surroundings (in terms of influence), then the clusters are S1 and S2. If the goal is to identify areas of homogeneous values, the clusters are A1 and A2.

essentially nonspatial, the spatial aspects exist because of the spatial autocorrelation that may exist in the attribute data. The clusters identified should be spatially homogeneous and not "speckled." These two interpretations of the clustering problem are formally defined as below:

> **DEFINITION 1. Given:** A set $S = \{s_1, \ldots, s_n\}$ of spatial objects (e.g., points) and a real-valued, nonspatial attributes f evaluated on S, (e.g., $f : S \rightarrow R$).

Find: Two disjoint subsets of S, C, and $NC = S - C$, where $C = \{s_1, \ldots, s_k\}$, $NC = \{nc_1, \ldots, nc_l\}$, and $k < n$.

Objective: $\min_{C \subset S} \sum_{j=1}^{l} | f(nc_j) - \sum_{i=1}^{k} \frac{f(c_i)}{(dist(nc_j, c_i))}|^2$

Where: $dist(a, b)$ is the Euclidean or some other distance measure.

Constraints:

1. The data set conforms to the theory of central places, which postulates that the influence of a central city decays as the square of the distance.
2. There is at most one nonspatial attribute.

DEFINITION 2. Given: (1) A set $S = \{s_1, \ldots, s_n\}$ of spatial objects (e.g., points) and a set of real-valued, nonspatial attributes f_i $i = 1, \ldots, I$ defined on S, (i.e., for each i, $f_k : S \rightarrow R$); and (2) neighborhood structure E on S.

Find: Find K subsets $C_k \subset S$, $k = 1, \ldots, K$ such that

Objective: $\min_{C_k \subset S} \sum_{C_k, s_i \in C_k, s_j \in C_k} dist(F(s_i), F(s_j)) + \sum_{i,j} nbddist(C_i, C_j)$

Where: (1) F is the cross-product of the $f_i's$, $i = 1, \ldots, n$; (2) $dist(a, b)$ is the Euclidean or some other distance measure; and (3) $nbddist(C, D)$ is the number of points in C and D which belong to E, i.e., pairs of neighbor mapped to different clusters.

Constraints: $|C_k| > 1$ for all $k = 1, \ldots, K$.

Categories of Clustering Algorithms

Cluster analysis is one of most often performed data analysis technique in many fields. This has resulted in a multitude of clustering algorithms, so it is useful to categorize them into groups. Based on the technique adopted to define clusters, the clustering algorithms can be categorized into four broad categories:

1. *Hierarchical* clustering methods start with all patterns as a single cluster, and successively perform splitting or merging until a stopping criterion is met. This results in a tree of clusters, called *dendograms*. The dendogram can be cut at different levels to yield desired clusters. Hierarchical algorithms can further be divided into *agglomerative* and *divisive* methods. Some of the hierarchical clustering algorithms are: balanced iterative reducing and clustering using hierarchies (BIRCH), clustering using representatives (CURE), and robust clustering using links (ROCK).

2. *Partitional* clustering algorithms start with each pattern as a single cluster and iteratively reallocates data points to each cluster until a stopping criterion is met. These methods tend to find clusters of spherical shape. *K-means* and *K-medoids* are commonly used partitional algorithms. Squared error is the most frequently used criterion function in partitional clustering. Some of the recent algorithms in this category are partitioning around medoids (PAM), clustering large applications (CLARA), clustering large applications based on randomized search (CLARANS), and expectation-maximization (EM).

3. *Density-based* clustering algorithms try to find clusters based on density of data points in a region. These algorithms treat clusters as dense regions of objects in the data space. Some of the density-based clustering algorithms are: density-based spatial clustering of applications with noise (DBSCAN), and density-based clustering (DENCLUE).

4. *Grid-based* clustering algorithms first quantize the clustering space into a finite number of cells and then perform the required operations on the quantized space. Cells that contain more than certain number of points are treated as dense. The dense cells are connected to form the clusters. Grid-based clustering algorithms are primarily developed for analyzing large spatial data sets. Some of the grid-based clustering algorithms are statistical information grid-based method (STING), STING+, WaveCluster, BANG-clustering, and clustering in quest (CLIQUE).

Sometimes the distinction among these categories is diminishing, and some algorithms can even be classified into more than one group. For example, CLIQUE can be considered as both a density-based and grid-based clustering method.

We now describe two well-known approaches to clustering, the *K-medoid* algorithm and mixture analysis using the EM algorithm. We also briefly discuss how the EM algorithm can be modified to account for the special nature of spatial data.

7.5.1   *K-medoid: An Algorithm for Clustering*

We restrict our attention to points in the two-dimensional space R^2, though the technique can be readily generalized to a higher dimensional space. Given a set P of n data points, $P = \{p_1, p_2, \ldots, p_n\}$ in R^2, the goal of *K-medoid* clustering is to partition the data points into k clusters such that the following objective function is minimized:

$$J(M) = J(m_1, \ldots, m_k) = \sum_{i=1}^{k} \sum_{p \in C_i} d(p, m_i)$$

In $J(C)$, m_i is the representative point of a cluster C_i. If m_i is restricted to be a member of P, then it is called a *medoid*. On the other hand, if m_i is the average of the cluster points and not necessarily a member of P, then it is called the *mean*. Thus the *K-mean* and the *K-medoid* approaches are intimately related. Even though the *K-mean* algorithm is more well known, we focus on the *K-medoid* approach because the medoid, unlike the median, is less sensitive to outliers.

The *K-medoids* characterize the K clusters, and each point in P belongs to its nearest medoid. Because we have restricted the ambient space to be R^2, the distance function d is the usual Euclidean distance.

$$d(p, m_i) = ((p(x) - m_i(x))^2 + (p(y) - m_i(y))^2)^{\frac{1}{2}}$$

Thus the K-medoid approach transforms the clustering problem into a search problem. The search space X is the set of all k-subsets M of P (i.e., $|M| = k$), and the objective function is $J(M)$. X can be modeled as a graph, where the nodes of the graph are the elements of X. Two nodes M_1 and M_2 are *adjacent* if $|M_1 \cap M_2| = k - 1$ (i.e.,+ they differ by one and only one data point).

The *K-medoid* algorithm consists of the following steps:

1. Choose an arbitrary node M_o in X.
2. Iteratively move from current node M_t to an adjacent node M_{t+1} such that $J(M_{t+1}) < J(M_t)$. The move from current node to adjacent node consists of replacing a current medoid m with a data point $p \in P$. Thus $M_{t+1} = M_t \cup \{p\} - \{m\}$.
3. Stop when $J(M_{t+1}) \geq J(M_t)$ for all adjacent nodes.

Step 2 is the heart of the algorithm. There are many options available to move from a node to its adjacent node. Table 7.6 lists some of the options. The table includes the name of each option as it is referred to in the literature, the strategy for moving, and whether the option will guarantee a local optima. All the options are examples of local search because only the adjacent nodes are explored.

TABLE 7.6: Four Options for Local Search in Clustering

Local Search	Strategy to move from M_t to $M_{t+1} = M_t \cup \{p\} - \{m\}$	Guarantee local optima
Global hill climbing (HC)	Move to the best neighbor	Yes
Randomized HC	Move to best of sampled neighbors	No
Local HC	Move to a new neighbor as soon as it is found	Yes
Distance-restricted HC	Move to best neighbor within a specified distance	No

7.5.2   Clustering, Mixture Analysis, and the EM Algorithm

One drawback of the *K-medoid* (or *K-mean*) approach is that it produces "hard" clusters, that is, each point is uniquely assigned to one and only one cluster. This can be a serious limitation because it is not known a priori what the actual clusters are. In the statistics literature, the clustering problem is often recast in terms of *mixture models*. In a mixture model, the data is assumed to be generated by a sequence of probability distributions where each distribution generates one cluster. The goal then is to identify the parameters of each probability distribution and their weights in the overall mixture distribution. In a mixture model, each instance of the database belongs to all the clusters but with a different grade of membership, which is quantified by the weights of the individual distributions in the mixture model. Thus the mixture model framework is more flexible than the *K-medoid* approach. Typically each probability distribution is represented as a normal distribution, and the challenge is to determine the mean, variance, and weight of each distribution. The assumption of normality is not as restrictive as it might appear because a statistics theorem guarantees that any probability distribution can be expressed as a finite sum of normal distributions.

A Finite Mixture Example

Consider the gray-scale 4×4 image shown in Figure 7.14. Assume we want to partition the set of pixels into two clusters, A and B, where each cluster is modeled as a Gaussian distribution. The finite mixture problem is to calculate the parameters $\mu_A, \mu_B, \sigma_A, \sigma_B, p_A, p_B$.

For the moment, assume the cluster membership of each pixel is given as shown in Figure 7.14(b). Then all the parameters can be easily calculated. For example,

$$\mu_A = \frac{12 + 10 + 2 + 18 + 11 + 5 + 7 + 9 + 13}{9} = 9.7$$

$$\sigma_A = \frac{(12 - \mu_1)^2 + (10 - \mu_1)^2 + \ldots + (13 - \mu_1)^2}{8} = 4.7$$

$$p_A = \frac{9}{16}$$

Similarly $\mu_B = 17.6$, $\sigma_B = 4.1$, and $p_A = \frac{5}{16}$. Computing the probability of a given pixel value belonging to cluster is then a simple exercise using Bayes's Theorem.

12	15	25	20
17	10	2	18
11	5	17	17
7	9	12	13

(a)

1	2	2	2
2	1	1	1
1	1	2	2
1	1	2	1

(b)

1	1	2	2
1	1	1	2
1	1	1	1
1	1	1	1

(c)

FIGURE 7.14. (a) A gray-scale 4×4 image. (b) The labels of the image generated using the EM algorithm. (c) The labels generated for the same image using the neighborhood EM algorithm. Notice the spatial smoothing attained by modifying the objective function.

For example, given a pixel value x, the probability that it belongs to cluster A is

$$P(A|x) = \frac{P(x|A)p_A}{P(x)}$$

$$= \frac{P(x|A)p_A}{P(x|A)p_A + P(x|B)p_B}$$

$$= \frac{N(x, \mu_A, \sigma_A)p_A}{N(x, \mu_A, \sigma_A)p_A + N(x, \mu_B, \sigma_B)p_B},$$

where

$$N(x, \mu_A, \sigma_A) = \frac{1}{\sqrt{(2\pi)}\sigma_A} \exp^{\frac{-(x-\mu_A)^2}{2\sigma^2}}$$

Now in our case the cluster labels are not known and neither are the distribution parameters. All we know is that there are two clusters and that each cluster is modeled as a Gaussian distribution. At first this problem may appear to be unsolvable because there are too many unknowns: cluster labels for each pixel and the distribution parameters of the cluster. Problems of this type can be solved using the EM algorithm. The EM algorithm, like the *K-medoid* algorithm, is an iterative algorithm which begins with the guess estimate of the distribution parameters. It then computes the "expected values" of the data given the initial parameters. The new, expected data values are then used to calculate the maximum likelihood estimate for the distribution parameters (see the appendix for a brief discussion of maximum likelihood estimation). This procedure is iterated until some convergence criterion is met. The EM algorithm guarantees that the maximum likelihood estimate will improve after each iteration, though the convergence can be slow. The steps of the EM algorithm follow:

1. Guess the initial model parameters: u_A^0, Σ_A^0 and p_A^0 and u_B^0, Σ_B^0 and p_B^0.
2. At each iteration j, calculate the probability that the data object x belongs to clusters A and B.

$$P(A|x) = \frac{p_A^j P^j(x|A)}{P^j(x)} \quad P(B|x) = \frac{p_B^j P^j(x|B)}{P^j(x)}$$

3. Update the mixture parameters on the basis of the new estimate:

$$p_A^{j+1} = \frac{1}{n} \sum_x P(A|x) \qquad p_B^{j+1} = \frac{1}{n} \sum_x P(B|x)$$

$$\mu_A^{j+1} = \frac{\sum_x x P(A|x)}{\sum_x P(A|x)} \qquad \mu_B^{j+1} = \frac{\sum_x x P(B|x)}{\sum_x P(B|x)}$$

$$\sigma_A^{j+1} = \frac{\sum_x P(A|x)(x - \mu_A^{j+1})^2}{\sum_x P(A|x)} \qquad \sigma_B^{j+1} = \frac{\sum_x P(B|x)(x - \mu_B^{j+1})^2}{\sum_x P(B|x)}$$

4. Compute the log estimate $E_j = \sum_x log(P^j(x))$. If for some fixed stopping criterion ϵ, $|E_j - E_{j+1}| \leq \epsilon$, then stop; else set $j = j + 1$.

The Neighborhood EM Algorithm

A careful reader may have noticed that the EM algorithm completely ignores the spatial distribution of the pixel; it only works with the pixel values. Thus if we rearrange the pixel values shown in Figure 7.14(a), the EM algorithm will still come up with the same cluster labeling and the same values of the distribution parameters.[2] Such a solution, as we know, does not take into account the spatial autocorrelation property inherent in spatial data. As we have mentioned before, the search space for spatially referenced data is a combination of a conceptual attribute space and the physical (geographic) space. The spatial autocorrelation property then implies that the clusters should vary gradually in the physical space.

In order to make the EM algorithm spatially sensitive, we first follow the recipe proposed by [Ambroise et al., 1997].

Step 1: The EM algorithm for mixture models is equivalent to the optimization of the following objective function:

$$D(c, \mu_k, \sigma_k, p_k) = \sum_{k=1}^{2} \sum_{i=1}^{n} c_{ik} \log(p_k N(x_i, \mu_k, \sigma_k)) - \sum_{k=1}^{2} \sum_{i=1}^{n} c_{ik} log(c_{ik}),$$

where $\mathbf{c} = \mathbf{c_{ik}}$, $\mathbf{i} = \mathbf{1}, \ldots, \mathbf{n}$ and $k = 1, \ldots K$ define a fuzzy classification representing the grade of membership of data point $\mathbf{x_i}$ into cluster k. The c_{ik}'s satisfy the constraints $(0 < c_{ik} < 1$, $\sum_{k=1}^{2} c_{ik} = 1, \sum_{i=1}^{n} c_{ik} > 0)$. Again we have two clusters $k = 1, 2$, and there are n data points.

Step 2: In order to account for spatial autocorrelation, we introduce a new term,

$$G(c) = \frac{1}{2} \sum_{k=1}^{2} \sum_{i=1}^{n} \sum_{j=1}^{n} c_{ik} c_{jk} w_{ij},$$

where $W = (w_{ij})$ is the contiguity matrix as defined before.

---

[2]Actually because of the randomness of the initial parameters, each run of the EM algorithm can potentially result in a different solution.

The new "spatially weighted" objective function is

$$U(c, \mu, \sigma) = D(c, \mu, \sigma) + \beta G(c),$$

where $\beta \geq 0$ is a parameter to control the spatial homogeneity of the dataset.

Step 3: Except for the new parameter c, which is an $n \times 2$ matrix, all the parameters are calculated exactly as before. The formula for $c'_{ik}s$ is

$$c_{ik}^{m+1} = \frac{p_k^m N(x_i, \mu_k, \sigma_k) \exp\{\beta \sum_{j=1}^{d=n} c_{jk}^{m+1} w_{ij}\}}{\sum_{l=1}^{2} p_l^m N(x_i, \mu_l^m, \sigma_l^m) \exp\{\beta \sum_{j=1}^{n} c_{jl}^{m+1} w_{ij}\}}$$

At each iteration m, the c'_{ik} can be solved using a fixed point iterative scheme.

We have carried out experiments using the neighborhood EM (NEM) algorithm on the bird data set. We assume two clusters corresponding to the presence/absence of nests. When $\beta = 0$, the NEM reduces to the classical EM algorithm. We varied the β parameters, and the results are shown in Figure 7.15. The results lead us to conclude that including spatial information in the clustering algorithm leads to a dramatic improvement of results (Figure 7.15[b] compared with Figure 7.15[a]), but overemphasizing spatial information leads to "oversmoothing" and degradation in accuracy.

7.5.3 Strategies for Clustering Large Spatial Databases

We now show how the *K-medoid* algorithm can be *scaled* by taking advantage of *spatial* index structures that were introduced in Chapter 4.

Assume we have a spatial database of n points which is too large for all the points to reside in the main memory at the same time. We make the following additional assumptions:

1. A spatial index structure such as the *R*-tree or Z-order is available in the SDBMS.
2. c is the average number of points stored in a disk page.
3. k is the number of clusters.
4. The cost of the *K-medoid* algorithm is dominated by Step 2, the computation of $J(M_{t+1}) - J(M_t)$.

Sampling via the R-Tree

The leaves of the *R*-tree correspond to collections of points associated with an MBR. We can choose a representative sample of the n points by selecting one sample point (e.g., mean or medoid) from each leaf node. A natural choice of the sample point is a data point *closest* to the centroid of the MBR. Thus instead of n points the algorithm only has to cluster, on the average, n/c points.

Choose Only Relevant Clusters

One way to compute $J(M_{t+1}) - J(M_t)$, is to loop over all the nonmedoid points and calculate the distance *afresh*. The cost associated with such a strategy can be prohibitive, given the large size of the database. Fortunately only the nonmedoid points associated with the old medoid m and new medoid p in $M_{t+1} = M_t \cup \{p\} - \{m\}$ contribute to $J(M_{t+1}) - J(M_t)$. Thus only the cluster points of m and p have to be fetched into the

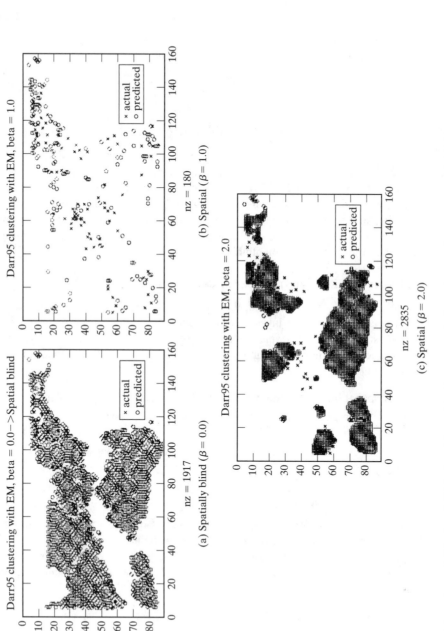

FIGURE 7.15. Using the neighborhood EM algorithm. (a) As expected clustering without any spatial information leads to poor results; (b) including spatial information ($\beta = 1.0$) leads to dramatic improvement of results; and (c) overemphasizing spatial information ($\beta = 2.0$) again leads to poor results.

main memory. The success of this approach is predicated upon the efficient retrieval of points corresponding to a cluster.

One way to efficiently retrieve the cluster points of a medoid is to observe that the *Voronoi polygons* associated with the medoids contain their cluster points. Thus a range query where the query region is the Voronoi polygon will retrieve all the cluster points of a medoid m. Such a query can be efficiently processed using either the R^*-tree or the Z-order index.

7.6 SPATIAL OUTLIER DETECTION

Global outliers have been informally defined as observations in a data set which appear to be inconsistent with the remainder of that set of data [Barnett and Lewis, 1994], or which deviate so much from other observations so as to arouse suspicions that they were generated by a different mechanism [Hawkins, 1980]. The identification of global outliers can lead to the discovery of unexpected knowledge and has a number of practical applications in areas such as credit card fraud, athlete performance analysis, voting irregularity, and severe weather prediction. This section focuses on spatial outliers, i.e., observations which appear to be inconsistent with their neighborhoods. Detecting spatial outliers is useful in many applications of geographic information systems and spatial databases. These application domains include transportation, ecology, public safety, public health, climatology, and location based services.

We model a spatial data set to be a collection of spatially referenced objects, such as houses, roads, and traffic sensors. Spatial objects have two distinct categories of dimensions along which attributes may be measured. Categories of dimensions of interest are spatial and non-spatial. Spatial attributes of a spatially referenced object includes location, shape, and other geometric or topological properties. Non-spatial attributes of a spatially referenced object include traffic-sensor-identifiers, manufacturer, owner, age, and measurement readings. A spatial neighborhood of a spatially referenced object is a subset of the spatial data based on a spatial dimension, e.g., location. Spatial neighborhoods may be defined based on spatial attributes, e.g., location, using spatial relationships such as distance or adjacency. Comparisons between spatially referenced objects are based on non-spatial attributes.

A spatial outlier is a spatially referenced object whose non-spatial attribute values are significantly different from those of other spatially referenced objects in its spatial neighborhood. Informally, a spatial outlier is a local instability (in values of non-spatial attributes) or a spatially referenced object whose non-spatial attributes are extreme relative to its neighbors, even though they may not be significantly different from those of the entire population. For example, a new house in an old neighborhood of a growing metropolitan area is a spatial outlier based on the non-spatial attribute house age.

We use an example to illustrate the differences between global and spatial outlier detection methods. In Figure 7.16(a), the X-axis is the location of data points in one dimensional space; the Y-axis is the attribute value for each data point. Global outlier detection methods ignore the spatial location of each data point, and fit the distribution model to the values of the non-spatial attribute. The outlier detected using a this approach is the data point G, which has an extremely high attribute value 7.9, exceeding the threshold of $\mu + 2\sigma = 4.49 + 2 * 1.61 = 7.71$, as shown in Figure 7.16(b). This test assumes a normal distribution for attribute values.

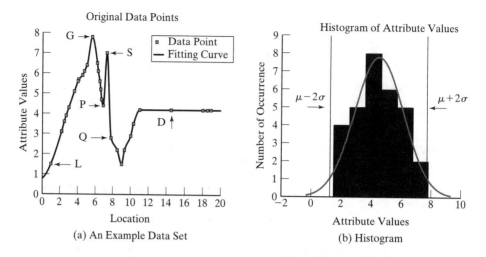

FIGURE 7.16. A Data Set for Outlier Detection.

Tests to detect spatial outliers seperate the spatial attributes from the non-spatial attributes. Spatial attributes are used to characterize location, neighborhood, and distance. Non-spatial attribute dimensions are used to compare a spatially referenced object to its neighbors. Spatial statistics literature provides two kinds of tests, namely graphical tests and quantitative tests. Graphical tests are based on visualization of spatial data which highlight spatial outliers. Example methods include variogram clouds and Moran scatterplots. Quantitative methods provide a precise test to distinguish spatial outliers from the remainder of data. Scatterplots [Luc, 1994] are a representative technique from the quantitative family.

A variogram-cloud displays data points related by neighborhood relationships. For each pair of locations, the square-root of the absolute difference between attribute values at the locations versus the Euclidean distance between the locations are plotted. In data sets exhibiting strong spatial dependence, the variance in the attribute differences will increase with increasing distance between locations. Locations that are near to one another, but with large attribute differences, might indicate a spatial outlier, even though the values at both locations may appear to be reasonable when examining the data set non-spatially. Figure 7.17(a) shows a variogram cloud for the example data set shown in Figure 7.16(a). This plot shows that two pairs (P, S) and (Q, S) in the left hand side lie above the main group of pairs, and are possibly related to spatial outliers. The point S may be identified as a spatial outlier since it occurs in both pairs (Q, S) and (P, S). However, graphical tests of spatial outlier detection are limited by the lack of precise criteria to distinguish spatial outliers. In addition, a variogram cloud requires non-trivial post-processing of highlighted pairs to separate spatial outliers from their neighbors, particularly when multiple outliers are present or density varies greatly.

A Moran scatterplot [Luc, 1995] is a plot of normalized attribute value $(Z[f(i)] = ((f(i) - \mu_f)/\sigma_f))$ against the neighborhood average of normalized attribute values $(W \cdot Z)$, where W is the row-normalized (i.e., $\sum_j W_{ij} = 1$) neighborhood matrix, (i.e., $W_{ij} > 0$ iff neighbor(i, j)). The upper left and lower right quadrants of Figure 7.17(b) indicate a spatial association of dissimilar values: low values surrounded by high value neighbors

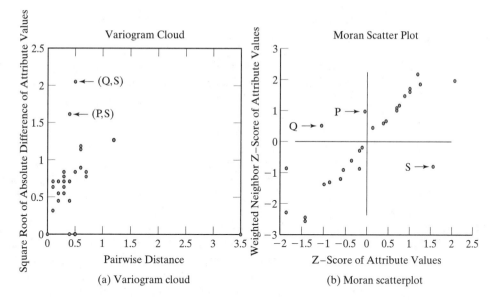

FIGURE 7.17. Variogram Cloud and Moran Scatterplot to Detect Spatial Outliers.

(e.g., points P and Q), and high values surrounded by low values (e.g., point S). Thus we can identify points(nodes) that are surrounded by unusually high or low value neighbors. These points can be treated as spatial outliers.

> **DEFINITION.** $Moran_{outlier}$ is a point located in the upper left and lower right quadrants of a Moran scatterplot. This point can be identified by $(Z[f(i)]) \times (\sum_j (W_{ij} Z[f(j)])) < 0$.

A scatterplot [Luc, 1994] shows attribute values on the X-axis and the average of the attribute values in the neighborhood on the Y-axis. A least square regression line is used to identify spatial outliers. A scatter sloping upward to the right indicates a positive spatial autocorrelation (adjacent values tend to be similar); a scatter sloping upward to the left indicates a negative spatial autocorrelation. The residual is defined as the vertical distance (Y-axis) between a point P with location (X_p, Y_p) to the regression line $Y = mX + b$, that is, residual $\epsilon = Y_p - (mX_p + b)$. Cases with standardized residuals, $\epsilon_{standard} = \frac{\epsilon - \mu_\epsilon}{\sigma_\epsilon}$, greater than 3.0 or less than -3.0 are flagged as possible spatial outliers, where μ_ϵ and σ_ϵ are the mean and standard deviation of the distribution of the error term ϵ. In Figure 7.18(a), a scatter plot shows the attribute values plotted against the average of the attribute values in neighboring areas for the data set in Figure 7.16(a). The point S turns out to be the farthest from the regression line and may be identified as a spatial outlier.

> **DEFINITION.** $Scatterplot_{outlier}$ is a point with significant standardized residual error from the least square regression line in a scatter plot. Assuming errors are normally distributed, then $\epsilon_{standard} = |\frac{\epsilon - \mu_\epsilon}{\sigma_\epsilon}| > \theta$ is a common test. Nodes with standardized residuals $\epsilon_{standard} = \frac{\epsilon - \mu_\epsilon}{\sigma_\epsilon}$ from regression line $Y = mX + b$ and greater than θ or less than $-\theta$ are flagged as possible spatial outliers. The μ_ϵ and σ_ϵ are the mean and standard deviation of the distribution of the error term ϵ.

A location may also be compared to its neighborhood using the function $S(x) = [f(x) - E_{y \in N(x)}(f(y))]$, where $f(x)$ is the attribute value for a location x, $N(x)$ is the set of neighbors of x, and $E_{y \in N(x)}(f(y))$ is the average attribute value for the neighbors of x. The statistic function $S(x)$ denotes the difference of the attribute value of a sensor located at x and the average attribute value of $x's$ neighbors.

Spatial Statistic $S(x)$ is normally distributed if the attribute value $f(x)$ is normally distributed. A popular test for detecting spatial outliers for normally distributed $f(x)$ can be described as follows: Spatial statistic $Z_{s(x)} = |\frac{S(x) - \mu_s}{\sigma_s}| > \theta$. For each location x with an attribute value $f(x)$, the $S(x)$ is the difference between the attribute value at location x and the average attribute value of $x's$ neighbors, μ_s is the mean value of $S(x)$, and σ_s is the value of the standard deviation of $S(x)$ over all stations. The choice of θ depends on a specified confidence level. For example, a confidence level of 95 percent will lead to $\theta \approx 2$.

Figure 7.18(b) shows the visualization of spatial statistic $Z_{s(x)}$ method using data set in Figure 7.16(a). The X-axis is the location of data points in one dimensional space; the Y-axis is the value of spatial statistic $Z_{s(x)}$ for each data point. We can easily observe that the point S has the $Z_{s(x)}$ value exceeding 3, and will be detected as spatial outlier. Note the two neighboring points P and Q of S have $Z_{s(x)}$ values close to -2 due to the presence of spatial outlier in their neighborhoods.

We now give an application domain case study of spatial outliers. The map shown in Figure 7.19 shows a network of sensor stations embedded in Interstate highways surrounding the Minneapolis-St. Paul (Twin Cities) metropolitan area in Minnesota, US. Each of the 900 stations (represented as polygons) measures the traffic volume and occupancy on a particular stretch of the highway at regular intervals. The natural notion of a neighborhood is defined in terms of graph connectivity rather than Euclidean distance. Our objective is to determine stations that are "outliers" based on the values of the traffic measurements (e.g., volume) from each station.

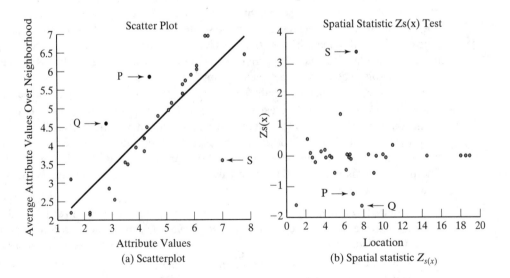

FIGURE 7.18. Scatterplot and Spatial Statistic $Z_{s(x)}$ to Detect Spatial Outliers.

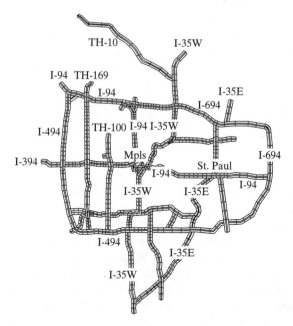

FIGURE 7.19. A network of traffic sensor stations.

The three neighborhood definitions we consider are shown in Figure 7.20. We consider spatio-temporal neighborhoods because time along with space are crucial for the discovery of spatial outliers. In Figure 7.20, $\{s_1, t_1\}$ and $\{s_3, t_3\}$ are spatial neighbors of $\{s_2, t_2\}$ if s_1, and s_3 are connected to s_2 in a spatial graph. Two data points $\{s_2, t_3\}$ are temporal neighbors of $\{s_2, t_2\}$ if t_1, t_2 and t_3 are consecutive time slots. In addition, we define a neighborhood based on both space and time series as a spatial-temporal

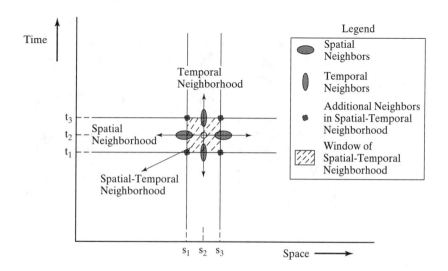

FIGURE 7.20. Spatial and temporal neighborhoods.

neighborhood. In Figure 7.20, $(s_1, t_1), (s_1, t_2), (s_1, s_3), (s_2, t_1)$ are the spatial-temporal neighbors of (s_2, t_2) if s_1 and s_3 are connected to s_2 in a spatial graph, and t_1, t_2 and t_3 are consecutive time slots.

The choice of the test statistic to probe the existence of outliers is the next task to consider. In this application we used $S(x) = [f(x) - E_{y \in N(x)}(f(y))]$, where $f(x)$ is the attribute value (e.g., volume) for neighbors of x. If $f(x)$ has a normal distribution, then it can be shown the $S(x)$ has a normal distribution too (see Exercises). A data point x is considered an outlier if the z-score

$$\frac{S(x) - \mu_s}{\sigma_s} > \theta$$

The choice of θ depends on the specified confidence interval. For example, a confidence interval of 95 percent will lead to $\theta = 2$.

The third and final task for detecting outliers is the design and application of an "efficient" algorithm to calculate the test statistic and apply the outlier detection test. This is a nontrivial task because the size of typical data sets are too large to fit in the primary memory. For example, in the traffic data there are approximately 4000 sensors, and they emit a reading every five minutes. Thus for a six-month time frame, and assuming each reading generates 100 bytes of data, the size of the data set is approximately $100 \times 12 \times 24 \times 180 \times 1000 = 5$ gigabytes. Thus it becomes imperative that I/O efficient algorithms be used to discover outliers.

The effectiveness of the $Z_{s(x)}$ method on the Twin-Cities traffic data set is illustrated in the following example. Figure 7.21 shows one example of traffic flow outliers. Figures 7.21(a) and (b) are the traffic volume maps for I-35W north bound and south bound, respectively, on 1/21/1997. The X-axis shows 5-minute time slots for the whole day and the Y-axis is the label of the stations installed on the highway, starting from 1 on the north end to 61 on the south end. The abnormal white line at 2:45PM and the white rectangle from 8:20AM to 10:00AM on the X-axis and between stations 29 to 34 on the Y-axis can be easily observed from both (a) and (b). The white line at 2:45PM is

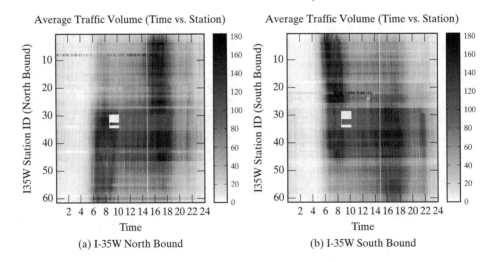

FIGURE 7.21. Spatial outliers in traffic volume data

an instance of temporal outliers, where the white rectangle is a spatial-temporal outlier. Both represent missing data. Moreover, station 9 in Figure 7.21(a) exhibits inconsistent traffic flow compared with its neighboring stations, and was detected as a spatial outlier. Station 9 may be a malfunctioning sensor.

7.7   SUMMARY

Data mining is a rapidly developing area that lies at the intersection of database management, statistics, and artificial intelligence. Data mining provides semiautomatic techniques for discovering unexpected patterns in very large quantities of data.

Spatial data mining is a niche area within data mining for the rapid analysis of spatial data. Spatial data mining can potentially influence major scientific challenges, including the study of global climate change and genomics.

The distinguishing characteristic of spatial data mining can be neatly summarized by the first law of geography: All things are related, but nearby things are more related than distant things. The implication of this statement is that the standard assumption of independence and identically distributed (iid) random variables, which characterize classical data mining, is not applicable for the mining of spatial data. Spatial statisticians have coined the word *spatial-autocorrelation* to capture this property of spatial data.

The important techniques in data mining are *association rules, clustering, classification*, and *regression*. Each of these techniques has to be modified before it can be used to mine spatial data. In general there are two strategies available to modify data mining techniques to make them more sensitive for spatial data: The underlying statistical model, which is based on the iid assumption, can be corrected, or the objective function, which drives the search, can be modified to include a spatial term. The spatial autoregressive regression technique is an example of the first approach, and the NEM algorithm is an example of the latter.

7.8   APPENDIX: BAYESIAN CALCULUS

Probability theory provides a mathematical framework to deal with uncertainty. It is also a cornerstone of data mining, because in data mining we are trying to *generalize* our findings on the basis of a finite, albeit large, database.

Given a set of *events* Ω, the *probability* P is a function from Ω into $[0, 1]$, which satisfies the following two axioms:

1. $P(\Omega) = 1$.
2. If A and B are mutually exclusive events (like the rolling of two dice), then

$$P(AB) = P(A)P(B)$$

7.8.1   Conditional Probability

The notion of *conditional* probability is central to data mining. A conditional probability, $P(A|B) = \alpha$, means that, given the event B has occurred, the probability of event A is α. Thus if event B has occurred and everything else is irrelevant to A, then $P(A) = \alpha$.

The basic rule for probability calculus is the following:

$$P(AB) = P(A|B)P(B) = P(B|A)P(A).$$

In words this statement says that the joint-probability $P(AB)$ is the product of the conditional $P(A|B)$ and the marginal $P(B)$. A simple manipulation of this rule results in Bayes's Theorem.

$$P(A|B) = \frac{P(B|A)P(A)}{P(B)}$$

In the context of Bayes's rule, $P(A|B)$ is called the *posterior* probability, and the $P(B)$ is called the *prior*. Bayes's rule allows the inversion of probabilities, which is the cornerstone of classification. For example, this allows probabilities to be calculated on the test data based on the probabilities calculated on the training data.

7.8.2 Maximum Likelihood

Suppose we know that a random variable A is governed by a normal distribution $N(\theta)$, where $\theta = (\mu, \sigma)$ are the mean and standard deviation of the distribution. The goal of probability theory is to study the chances of A in a sample space, given that θ is fixed. In statistics, we invert the problem (using Bayes's Theorem) and study the chances of the parameter θ, given that A has happened (fixed). The normal distribution (or any other distribution) $N(A, \theta)$ as a function of θ (not x) is the likelihood function of θ. We then want to choose θ that has the *maximum likelihood* of generating the data A. This point of view connects a statistical problem with differential calculus.

BIBLIOGRAPHIC NOTES

7.1 Data mining is a rapidly developing area that lies at the intersection of database management, artificial intelligence, and statistics. Spatial data mining is an important but evolving area within data mining. [Han et al., 1997] designed a system prototype of spatial data mining.

7.2 The data for the Darr and Stubble wetlands was collected by [Ozesmi and Ozesmi, 1999]. Classical data-mining techniques, such as logistic regression and neural networks, were applied to predict the location of bird nests.

Spatial statisticians have grappled with spatial data for a long time. They have identified and coined terms such as *spatial autocorrelation* and *spatial heterogeneity* to identify the unique properties of spatial data. A good deal of spatial statistical methods can be found in [Cressie, 1993].

7.3 For an overview of classical data-mining techniques consult [Han and Kamber, 2000]. Spatial regression has been extensively discussed in [Anselin, 1988; LeSage, 1997]. LeSage has also provided an excellent MATLAB toolbox on the Web for different spatial regression models.

7.4 The *Apriori* algorithm was introduced by [Agrawal and Srikant, 1994]. [Koperski and Han, 1995] carried out the first known extensions for spatial data.

7.4.3 For a more detailed discussion of spatial colocation patterns, consult [Shekhar and Huang, 2001].

7.4.5 More description of classical methods (Regression, Bayesian) and their spatial extensions (SAR, MRF) can be found in [Shekhar et al., 2002]. This paper provides comparisons between these models using a probabilistic and an experimental framework.

7.5 Our discussion of the *K-medoid* algorithm is from [Estivill-Castro and Murray, 1998]. The EM algorithm is due to [Dempster et al., 1977], and the extensions for spatial data are due to [Ambroise et al., 1997]. [Ordonez and Cereghini, 2000] present an efficient SQL implementation of the EM algorithm to perform clustering in very large databases. For spatial clustering based on wavelet transforms, consult [Sheikholeslami et al., 1998]. [Wang et al., 1997] discuss a hierarchical statistical information grid based approach for clustering and region oriented queries.

EXERCISES

1. Consider the following database (see Table 7.7) about entertainment facilities in different cities.

TABLE 7.7: Database
of Facilities

CityID	Facilities
1	a,b,e
2	b,c,d
3	c,e
4	d,c
5	d,e
6	a,c,e
7	a,b,c,e
8	a,b,c,d,e

(a) Compute the support for item sets $\{a, b\}$, $\{c\}$, and $\{a, b, c\}$.
(b) Compute the confidence for the association rules $\{a, b\} \rightarrow \{c\}$.
(c) Compute the confidence for the association rules $\{c\} \rightarrow \{a, b\}$.
(d) Why is the confidence not symmetric but support is?
(e) Extract spatial association rules with a support more than 30 and a confidence more than 70 percent from the following table. X represents lakes in the database (the total number of lakes is 100). For each rule, write the support and the confidence.

spatial predicate	count
near(X,forest)	45
inside(X,state_park)	90
adjacent(X,federal_land)	50
near(X,forest) and inside(X,state_park)	30
near(X,forest) and adjacent(X,federal_land)	20
near(X,forest) and inside(X,state_park) and adjacent(X,federal_land)	10

Rule	support	confidence
lake(X) $\Rightarrow$ near(forest)		
lake(X) and inside(X, state_park) $\Rightarrow$ near(X, forest_land)		
lake(X) and inside(X, state_park) $\Rightarrow$ adjacent(X,federal_land)		
lake(X) and inside(X, state_park) and adjacent(X,federal_land) $\Rightarrow$ near(forest)		

(f) In the computation of $J(M_{t+1}) - J(M_t)$ in the K-*medoid* algorithm, why do only the nonmedoid points of the m_o(medoid-old) and m_n(medoid-new) in $M_{t+1} = M_t \cup \{m_n\} - \{m_o\}$ have to be fetched in the main memory?

Hint: All the nonmedoid points satisfy one of the four following cases:

    (i) $p \ni C_{m_o} \wedge \exists m \in M_t$ such that $d(p, m) < d(p, m_n) \Rightarrow p \in C(m) in$ M_{t+1}.

    (ii) $p \ni C_{m_o} \wedge \forall m \in M_t, d(p, m) < d(p, m_n) \Rightarrow p \in C(m_n) in M_{t+1}$.

    (iii) $p \ni C_{m_o} \wedge \exists m_1 \in M_t$ such that $d(p, m_1) < d(p, m_n) \Rightarrow p \in C(m_1) in$ M_{t+1}.

    (iv) $p \ni C_{m_o} \wedge \exists m_1 \in M_t$ such that $d(p, m_1) > d(p, m_n) \Rightarrow p \in C(m_n) in$ M_{t+1}.

(g) Assume all the clusters have the same size. What is the performance gain due to the above approach?

2. Consider a data set with N features and T transactions. How many distinct associations can be enumerated, and how may distinct association rules can be found?

3. Which data mining technique would you use for following scenarios:

    (a) An astronomer wants to determine if an unknown object in the sky is a special kind of galaxy (i.e., bent-double galaxy).

    (b) A meteorologist wants to predict the weather (temperature and precipitation) for the Thanksgiving weekend.

    (c) A urban planner who is designing a shopping mall wants to determine which categories of stores tend to be visited together.

    (d) A political analyst wants to group cities according to their voting history in the last twenty years.

    (e) In order to plan police patrols, the public safety department wants to identify hot spots on a city map.

    (f) Epidemiologists want to predict the spread and movement of the Blue Nile virus.

    (g) Doctors want to determine if spatial location has an affect on the cancer rate.

    (h) Natural resource planners want to assess the total area of pine forest stands using remotely sensed images.

    (i) A judge wants to redistrict the congressional districts based on new census data.

4. Compare and contrast:

    (a) association rules versus statistical correlation.

    (b) autocorrelation versus cross-correlation.

    (c) classification versus location prediction.

    (d) hotspots versus clusters.

    (e) clustering versus classification

    (f) association *versus* clustering

5. Consider the following set of nine points: $(0, 0), (0, 1), (1, 1), (1, 0), (2, 3) (5, 5)$, $(5, 6), (6, 6), (6, 5)$.

    (a) Assume all the points belong to a single cluster. Calculate the mean and the medoid of the cluster.

    (b) Compare the mean and the medoid as the most representative point of the cluster. Use the average distance from the representative point to all points in the cluster as a comparison metric.

    (c) Consider the scenario when the first four points are in one cluster and the last four are in the second cluster. Compute means as representative points for these clusters. Which cluster should the remaining point $((2, 3))$ be assigned to?

6. What is special about spatial data mining relative to mining relational data? Is it adequate to materialize spatial features to be used as input to classical data mining algorithms/models?

7. What is special about spatial statistics relative to statistics?

8. Which of the following spatial features show positive spatial auto correlation? Why? (Is there a physical/scientific reason?)
   Elevation slope, water content, temperature, soil type, population density, annual precipitation (rain, snow).

9. Classify the following spatial point functions into classes of positive spatial autocorrelation, no spatial autocorrelation, and negative spatial autocorrelation:
   (a) $f(x, y) = 1$
   (b)
   $$f(x, y) = \begin{cases} 1, & \text{if } |x + y| \text{ is even,} \\ 0, & \text{otherwise} \end{cases}$$

   (c) $f(x, y) = (x - x_0)^2 + (y - y_0)^2$
   (d) $f(x, y)$ is a random number from $[0, 1]$

10. Discuss the following assertion from an expert on marketing data analysis about mining numeric data sets: "The only data mining techniques one needs is linear regression, if features are selected carefully." Hint: Feature selection can simplify models.

11. Compute Moran's I for the gray-scale image shown in Figure 7.14(a), and matrices in Figure 7.6(b) and 7.6(c).

12. Compare and contrast the concepts in the following pairs:
   (i) Spatial outliers vs. global outliers
   (ii) SAR vs. MRF Bayesian classifiers
   (iii) Colocations vs. spatial association rules
   (iv) Classification accuracy vs. spatial accuracy

13. Spatial data can be mined either via custom methods (e.g., colocations, spatial outliers detection, SAR) or via classical methods (e.g., association rules, global outliers, regression) after selecting relevent spatial features. Compare and contrast these approaches. Where would you use each approach?

14. Spatial outlier detection computation may be modeled as a spatial self-join query. Write SQL3/OGIS expression to identify spatial outliers using $Z_s(x)$ method. Assume that the following tables were given:
   (a) neighbor(location, location)
   (b) observation(sensor-id, location, value)

15. Identify 2 clusters identified by K-medoid algorithm for following set of points:
   (i) (0,0), (1,1), (1,0), (0,1), (6,6), (7,6), (6,7), (7,7)
   (ii) (0,0), (1,1), (1,0), (0,1)

16. Clustering records retrieved together by frequent queries into common disk pages is an important storage issue for spatial databases. Can the clustering methods discussed in this chapter help spatial storage methods in that problem?

17. Define scale-dependent and scale-independent spatial patterns. Provide examples.

18. Study the notion of spatial accuracy discussed in Sections 7.3.3 and 7.3.4. Propose measures of spatial accuracy given a map of predicted nest locations and actual nest locations. How can a classification algorithm use proposed measures?

19. Consider spatial patterns based on shapes of spatial objects, for example, country boundaries. Example patterns include identification of most common or unusual shapes. Discuss how one may formalize the notion of shape and discover such patterns.

20. Consider sample data and co-location patterns in Figure 7.12. Discuss computational approaches to find the co-location patterns from sample data. How would one define conditional probability of a co-location rule? How would one define support for a co-location? (Hint: spatial join on neighbor relation)

21. Consider the problem of detecting multiple spatial outliers. Discuss how one should extend the techniques discussed in Section 7.6. Note that a true spatial outlier can make its neighbor be flagged as spatial outliers by some of the tests discussed in Section 7.6.

C H A P T E R   8

Trends in Spatial Databases

8.1   DATABASE SUPPORT FOR FIELD ENTITIES
8.2   CONTENT-BASED RETRIEVAL
8.3   INTRODUCTION TO SPATIAL DATA WAREHOUSES
8.4   SUMMARY

In this chapter, we discuss some of the emerging database issues related to spatial information systems. In particular we focus on the raster database management, content-based retrieval, and spatial data warehouses.

Remote sensing images from satellites and scanning of topographic and thematic maps have resulted in large amounts of raster data. We need efficient SDBMS support for entities that are modeled as *fields*. Data warehouses process large volumes of data obtained from operational and legacy systems. Data warehouses clean and transform the data so that changes and trends can be inferred from it. This data analysis is used in decision-support systems, which have become critical to many organizations. The volume of data in these data warehouses is very large, due to its historical nature. This data is often modeled and processed as multidimensional data. Even though the volume processed in such queries is high, the query-response time has to be low to support interactive and iterative data analysis to facilitate the data mining and discovery process.

In Section 1 we introduce important raster image operations. We also look into storage and indexing schemes for raster data. Section 2 deals with content-based retrieval (CBR). Section 3 provides an introduction to data warehousing terminology and concepts as applicable to spatial data.

8.1   DATABASE SUPPORT FOR FIELD ENTITIES

SDB management systems must provide support for spatial entities, which are modeled as *fields*. Examples of such entities include temperature, elevation, rainfall, and pressure. The underlying commonality between these entities is that they are *continuous:* if two points in their domains are close to each other, then so are the values of the field at those points.

Theoretically, a field model can be transformed into an object model by inverting the field function. For example, if f is the temperature field, then all areas that are experiencing temperatures of greater than 40°C can be characterized as

$$f^-(x) = \{x \in Domain \,|\, f(x) \geq 40\}.$$

From a computational point of view, calculating the inverse of (nonlinear) functions is extremely difficult. It is more practical to deal with field entities directly.

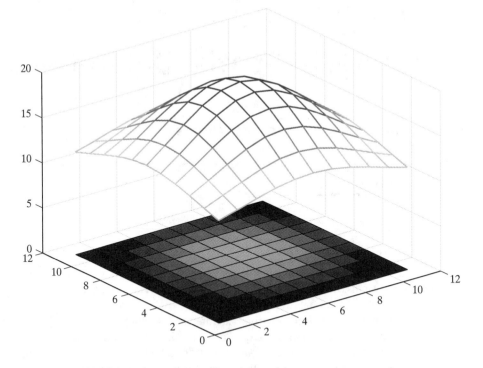

FIGURE 8.1. A continuous function and its raster representation.

But how can a field function be represented in a database? An important consequence of the continuity of fields is that a relatively small sample of *averaged* field values can be used to represent the whole function. For example, consider the function shown in Figure 8.1. Each cell in the grid is assigned a color (or gray value) based on the average value of a finite sample of points in that cell. The continuity of the field function ensures that the distribution of averaged values is a good representation of the original function. Thus a field function can be represented by a *matrix* of representative values. In GIS this matrix is called a *raster*, and each cell of the raster is called a *pixel*, which is short for *picture element*.

Another reason why database support for raster data is indispensable is that data collected from satellites, aerial-photography, and digital elevation maps (DEMs) is already in raster form.

8.1.1   Raster and Image Operations

Map algebra, first introduced by Tomlin [Tomlin, 1990], is a systematic framework for organizing the vast array of operations used in raster analysis. Map algebra was initially developed for the cartographic community but has now evolved as the preeminent *language* for dealing with raster data. Many GIS commercial software products support some form of map algebra. It is important to keep in mind that map algebra is a framework for raster analysis rather than raster querying. Similar to map algebra, but more formal, is the set of image-processing operations known as image algebra. Lately there has been an attempt to formalize and extend the functionality of map algebra with techniques borrowed from image algebra. The result is called *Geo-Algebra*!

An *algebra* is a mathematical structure consisting of two distinct sets of elements; (Ω_a, Ω_o). Ω_a is the set of *operands*, and Ω_o is the set of *operations*. There are many axioms that an algebra must satisfy, but the most crucial is closure, that is, the result of an *operation* on an *operand* must remain in Ω_a. A simple example of an algebra is the set of natural numbers with operations *addition* and *multiplication*.

In map algebra the *operand* is the raster matrix, and the operations can be divided into four classes: *local, focal, zonal,* and *global*. We describe each of these classes with the help of examples.

Local Operations

A local operation maps a raster into another raster such that the value of a *cell* in the *new* raster depends only on the value of that cell in the *original* raster. An example of a local operation is shown in Figure 8.2.

The value of each cell of a raster is set to 0 or 1 depending on whether the value of that cell in the original raster is below or above some user-defined value. In the figure, all cells whose value is less than 3 are set to 0, and all those whose value is 3 or more are set to 1. This operation is known as *thresholding*. For example, in a DEM, the thresholding operation is used to identify cells that are above a certain height.

Focal Operations

In a focal operation, the value of a cell in the *new* raster is dependent on the values of the cell and its neighboring cells in the *original* raster. There are three common definitions of what constitutes the *neighborhood* of a cell. These are shown in Figure 8.3(a). Borrowing an analogy from chess, these neighborhoods are called Rook, Bishop, and Queen. In Figure 8.3(b) the value of a cell in the *new* raster is the sum of the values of the cells in the *original* raster belonging to the Queen neighborhood. Example of focal operations include slope, gradient, continuity etc., for fields. Figure 8.3(b) shows a focal operation, namely focal sum using Queen neighborhood.

Zonal Operations

In a zonal operation, the value of a cell in the *new* raster is a function of the value of that cell in the *original* layer and the values of other cells which appear in the same zone specified in another raster. For example, in Figure 8.4, the value of the top left cell (12) in the *new* raster is the sum of all cells in the *original* raster which are in the same

FIGURE 8.2. Example of a local operation: Thresholding.

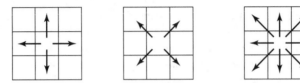

(a) Rook, Bishop and Queen neighborhoods

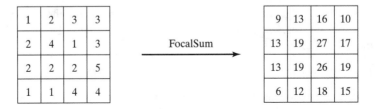

(b) Example of a focal operation: FocalSum

FIGURE 8.3. Neighborhoods of a cell and an example of a focal operation: FocalSum.

zone A, as specified in the zonal map. This information can alternatively be represented as a table with one row for each zone showing the sum of all cells for each zone. As the example shows, the zones do not have to be contiguous, and they do not have to cover all the cells of the input map.

Global Operations

In a global operation, the value of a cell in the *new* raster is a function of the location or values of *all* cells in the *original* or another raster. Figure 8.5 shows an example of a global operation. In the *original* raster, the locations of sources $S1$ and $S2$ are given. Each cell in the *new* raster records the distance of that cell from the *nearest* source. Two adjacent cells in the horizontal and vertical directions are separated by unit distance and two adjacent cells in diagonal locations are separated by distance equal to the square root of 2.

Image Operations

Besides the four classes of operations that we have described, there are two other operations which are of particular interest in image processing. These are the *trim* and *slice* operations. A *trim* operation extracts an axis-aligned subset of the original raster. An example is shown in Figure 8.6. The *slice* operation is of particular interest in the area

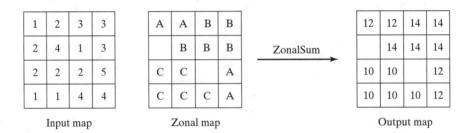

FIGURE 8.4. Example of a zonal operation: ZonalSum.

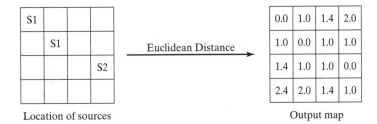

Location of sources   Output map

FIGURE 8.5. Example of a global operation.

of medical imaging. A slice operation projects a higher-dimensional raster image into one or a sequence of lower-dimensional raster images. The example shown in Figure 8.7 projects a three-dimensional raster into a sequence of three two-dimensional raster images projected onto the underline z-axis.

8.1.2 Storage and Indexing

For querying and other database support, it is important that raster images be stored within the database and not as files in the file system. Because the raster images occupy a much greater fraction of the disk block space than other attributes, it is important to have a separate storage strategy for them. For instance, if they are stored just as the other attributes, then there is a danger of dramatically increasing the seek time of the tuples in the relations because the blocking factor (number of record per disk block) will be small.

One strategy is to just store important information about the array with the other attributes in a table and store the actual raw image in a separate table. In order to keep track of the raw image a foreign key reference to the table containing the raw image is included in the first relation.

For very large arrays, one efficient strategy is to decompose the arrays into tiles and store the tiles individually as separate tuples in a relation. This is particularly useful when a query requests only a subset of the original array, as in the *trim* operation.

For example, consider the raster image shown in Figure 8.8(a). If a query region A wants to access a portion of the array, then the way in which the raster is partitioned into disk pages can lead to dramatically different results. Assume that the raster is an array of size $16,000 \times 16,000$, each pixel requires one byte of storage, the size of the disk page is $16Kb = 16,000$ bytes, and the size of query region A is 700×800.

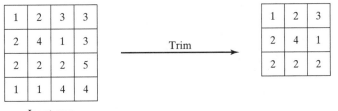

Input map

FIGURE 8.6. The `trim` operation: dimension preserving.

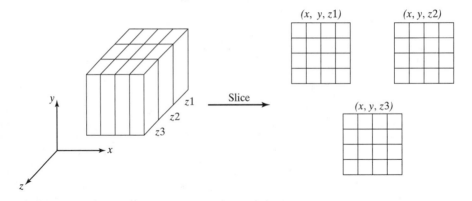

FIGURE 8.7. The `slice` operation: dimension reduction.

Linear Allocation

In this default strategy, each row of the array is assigned to one disk page, that is, the array is partitioned into subarrays of size $1 \times 16{,}000$. To retrieve the elements that overlap query region A requires 700 disk accesses. Because query region A corresponds to thirty disk pages, this is prohibitively excessive.

Tiling

In this strategy the array is partitioned into subarrays of size 160×100. Thus, assuming the query region is aligned with the tiles, the number of disk pages accessed is $5 \times 8 = 40$. Thus this tiling strategy dramatically reduces the number of page accesses for this particular query. Obviously different query sizes will require a different optimal tiling strategy. The tiling strategy and parameters can be fine-tuned by keeping track of the query statistics. Furthermore an R-tree index can be built on the tiles for faster access to the tiles matched by the query region.

Another strategy is based on data compression. A collection of images on a common geographic area can be approximated by a smaller collection of orthogonal images. Individual images can be compressed using techniques such as run-length encoding, vector quantization, subband coding. Compression reduces the disk space needed to store a collection of images.

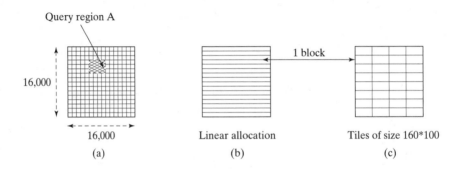

FIGURE 8.8. Different strategies for storing arrays.

8.2   CONTENT-BASED RETRIEVAL

From a database perspective, the operations of map algebra are of secondary interest because they deal with *data analysis* as opposed to *data querying*. The key database challenge is to efficiently retrieve images from a database that satisfies predicates specified in the user query. Search predicate can be based on meta-data or content. Meta-data is a description of an image using simpler datatypes (e.g., numeric, text). For example, coordinates (latitude, longitude), place names, date, sensor type, are often attached to each raster data-item. Images can be retrieved using predicates based on meta-data. Such queries can be processed by the techniques discussed in Chapter 5. In contrast, content of an image refers to full semantics of image beyond what is documented in meta-data. Examples include color, texture, and spatial configuration of objects in the images. Consider a search predicate to identify all raster images similar to a given (example) image with a highway passing through urban areas and touching a lake. This kind of querying is often called content-based retrieval because the result of the query is dependent on the implicit content and relations embedded in the image. Examples of potentially important content-based queries follow:

1. Find all images which have an ocean in the background and a beach in the foreground.
2. Locate a photograph of a river in Minnesota with trees nearby.
3. Find all images of state parks which have a lake *within* them, are within a radius of one hundred miles from Chicago, and are southwest of Chicago.
4. Retrieve countries shaped like ladies boots or tear drops.
5. Retrieve pairs of molecules or continents whose shapes fit like pieces of a jig-saw puzzle.

The third query is significant for spatial databases because it involves all three classes of spatial predicates, namely, `topological` (lake *within* forest), `directional` (*southwest* of Chicago), and `metric` (within one hundred miles of Chicago). The last two queries are based on shapes which has not been modelled by OGIS data model yet. The ability to query image databases on the basis of spatial constraints is clearly a nontrivial task and is a topic of intense current research.

The general methodology in content-based retrieval consists of five steps and is shown in Figure 8.13. We briefly discuss the basic concepts used in this methodology.

8.2.1   Topological Similarity

We have discussed topological relations in detail in Chapters 2 and 3. There we noted that topological relations can be expressed using Egenhofer's nine-intersection model. This model is the basis of the OGIS extension of SQL that was presented in Chapter 3. For polygonal objects, we can intuitively define a concept of *neighborhood* for topological relations.

Two topological relations T_1 and T_2 are *neighbors* if $T_1(T_2)$ can be continuously transformed in $T_2(T_1)$ without going through an intermediate topological relation. Thus `Disjoint` and `Touch` are neighbors but `Disjoint` and `Overlap` are not: `Disjoint` is first transformed into `touch` and then into `overlap`. The neighborhood graph of the

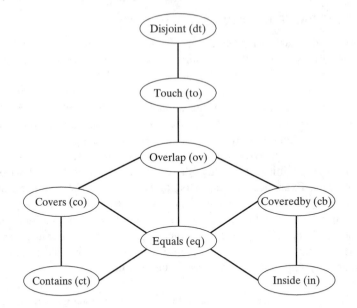

FIGURE 8.9. The topological neighborhood graph [Ang et al., 1998]. The distance between two relations is the shortest path on this graph.

topological relations is shown in Figure 8.9. Formally, the distance $D_{top}(T_1, T_2)$ between two relations T_1 and T_2 is defined as

$$D_{top}(T_1, T_2) \text{ equals the numbers of edges in the shortest path on the neighborhood graph between } T_1 \text{ and } T_2.$$

8.2.2 Directional Similarity

A notion similar to topological relations can be defined for *directional* relations. The eight well-known directions follow:

{North (N), Northwest (NW), West (W), Southwest (SW), South (S), Southeast (SE), East (E), Northeast (NE)}

The only difference is that for extended objects such as `line` and `polygon` the directional relations are not well defined. For example, where does *northwest* end and *north* begin? For content-based retrieval, a sort of *fuzzy* notion of directional relationships is usually the preferred approach.

One approach is to use the neighborhood graph shown in Figure 8.10. The solid lines are used to compute the distance between the two nodes, and the dotted lines indicate that the distance between those two nodes is zero. Thus the distance $D_{dir}(D_1, D_2)$ between two directional relations D_1 and D_2 is

$$D_{dir}(D_1, D_2)$$
$$= \begin{cases} \text{shortest path on graph} & \text{if } D_1 \text{ and } D_2 \text{ are connected by a solid line path} \\ 0 & \text{if } D_1 \text{ and } D_2 \text{ are connected by a dotted line} \end{cases}$$

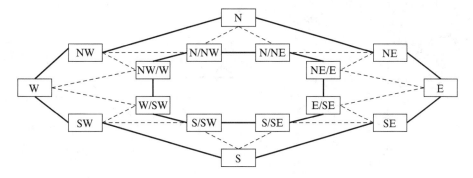

FIGURE 8.10. The directional neighborhood graph [Ang et al., 1998]. The distance be-tween two relations is the shortest solid line path on this graph.

8.2.3 Distance Similarity

In some sense similarity based on distance is the least important of the three classes of spatial relationships: topological, directional, and metric. This is particularly true if the topological and directional relations remain unchanged. For example, consider the two images shown in Figure 8.11. Image P is, at least visually, more similar to Q than to R, even though, in terms of pure *distance,* P and R are closer.

For *distance* similarity, we will take the standard Euclidean square distance between the centroids of the objects.

8.2.4 Attribute Relational Graphs

Attribute relational graphs (ARGs) are completely connected graphs which capture in-formation about objects and their relationships. For example, an image and its ARG are shown in Figure 8.12. The nodes of the ARG are annotated with object labels, and the edges between two nodes are labeled with information about the relationships between the two nodes. For example, the edge between the two nodes O_1 and O_2 is labeled (D, 61, 5.2). This means that between O_1 and O_2 the topological relationship is *disjoint*, the angle between them is 61° (measured in increasing subscript order), and the distance is 5.2 units.

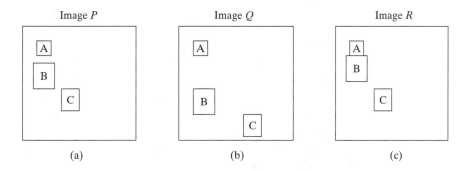

FIGURE 8.11. Visual perspective: distance as the least discriminating spatial predicate.

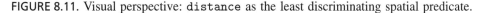

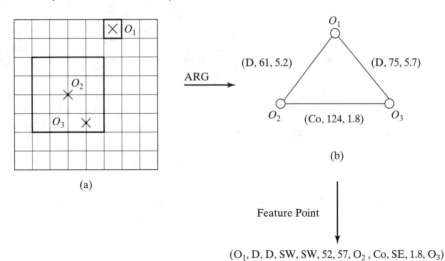

(a)

ARG →

(D, 61, 5.2) (D, 75, 5.7)

O_2 (Co, 124, 1.8) O_3

(b)

Feature Point

$(O_1, D, D, SW, SW, 52, 57, O_2, Co, SE, 1.8, O_3)$

FIGURE 8.12. An image and its ARG [Petrakis and Faloutsos, 1997]. The ARG is mapped onto an N-dimensional feature point.

After the ARG has been created for each image, it is mapped into a multidimensional point in a feature space. The points in this feature space are organized in some prespecifed order: the first object followed by all the relationships between this and all other objects, followed by the second object and all its relationships with subsequent objects. At this stage the directional *angles* are also transformed into *directional* predicates. For example the angle of $61°$ between O_1 and O_2 is mapped into southwest.

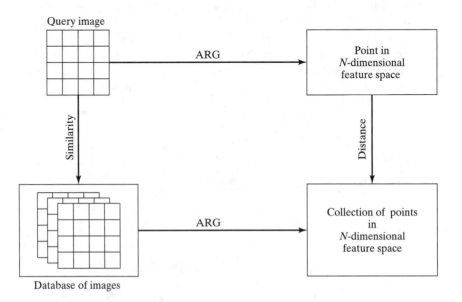

FIGURE 8.13. The general methodology of content-based retrieval.

8.2.5   Retrieval Step

1. Map all the images in the image database into points in a multidimensional feature space. This mapping is done by first constructing an ARG for each image in the database.

2. Define a distance metric corresponding to each criterion of *similarity* between images. Possible examples of similarity criteria are the shape of the objects in the image, brightness, color, texture, and spatial relationships. If a search is to be conducted based on multiple similarity criteria, then the resulting distance metric is an aggregation (e.g., sum) of the individual components. This task is usually performed by a domain expert.

3. Build a storage method (e.g., an R-tree) to cluster and index the multidimensional feature points.

4. Map the query image into a point or a region in the feature space and select points which are *near* the query point, or within the query region. This step may use nearest neighbor finding algorithms, or range query processing algorithms.

5. Return the images corresponding to the selected points as the result.

8.3   INTRODUCTION TO SPATIAL DATA WAREHOUSES

A data warehouse (DW) is a collection of decision support technologies aimed at enabling knowledge workers (executives, managers, analysts) to make better and faster decisions. DWs contain large amounts of information collected from a variety of independent sources and often maintained separately from the operational databases. Traditionally, operational databases are optimized for OLTP, where consistency and recoverability are critical. Transactions are typically small and access a small number of records based on the primary key. Operational databases maintain current state information. In contrast, DWs maintain historical information and are designed for OLAP, where queries aggregate large volumes of data in order to detect trends and anomalies. Dimensions, measures, and aggregation hierarchies are the core concepts in data warehouses. Dimensions are used to define the context of the measures, and can be viewed as independent variables (or keys) which determine the values of measures (dependent variables). There are two kinds of aggregation hierarchies, namely, a dimension power-set hierarchy and a per-dimension concept hierarchy. To facilitate complex analysis, the data in the warehouse is often modeled as a multidimensional data cube. For example, in a census data warehouse, the age group, income type, race category, and time (year) are some of the dimensions of interest. A data cube is an aggregate operator which generalizes the `group-by` SQL queries in an N-dimensional space.

Spatial DWs contain geographic data (e.g., satellite images, aerial photography), in addition to nonspatial data. Examples of spatial DWs include the U.S. census dataset, EOS archives of satellite imagery, Sequoia 2000, and highway traffic measurement archives. A major difference between conventional and spatial DWs lies in the visualization of the results. Conventional DW OLAP results are often shown as summary tables or spreadsheets of text and numbers, whereas spatial DW results may be a mosaic of maps. Another difference is related to choice and standardization (or lack of it) for the aggregate operators on geometry data types (e.g., point, line, polygon). Neither existing databases nor the emerging standard for geographic data, OGIS, has addressed this issue. In the

TABLE 8.1: Aggregation Operations

Data Type	Aggregation Function		
	Distributive Function	Algebraic Function	Holistic Function
Set of numbers	Count,Min,Max,Sum	Average, Standard Deviation, MaxN, MinN	Median, MostFrequent, Rank
Set of points, lines, polygons	Convex Hull, Geometric Union, Geometric Intersection	Centroid, Center of mass, Center of gravity	Nearest neighbor index, Equi-partition

remainder of the section, we overview important DW operations and their counterparts in the spatial context.

8.3.1 Aggregate Operations

A data cube consists of a lattice of cuboids, each of which represents a certain level of hierarchy. Aggregate functions compute statistics for a given set of values within each cuboid. Examples of aggregate functions include sum, average, and centroid. Aggregate functions can be grouped into three categories, namely, distributive, algebraic, and holistic as suggested by [Gray et al., 1997]. We define these functions in this section and provide some examples from the GIS domain. Table 8.1 shows all of these aggregation functions for different data types.

Distributive

An aggregate function F is called distributive if there exists a function G such that the value of F for an N-dimensional cuboid can be computed by applying a G function to the value of F in an $(N+1)$–dimensional cuboid. For example, when $N = 1$, $F(M_{ij}) = G(F(C_j)) = G(F(R_i))$, where M_{ij} represents the elements of a two-dimensional matrix, C_j denotes each column of the matrix, and R_i denotes each row of the matrix. Consider the aggregate functions Min and Count as shown in Figure 8.14. In the first example, $F = Min$, then $G = Min$, because $Min(M_{ij}) = Min(Min(C_j)) = Min(Min(R_i))$. In the second example, $F = Count$, $G = Sum$, because $Count(M_{ij}) = Sum(Count(C_j)) = Sum(Count(R_i))$. Other distributive aggregate functions include Max and Sum. Note that "null"-valued elements are ignored in computing aggregate functions.

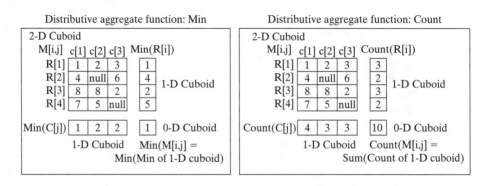

FIGURE 8.14. Computation of distributive aggregate function.

Distributive GIS aggregate operations include convex hull, geometric union, and geometric intersection. The convex hull of a set Q of points is the smallest convex polygon P for which each point in Q is either on the boundary of P or in its interior. Intuitively, the convex hull is the shape formed by a tight rubber band that surrounds all the nails. The geometric intersection is a binary operation that takes two sets of geometric areas and returns the set of regions that are covered by both of the original areas. The geometric union is a binary operation that takes two sets of geometric areas and returns the set of regions that are covered by at least one of the original areas. For all these aggregations, the operator aggregates the computed regions of the subset, and then computes the final result.

Algebraic

An aggregate function F is algebraic if F of an N-dimensional cuboid can be computed using a fixed number of aggregates of the $(N+1)$–dimensional cuboid. Average, variance, standard deviation, max$N$, and min$N$ are all algebraic. In Figure 8.15, for example, the computations of average and variance for the matrix M are shown. The average of elements in the two-dimensional matrix M can be computed from sum and count values of the 1-D sub-cubes (e.g., rows or columns). The Variance can be derived from Count, Sum (i.e., $\sum_i X_i$), and Sum of Sq (i.e., $\sum_i X_i^2$) of rows or columns. Similar techniques apply to other algebraic functions.

An algebraic aggregate operation in GIS is center. The center of n geometric points $\vec{V}^i = (V_x^i, V_y^i)$ is defined as $Center = \frac{1}{n} \sum \vec{V}_i$, $C_x = \frac{\sum V_x}{n}$, $C_y = \frac{\sum V_y}{n}$. Both the center and the count are required to compute the result for the next layer. The center of mass and the center of gravity are other examples of algebraic aggregate functions.

Holistic

An aggregate function F is called holistic if the value of F for an N-dimensional cuboid cannot be computed from a constant number of aggregates of the $(N + 1)$–dimensional cuboid. Examples of holistic functions include Median, MostFrequent, and Rank.

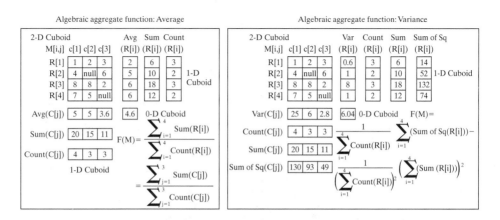

FIGURE 8.15. Computation of algebraic aggregate function.

Holistic GIS aggregate operations include equipartition and nearest-neighbor index. Equipartition of a set of points yields a line L such that there are the same number of point objects on each side of L. Nearest-neighbor index measures the degree of clustering of objects in a spatial field. If a spatial field has the property that like values tend to cluster together, then the field exhibits a high nearest-neighbor index. When new data is added, many of the tuples in the nearest-neighbor relationship may change. Therefore, the nearest-neighbor index is holistic. The line of equipartition could be changed with any new added points. To compute the equipartition or nearest neighbor-index in all levels of dimensions, we need the base data.

The computation of aggregate functions has graduated difficulty. The distributive function can be computed from the next lower level of dimension values. The algebraic function can be computed from a set of aggregates of the next lower level of data. Distributive and algebraic aggregates for a very large disk-resident dataset can be computed using a small number of main memory buffers. The holistic function needs the base data to compute the result in all levels of dimension.

8.3.2   An Example of Geometric Aggregation

Figure 8.16 shows the results from the aggregation operation of geometric union. The base table, Election-Base, has the following attributes: State Name, Governor Political Party (GPP), majority Legislator Political Party (LPP), Boundary, and Delegates. The Boundary is a foreign key pointing to another table which describes the geometric polygon representing the state boundary polygon. From the base table and its corresponding map, we issue the queries GQ1, GQ2, GQ3, GQ4, and GQ5 as listed in Table 8.2. If the neighboring polygons have the same value in the attributes of the GROUP-BY clause, the Geometric-Union-by-Continuous-Polygon operator merges them into one large polygon. These queries have the same effect as the GIS reclassify map operation. For example, the query GQ1 generates the same result as Base-Map reclassified by attributes GPP and LPP. The map interpretation of these queries is shown in the left portion of Figure 8.16. The boundaries of regions $Q1, Q2, \ldots, Q8$ are derived from the geometric union of smaller regions $P1, P2, \ldots, P12$ in the Base-Map. For example, $Q2$ represents the geometric union of $P2$ and $P3$ as they have same value for the grouping attribute set <LPP,GPP>. Similarly, regions $A1, A2, A3$ in Map-L2-A and regions $B1, B2, B3$ in Map-L2-B are derived from the geometric-union of smaller regions in Map-L1 (or Base-Map). For example, region $A1$ in Map-L2-A is the geometric union of region $Q1$ and $Q4$ from Map-L1.

TABLE 8.2: SQL Queries for Map Reclassification

GQ1	SELECT GPP, LPP, Geometric-Union-by-Continuous-Polygon (Boundary) FROM Election-Base **GROUP BY** GPP, LPP
GQ2	SELECT GPP, Geometric-Union-by-Continuous-Polygon (Boundary) FROM Election-L1 **GROUP BY** GPP
GQ3	SELECT LPP, Geometric-Union-by-Continuous-Polygon (Boundary) FROM Election-L1 **GROUP BY** LPP
GQ4	SELECT GPP, Geometric-Union-by-Continuous-Polygon (Boundary) FROM Election-Base **GROUP BY** GPP
GQ5	SELECT LPP, Geometric-Union-by-Continuous-Polygon (Boundary) FROM Election-Base **GROUP BY** LPP

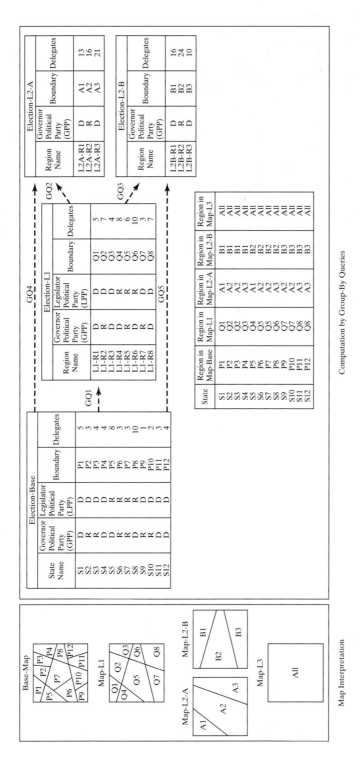

FIGURE 8.16. An example of GIS aggregate function, geometric-union.

241

8.3.3 Aggregation Hierarchy

The CUBE operator generalizes the histogram, cross-tabulation, roll-up, drill-down, and subtotal constructs. It is the N-dimensional generalization of simple aggregate functions. Figure 8.17 shows the concept for aggregations up to three dimensions. The dimensions are Year, Company, and Region. The measure is sales. The 0-D data cube is a point that shows the total summary. There are three 1-D data cubes: Group-by Region, Group-by Company, and Group-by Year. The three 2-D data cubes are cross tabs, which are a combination of these three dimensions. The 3-D data cube is a cube with three intersecting 2-D cross tabs. Figure 8.18 shows the tabular forms of the total elements in a 3-D data cube after a cube operation. Creating a data cube requires generating a power set of the aggregation columns.

A tabular view of the individual subspace data-cubes of Figure 8.17 is shown in Figure 8.19. The union of all the tables in Figure 8.19 yields the resulting table from the

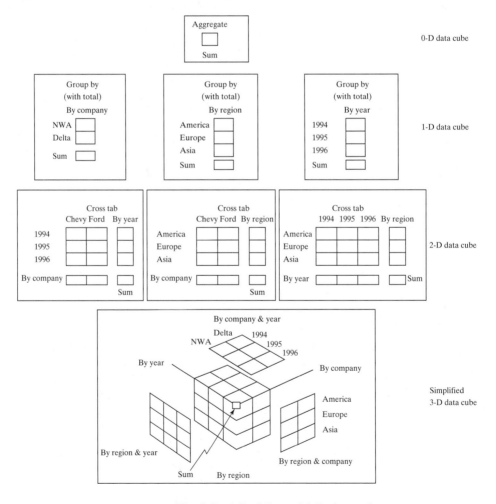

FIGURE 8.17. The 0-D, 1-D, 2-D, and 3-D data cubes.

Cube-query

```
SELECT  Company, Year, Region,
        Sum(Sales) AS Sales
FROM  SALES
GROUP BY  CUBE Company, Year, Region
```

SALES			
Company	Year	Region	Sales
NWA	1994	America	20
NWA	1994	Europe	15
NWA	1994	Asia	5
NWA	1995	America	12
NWA	1995	Europe	6
NWA	1995	Asia	18
NWA	1996	America	7
NWA	1996	Europe	20
NWA	1996	Asia	17
Delta	1994	America	15
Delta	1994	Europe	3
Delta	1994	Asia	12
Delta	1995	America	9
Delta	1995	Europe	14
Delta	1995	Asia	20
Delta	1996	America	15
Delta	1996	Europe	8
Delta	1996	Asia	16

Base table

CUBE →

Data Cube			
Company	Year	Region	Sales
ALL	ALL	ALL	232
NWA	ALL	ALL	120
Delta	ALL	ALL	112
ALL	1994	ALL	70
ALL	1995	ALL	79
ALL	1996	ALL	83
ALL	ALL	America	78
ALL	ALL	Europe	66
ALL	ALL	Asia	88
NWA	1994	ALL	40
NWA	1995	ALL	36
NWA	1996	ALL	44
Delta	1994	ALL	30
Delta	1995	ALL	43
Delta	1996	ALL	39
NWA	ALL	America	39
NWA	ALL	Europe	41
NWA	ALL	Asia	40
Delta	ALL	America	39
Delta	ALL	Europe	25
Delta	ALL	Asia	48
ALL	1994	America	35
ALL	1994	Europe	18
ALL	1994	Asia	17
ALL	1995	America	21
ALL	1995	Europe	20
ALL	1995	Asia	38
ALL	1996	America	22
ALL	1996	Europe	28
ALL	1996	Asia	33
.	.	.	.
.	.	.	.
.	.	.	.
.	.	.	.

Resulting table from cube operator
(aka data cube)

FIGURE 8.18. An example of a data cube.

data cube operator. The 0-dimensional subspace cube labeled "Aggregate" in Figure 8.17 is represented by Table "SALES-L2" in Figure 8.19. The one-dimensional subspace cube labeled "By Company" in Figure 8.17 is represented by Table "SALES-L1-C" in Figure 8.19. The two-dimensional cube labeled "By Company & Year" is represented by Table "SALES-L0-C" in Figure 8.19. Readers can establish the correspondence between the remaining subspace cubes and tables.

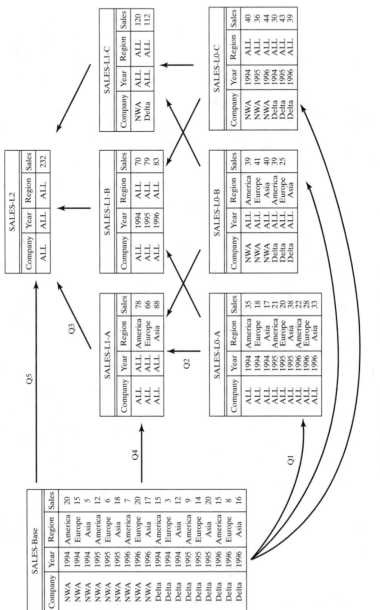

FIGURE 8.19. An example of using the group–by operator.

TABLE 8.3: Table of GROUP-BY Queries

Q1	SELECT 'ALL', Year, Region, SUM(Sales) FROM SALES-Base group-by Year,Region
Q2	SELECT 'ALL', 'ALL', Region SUM(Sales) FROM SALES-L0-A group-by Region
Q3	SELECT 'ALL', 'ALL', 'ALL' SUM(Sales) FROM SALES-L1-A
Q4	SELECT 'ALL', 'ALL', Region, SUM(Sales) FROM SALES-Base group-by Region
Q5	SELECT 'ALL', 'ALL', 'ALL', SUM(Sales) FROM SALES-Base

The cube operator can be modeled by a family of SQL queries using GROUP-BY operators and aggregation functions. Each arrow in Figure 8.19 is represented by an SQL query. Table 8.3 provides the corresponding queries for the five arrows labeled $Q1, Q2, \ldots, Q5$ in Figure 8.19. For example, query $Q1$ in Table 8.3 aggregates "Sales" by "Year" and "Region," and generates Table "SALES-L0-A" in Figure 8.19.

The GROUP-BY clause with CUBE operator specifies the grouping attributes which should also appear in the SELECT clause, so that the value resulting from applying each function to a group of tuples appears along with the value of the grouping attribute(s). Figure 8.18 shows a SQL query with CUBE operator in the top left corner. SQL also provides a ROLLUP operator for use in GROUP BY clause.

8.3.4   What Is an Aggregation Hierarchy Used For?

To support OLAP, the data cube provides the following operators : roll-up, drill-down, slice and dice, and pivot. We now define these operators.

- **Roll-up**: Increasing the level of abstraction. This operator generalizes one or more dimensions and aggregates the corresponding measures. For example, Table SALES-L0-A in Figure 8.19 is the roll-up of Table SALES-Base on the Company dimension. Many commercial implementations of SQL support ROLLUP operator as an extension of GROUP BY clause. For example, ROLLUP(Year, Region) on SALES-Base table will return a union of SALES-L0-C (aggregate away Region) and SALES-L1-C (aggregate away both Year and Region) with the SALES-Base table.

- **Drill-down**: Decreasing the level of abstraction or increasing detail. It specializes in one or a few dimensions and presents low-level aggregations. For example, Table SALES-L0-A in Figure 8.19 is the drill-down of Table SALES-L1-A on the Year dimension.

- **Slice and dice**: Selection and projection. Slicing into one dimension is very much like drilling one level down into that dimension, but the number of entries displayed is limited to that specified in the slice command. A dice operation is like a slice on more than one dimension. On a two-dimensional display, for example, dicing means slicing on both the row and column dimensions.

Table 8.4 shows the result of slicing into the value of "America" on the Year dimension from the Table SALES-L2 in Figure 8.19.

TABLE 8.4: Slice on the Value "America" of the Region Dimension

Company	Year	Region	Sales
ALL	ALL	America	78

TABLE 8.5: Dice on the Value "1994" of the
Year Dimension and the Value "America" of
the Region Dimension

Company	Year	Region	Sales
ALL	1994	America	35

Table 8.5 shows the result of dicing into the value of "1994" on the Year dimension and the value of "America" on the Region dimension from Table SALES-L2 in Figure 8.19.

- **Pivoting**: Reorienting the multidimensional view of data. It presents the measures in different cross-tabular layouts. This function is often available in spreadsheet software, for example, MS Excel.

8.4   SUMMARY

Recent advances in remote sensing technology are yielding an increasingly large amount of spatial data in raster form. Raster databases are becoming extremely important as much of the remote sensing data may never be converted to vector format. Raster data can be modeled as *fields*. Map algebra provides a set of operators for manipulating raster datasets. Tiling is a popular storage method for raster datasets.

Raster data-items can be queried by metadata or content. Queries specified by metadata (e.g., recording date, sensor type, spatial location) can be processed using the techniques discussed in earlier chapters. CBR requires new techniques for specifying and processing the queries. CBR queries often look for most similar raster data items instead of finding the raster data items that satisfy all query predicates. Spatial similarity among raster data items can be specified in terms of an ARG, which models spatial objects in respective raster data items along with their spatial relationships (e.g., topological, directional, distance). CBR queries can be processed by finding ARGs most similar to query ARGs. Efficient processing of CBR queries is still an active area of research.

A spatial DW is a special kind of database designed to efficiently support statistical aggregate summary queries. Aggregate operations can be classified into three groups, namely, distributive, algebraic, and holistic. Distributive and algebraic aggregate functions can be computed using a small number of memory buffers using a single scan of data sets, even when the data sets are too large to fit in the main memory. DW often deals with a single fact table and a set of dimension tables where fact table is related to all dimension tables. Summaries of interest can be specified in terms of subsets of dimensions. Given N dimensions, there are power(2, N) interesting summary tables, each of which may be computed using SQL queries with group by clauses. The CUBE operator is a generalization of SQL group by clause to specify computation of all the power(2, N) summary table via a single statement. The summary tables generated by the CUBE operators can be explored using operations such as pivot, roll-up, drill-down, and slice and dice.

BIBLIOGRAPHIC NOTES

8.1 The vector-raster dichotomy is discussed in detail in [Couclelis, 1992]. Map algebra for cartographic modeling was introduced in [Tomlin, 1990], image algebra for image processing in Ritter [Ritter et al., 1990], and geo-algebra for dynamic spatial modeling in [Takeyama and Couclelis, 1997]. For a database perspective, see [Baumann, 1994].

8.2 Lately there has been a lot of focus on content-based retrieval. [Yoshitaka and Ichikawa, 1999] provides a recent survey on CBR for multimedia databases. For a spatial perspective, see [Papadias et al., 1999] and [Ang et al., 1998]. For indexing of attributed relational graphs, see [Petrakis and Faloutsos, 1997]. A Spatial-Query-by-Sketch based system for GIS is given in [Egenhofer, 1997]. Texture based aerial images retrieval can be found in [Ma and Manjunath, 1998].

8.3 The concept of data cube and aggregate operations over it can be found in [Gray et al., 1997]. See [Sarawagi and Stonebraker, 1994] for a detailed discussion on the storage of multidimensional arrays in secondary and tertiary storage media. See [Keim, 1999] for a similarity search of 3D spatial databases. For an example of spatial data warehouse, see [Barclay et al., 2000; Shekhar et al., 2001b].

EXERCISES

1. Let R be the raster layer shown in Figure 8.2(a). Compute a new layer R_{lp} by applying the **FocalMean** operation. The `FocalMean` operation is defined as

$$R_{lp}(x) = \frac{1}{|nbd(x)|} \sum_{y \in nbd(x)} R(y).$$

Here x and y are pixels and $nbd(x)$ is the set of neighboring pixels of x. Use the `Queen` neighborhood template for $nbd(x)$. The new raster layer R_{lp} is a "blurred" image of the original layer R. This is the reason the **FocalMean** operation is sometimes called a *low-pass* filter.

2. Calculate a new layer R_{hp} as
$$R_{hp} = R - R_{lp}$$

The R_{hp} recovers the sharp edges (if any) in the original layer R. This is called a *high-pass* filter. This is an example of a binary local operation.

3. The raster maps shown above represent the *nitrogen* content and the *soil type* at each pixel. Calculate the average nitrogen content of each soil type and classify the operation as either local, focal, zonal, or global.

1	2	3	3
2	4	1	3
2	2	2	5
1	1	4	4

Nitrogen content

A	A	B	B
	B	B	B
C	C		A
C	C	C	A

Soil map

H	H	B	H
H	H	H	H
H	H	H	H
H	B	H	H

Locations of Banks and Households

4. The raster layer R shows the location of households (H) and Banks (B). Assume each household does business with both the banks. A survey of the last thirty visits by

members of the household was conducted which showed that a household interacted with the *nearest* bank 60 percent of the time. What was the average distance that members of the household traveled to banks in the last thirty days? Assume a distance of one to horizontal and vertical neighbors, and 1.4 to diagonal neighbors.

5. From a database perspective, which sequence of operations is more efficient: *trim∘slice* or *slice ∘ trim*? Assume right to left order of evaluation for operators.

6. For the binary raster image shown below, calculate the storage space required for the following three data structures. Assume one byte is required for each number or pointer.

   - matrix representation.
   - run-length encoding.
   - quadtree.

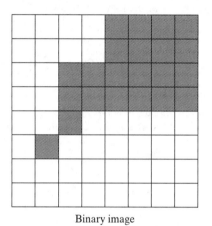

Binary image

7. The vector versus raster dichotomy can be compared with the "what" and "where" in natural language. Discuss.
8. Is topology implicit or explicit in raster DBMS ?
9. Compute the storage-space needed to store a raster representation of a 20km × 20km rectangular area at a resolution of
   (a) 10m × 10m pixels.
   (b) 1m × 1m pixels.
   (c) 1cm × 1cm pixels.
10. Study the raster data model proposed by OGIS. Compare it with the map algebra model discussed in this chapter.
11. Define the "closure" property of algebra. Evaluate OGIS model for vector spatial data for closure.
12. What is special about data warehousing for geospatial applications (e.g., census)?
13. Compare and contrast:
    (a) measures versus dimensions
    (b) data mining versus data warehousing.
    (c) Rollup versus Drill down
    (d) SQL2 GROUP BY aggregate queries versus GROUP BY aggregate queries with CUBE operator.
    (e) CUBE versus ROLLUP.
14. Classify following aggregate spatial functions into distributive, algebraic, and holistic functions: mean, medoid, autocorrelation (Moran's I), minimum bounding orthogonal

rectangle and minimum bounding circle, minimum bounding convex polygon, spatial outlier detection tests in Section 7.4.

15. Map algebra is typically defined on raster maps of scalar features, that is, each cell in the raster has a scalar value. Generalize map algebra to raster maps with vector features for application in wind-velocity maps and elevation gradient maps for flood analysis.

16. Some researchers in content based retrieval consider ARGs to be similar to the Entity Relationship Models. Do you agree? Explain with a simple example.

17. Can ARG model raster images with amorphous phenomenon, e.g. clouds, smoke aerosol? Explain.

18. Any arbitrary pair of spatial objects would always have some spatial relationship, e.g. distance. This can lead to clique like ARGs with large number of edges to model all spatial relationships. Suggest ways to sparsify ARGs for efficient content based retrievals.

19. Consider the content based query to retrieve countries with a given shape (e.g. tear drop, ladies boot, duck) of boundaries. Discuss how one may model shapes of spatial objects and similarity between shapes.

20. Consider Figure 8.19. Write SQL aggregate queries for the unlabeled edges between the tables.

21. Explore a spreadsheet software, for example, MS excel, to find pivot operation. Create an example data-set and illustrate the effect of pivot operation.

22. Study the census data-set and model it as a data warehouse. List the dimensions, measures, aggregation operations, and hierarchies.

23. Consider a table FACT (routenumber, stopid, rank, fare-collected, number-boarded, number-disboared) extending the RouteStop given in Table 6.2. Use DW operations and SQL to process following reports:
    (i) Total fare-collected by stops
    (ii) Total fare collected by routes
    (iii) Average activity (boarding + disboarding) by stops
    (iv) Busiest stops in each route

Bibliography

Acharya, S., Poosala, V., and Ramaswamy, S. (1999). Selectivity estimation in spatial databases. In *SIGMOD 1999, Proceedings ACM SIGMOD International Conference on Management of Data, June 1–3, 1999, Philadephia, Pennsylvania, USA*, pages 13–24. ACM Press.

Adam, N. and Gangopadhyay, A. (1997). *Database issues in Geographical Information Systems*. Kluwer Academics.

Agrawal, R. and Srikant, R. (1994). Fast algorithms for mining association rules. In Bocca, J. B., Jarke, M., and Zaniolo, C., editors, *Proc. 20th Int. Conf. Very Large Data Bases, VLDB*, pages 487–499. Morgan Kaufmann.

Albrecht, J. (1998). Universal analytical gis operations - a task-oriented systematization of data-structure-independent gis functionality. In *Geographic information research: transatlantic perspectives, M. Craglia and H. Onsrud (Eds.)*, pages 557–591. Tylor & Francis.

Ambroise, C., Dang, V., and Govaert, G. (1997). Clustering of spatial data by the EM algorithm. *Quantitative Geology and Geostatistics*, 9:493–504.

Ang, C., Ling, T., and Zhou, X. (1998). Qualitative spatial relationships represenation and its retrieval. In *Database and Expert Systems Applications(DEXA)*, volume 1460, pages 65–77. Springer-Verlag.

Anselin, L. (1988). *Spatial econometrics: Methods and models*. Kluwer.

Aref, W. and Samet, H. (1994). A cost model for query optimization using R-trees. In *The Proceedings of the Second ACM Workshop on Advances in Geographic Information Systems, ACM Press*.

Arge, L., Procopiuc, O., Ramaswamy, S., Suel, T., and Vitter, J. S. (1998). Scalable sweeping-based spatial join. In *VLDB '98, Proceedings of 24rd International Conference on Very Large Data Bases, August 24–27, 1998, New York City, New York, USA*, pages 570–581. Morgan Kaufmann.

Asano, T., Ranjan, D., Roos, T., Wiezl, E., and Widmayer, P. (1997). Space filling curves and their use in the design of geometric data structures. *Theoretical Computer Science*, 181(1):3–15.

Bailey, D. (1998). *Java structures*. WCB McGraw-Hill.

Bailey, T. C. and Gatrell, A. (1995). *Interactive spatial data analysis*. Longman Scientific & Technical.

Barclay, T., Slutz, D. R., and Gray, J. (2000). Terraserver: A spatial data warehouse. *SIGMOD Record*, 29(2):307–318.

Barnett, V. and Lewis, T. (1994). *Outliers in Statistical Data*. John Wiley, New York, 3rd edition.

Baumann, P. (1994). Management of multidimensional discrete data. *The VLDB Journal*, 3(4):401–444.

Beckmann, N., Kriegel, H., Schneider, R., and Seeger, B. (1990). The R*-tree: An efficient and robust access method for points and rectangles. In *Proceedings of the 1990 ACM SIGMOD International Conference on Management of Data*. ACM Press.

Biskup, J., Rasch, U., and Stiefeling, H. (1990). An extension of sql for querying graph relations. *Computer Languages*, 15(2):65–82.

Blyth, T. and Robertson, E. (1999). *Basic Linear Algebra*. Springer-Verlag.

Booch, G., Rumbaugh, J., and Jacobson, I. (1999). *The unified modeling language user guide*. Addison Wesley.

Brinkhoff, T., Kriegel, H., Schneider, R., and Seeger, B. (1994). Multi-step processing of spatial joins. In *Proceedings of ACM SIGMOD Int. Conf. on Management of Data*, pages 197–208. ACM Press.

Brinkhoff, T., Kriegel, H., and Seeger, B. (1993). Efficient processing of spatial joins using r-trees. In *Proceedings of ACM SIGMOD Int. Conf. on Management of Data*, pages 237–246. ACM Press.

Brinkhoff, T. and Kriegel, H.-P. (1994). The impact global clustering on spatial database systems. In *Proceedings of the 20th International Conference on Very Large Data Bases, (VLDB '94)*. Morgan Kaufmann.

Brodeur, J., Bedard, Y., and Proulx, M.-J. (2000). Modelling geospatial application databases using uml-based repositories aligned with international standards in geomatics. In *ACM-GIS 2000, Proceedings of the Eighth ACM Symposium on Advances in Geographic Information Systems, November 10–11, 2000, Washington, D.C., USA*, pages 39–46. ACM.

Chakrabarti, K. and Mehrotra, S. (1999). Efficient concurrency control in multidimensional access methods. In *SIGMOD 1999, Proceedings ACM SIGMOD International Conference on Management of Data, June 1–3, 1999, Philadephia, Pennsylvania, USA*, pages 25–36. ACM Press.

Chaudhuri, S. and Shim, K. (1996). Optimization of queries with user-defined predicates. In *VLDB '96, Proceedings of 22nd International Conference on Very Large Data Bases*, pages 87–98. Morgan Kaufmann.

Chou, H.-T. and DeWitt, D. J. (1985). An evaluation of buffer management strategies for relational database systems. In *VLDB '85, Proceedings of 11th International Conference on Very Large Data Bases*, pages 127–141. Morgan Kaufmann.

Chrisman, N. (1997). *Exploring geographic information systems*. John Wiley and Sons.

Clementini, E. and Felice, P. D. (1995). A comparison of methods for representing topological relationships. *Information Sciences*, 3.

Clementini, E., Felice, P. D., and van Oosterom, P. (1993). A small set of formal topological relationships suitable for end-user interaction. In *Lecture Notes in Computer Science, Vol. 692*, pages 277–295. SSD '93, Springer-Verlag.

Corral, A., Manolopoulos, Y., Theodoridis, Y., and Vassilakopoulos, M. (2000). Closest pair queries in spatial databases. In *Proceedings of the 2000 ACM SIGMOD International Conference on Management of Data, May 16–18, 2000, Dallas, Texas, USA*, pages 189–200. ACM.

Couclelis, H. (1992). People manipulate objects (but cultivate fields): beyond on the raster-vector debate in gis. In *Theories and Methods of Spatio-temporal Reasoning in Geographic Space*, pages 65–77.

Cressie, N. A. (1993). *Statistics for spatial data*. Wiley Series in Probability and Statistics.

de La Beaujardiere, J., Mitchell, H., Raskin, R. G., and Rao, A. (2000). The nasa digital earth testbed. In *ACM-GIS 2000, Proceedings of the Eighth ACM Symposium on Advances in Geographic Information Systems, November 10–11, 2000, Washington, D.C., USA*, pages 47–53. ACM.

Delis, V., Hadzilacos, T., and Tryfona, N. (1994). An introduction to layer algebra. In *Proceedings of Advances in GIS Research*. Taylor and Francis.

Dempster, A., Laird, N., and Rubin, D. (1977). Maximum likelihood from incomplete data using the EM algorithm. *Journal of the Royal Statistical Society*, 39(B).

den Bercken, J. V., Seeger, B., and Widmayer, P. (1997). A generic approach to bulk loading multidimensional index structures. In *VLDB '97, Proceedings of 23rd International Conference on Very Large Data Bases, August 25–29, 1997, Athens, Greece*, pages 406–415. Morgan Kaufmann.

Egenhofer, M. (1991a). Extending SQL for geographical display. *Cartography and Geographic Information Systems*, 18(4):230–245.

Egenhofer, M. (1991b). Reasoning about binary topological relations. In *SSD '91, Advances in Spatial Databases, Second International Symposium*, pages 143–160. Springer-Verlag.

Egenhofer, M. (1994). Spatial SQL: A Query and Presentation Language. *IEEE TKDE*, 6(1):86–95.

Egenhofer, M. (1997). Query Processing in Spatial-Query-by-Sketch. *Journal of Visual Languages and Computing*, 8(4):403–424.

Egenhofer, M., Frank, A. U., and Jackson, J. P. (1989). A topological data model for spatial databases. In *SSD '89, Design and Implementation of Large Spatial Databases, First Symposium*, pages 47–66. Springer-Verlag.

Elmasri, R. and Navathe, S. (2000). *Fundamentals of database systems*. Addison Wesley & Benjamin Cummings.

ESRI (1991). *Network analysis: Modeling network systems*. Environmental Systems Research Institute, Inc.

Estivill-Castro, V. and Murray, A. (1998). Discovering associations in spatial data—an efficient medoid based approach. In *Research and Development in Knowledge Discovery and Data Mining (PAKDD-98)*, volume 1394, pages 110–121. Springer.

Faloutsos, C. and Kamel, I. (1994). Beyond uniformity and independence: Analysis of r-tree using the concept of fractal dimension. In *Proceeding 13th ACM-SIGACT-SIGMOD-SIGART Symposium on Principles of Database Systems*, pages 4–13. ACM Press.

Faloutsos, C. and Roseman, S. (1989). Fractals for secondary key retrieval. In *Proceedings of the ACM conference on Principles of Database Systems*, pages 247–252.

Faloutsos, C., Seeger, B., Traina, A. J. M., and Jr., C. T. (2000). Spatial join selectivity using power laws. In *Proceedings of the 2000 ACM SIGMOD International Conference on Management of Data, May 16–18, 2000, Dallas, Texas, USA*, pages 177–188. ACM.

Faloutsos, C. and Sellis, T. (1987). Analysis of object oriented spatial access methods. In *Proceedings of the 1987 ACM SIGMOD International Conference on Management of Data*, pages 426–439. ACM Press.

Fischer, M. and Getis, A. (1997). *Recent developments in spatial analysis*. Springer Verlag.

Fotheringham, A. S. and Rogerson, P. A. (1994). *Spatial Analysis and GIS*. Taylor and Francis.

Gaede, V. and Gunther, O. (1998). Multidimensional access methods. *ACM Computing Surveys*, 30(2):170–231.

Goldstein, J. and Ramakrishnan, R. (2000). Contrast plots and p-sphere trees: Space vs. time in nearest neighbour searches. In *VLDB 2000, Proceedings of 26th International Conference on Very Large Data Bases, September 10–14, 2000, Cairo, Egypt*, pages 429–440. Morgan Kaufmann.

Goodchild, M. F. (1986). *Spatial Autocorrelation*. CATMOG 47, GeoBooks.

Gray, J., Chaudhuri, S., Bosworth, A., Layman, A., Reichart, D., Venkatrao, M., Pellow, F., and Pirahesh, H. (1997). Data Cube: A Relational Aggregation Operator Generalizing Group-By, Cross-Tab, and Sub-Totals. *Data Mining and Knowledge Discovery*, 1(1):29–53.

Griffith, D. (1999). Statistical and mathematical sources of regional science theory: Map pattern analysis as an example. *Papers in Regional Science*, 78(1):21–45.

Guting, R. (1994a). An Introduction to Spatial Database Systems. *The VLDB Journal*, 3(4):357–399.

Guting, R. (1994b). Graph DB: Modeling and querying graphs in databases. In *VLDB '94, Proccdings of 20th International Conference on Very Large Data Bases*. Morgan Kaufmann.

Guttman, A. (1984). R-tree: A dynamic index structure for spatial searching. In *SIGMOD '84, Proceedings of the ACM SIGMOD Conference*. ACM Press, ACM Press.

Hadzilacos, T. and Tryfona, N. (1997). An extended entity-relationship model for geographic applications. *SIGMOD Record*, 26(3).

Hagen, L. and Kahng, A. (1991). Fast spectral methods for ratio cut partitioning and clustering. In *Proceedings of IEEE International Conference on Computer Aided Design*, pages 10–13.

Han, J. and Kamber, M. (2000). *Data Mining: Concepts and Techniques*. Morgan Kaufmann.

Han, J., Koperski, K., and Stefanovic, N. (1997). Geominer: A system prototype for spatial data mining. In *SIGMOD 1997, Proceedings ACM SIGMOD International Conference on Management of Data, May 13–15, 1997, Tucson, Arizona, USA*, pages 553–556. ACM Press.

Hand, D. J. (1999). Statistics and Data Mining: Intersecting Disciplines. *SIGKDD Explorations*, 1(1):16–19.

Hawkins, D. (1980). *Identification of Outliers*. Chapman and Hall.

Hellerstein, J. and Stonebraker, M. (1993). Predicate migration: Optimizing queries with expensive predicates. In *SIGMOD '93, Proceedings of the ACM SIGMOD International Conference on Management of Data*, pages 267–276. ACM Press.

Herring, J. (1991). The mathematical modeling of spatial and non-spatial information in geographic information systems. In Mark, D. and Frank, U., editors, *Cognitive and Linguisitic Aspects of Geographic Space*, pages 313–350.

Jiang, B. (1991). Traversing graphs in a paging environment, bfs or dfs? *Information Processing Letters*, 37(3):143–147.

Jing, N., Huang, Y., and Rundensteiner, E. (1998). Hierarchical encoded path views for path query processing: An optimal model and its performance evaluation. *IEEE Transactions on Knowledge and Data Engineering*, 10(3):409–432.

Kamel, I. and Faloutsos, C. (1993). On packing r-trees. In *CIKM'93, Proceedings of the Second International Conference on Information and Knowledge Management*, pages 490–499. ACM Press.

Kanth, K. V. R., Ravada, S., Sharma, J., and Banerjee, J. (1999). Indexing medium-dimensionality data in oracle. In *SIGMOD 1999, Proceedings ACM SIGMOD International Conference on Management of Data, June 1–3, 1999, Philadephia, Pennsylvania, USA*, pages 521–522. ACM Press.

Karypis, G., Aggarwal, R., Kumar, V., and Shekhar, S. (1998). hmetis home page. http://www-users.cs.umn.edu/ ~karypis/metis/hmetis/main.html.

Karypis, G. and Kumar, V. (1998). Metis home page. http://www-users.cs.umn.edu/~karypis/metis/metis/main.html.

Keim, D. A. (1999). Efficient geometry-based similarity search of 3d spatial databases. In *SIGMOD 1999, Proceedings ACM SIGMOD International Conference on Management of Data, June 1–3, 1999, Philadephia, Pennsylvania, USA*, pages 419–430. ACM Press.

Kernighan, B. W. and Lin, S. (1970). An efficient heuristic procedure for partitioning graphs. *Bell System Technical Journal*, 49(2):291–307.

Khoshafian, S. and Baker, A. (1998). *MultiMedia and Imaging Databases*. Morgan Kaufmann.

Koperski, K. and Han, J. (1995). Discovery of spatial association rules in geographic information systems. In *Advances in Spatial Databases, 4th International Symposium(SSD '95)*, pages 47–66. Springer-Verlag.

Korn, F. and Muthukrishnan, S. (2000). Influence sets based on reverse nearest neighbor queries. In *Proceedings of the 2000 ACM SIGMOD International Conference on Management of Data, May 16–18, 2000, Dallas, Texas, USA*, pages 201–212. ACM.

Kornacker, M. and Banks, D. (1995). High-concurrency locking in R-trees. In *VLDB '95, Proceedings of 21th International Conference on Very Large Data Bases*. Morgan Kaufmann.

Kriegel, H.-P., Muller, A., Potke, M., and Seidl, T. (2001). Spatial data management for computer aided design. In *ACM SIGMOD International Conference on Management of Data*, page 614. ACM Press.

Laurini, R. and Thompson, D. (1992). *Fundamentals of spatial information systems*. Academic Press.

Lehman, P. and Yao, S. (1981). Efficient locking for concurrent operations on b-trees. *ACM TODS*, 6(4).

LeSage, J. (1997). Regression analysis of spatial data. *Journal of Regional Analysis and Policy (Publisher: Mid-Continent Regional Science Association and UNL College of Business Administration)*, 27(2):83–94.

Leutenegger, S. T. and Lopez, M. A. (2000). The effect of buffering on the performance of r-trees. *IEEE Transactions on Knowledge and Data Engineering*, 12(1):33–44.

Lin, H. and Huang, B. (2001). Sql/sda: A query language for supporting spatial data analysis and its web-based implementation. *IEEE Transactions on Knowledge and Data Engineering*, 13(4):671–682.

Lo, M. and Ravishankar, C. (1996). Spatial hash joins. In *ACM SIGMOD International Conference on Management of Data*, pages 247–258. ACM Press.

Luc, A. (1994). Exploratory Spatial Data Analysis and Geographic Information Systems. In Painho, M., editor, *New Tools for Spatial Analysis*, pages 45–54.

Luc, A. (1995). Local Indicators of Spatial Association: LISA. *Geographical Analysis*, 27(2):93–115.

Ma, W. and Manjunath, B. (1998). A texture thesaurus for browsing large aerial photographs. *Journal of the American Society for Information Science*, 49(7):633–48.

Mamoulis, N. and Papadias, D. (1999). Integration of spatial join algorithms for processing multiple inputs. In *SIGMOD 1999, Proceedings ACM SIGMOD International Conference on Management of Data, June 1–3, 1999, Philadephia, Pennsylvania, USA*, pages 1–12. ACM Press.

Mannino, M. and Shapiro, L. (1990). Extensions to query languages for graph traversal problem. *IEEE TKDE*, 2(3):353–363.

Merrett, T., Kimbayasi, Y., and Yasuura, H. (1981). Scheduling of page-fetches in join operations. In *Proceedings of the 7th International Conference on Very Large Data Bases*. Morgan Kaufmann.

Moon, B., Jagadish, H., Faloutsos, C., and Saltz, J. H. (1996). Analysis of the clustering properties of hilbert space-filling curve. Technical Report UMIACS-TR-96-20, CS dept., University of Maryland.

Murray, J. D. and van Ryper, W. (1999). *Encyclopedia of Graphics File Formats*. O'REILLY.

Nievergelt, J., Hinterberger, H., and Sevcik, K. (1984). The grid file: An adaptable, symmetric multikey file structure. *ACM Transactions on Database Systems*, 9(1):38–71.

OGIS (1999). Open GIS consortium: Open GIS simple features specification for SQL (Revision 1.1). In *URL: http://www.opengis.org/techno/specs.htm*.

OGIS (2000). Web map server interfaces implementation specification. In *URL: http:// www. opengis.org/techno/specs/00-028.pdf*.

OpenGIS (1998). *Open GIS simple features specification for SQL*. Open GIS Consortium, Inc., http://www.opengis.org.

Ordonez, C. and Cereghini, P. (2000). Sqlem: Fast clustering in sql using the em algorithm. *SIGMOD Record*, 29(2):559–570.

Orenstein, J. (1986). Spatial query processing in an object-oriented database. In *Proceedings of the 1986 ACM SIGMOD International Conference on Management of Data*. ACM Press.

Orenstein, J. and Manola, F. (1988). PROBE spatial data modeling and query processing in an image database application. *IEEE Trans on Software Engineering*, 14(5):611–629.

Ozesmi, S. and Ozesmi, U. (1999). An artificial neural network approach to spatial habitat modeling with interspecific interation. *Ecological Modeling*, 116:15–31.

Pagel, B.-U., Six, H.-W., and Toben, H. (1993a). The transformation technique for spatial objects revisited. In *SSD, Lecture Notes in Computer Science, Vol. 2121*, pages 73–88. Springer-Verlag.

Pagel, B.-U., Six, H.-W., Toben, H., and Widmayer, P. (1993b). Towards an analysis of range query performance in spatial data structures. In *Proceedings of the Twelfth ACM SIGACT-SIGMODSIGART Symposium on Principles of Database Systems*, pages 214–221. ACM Press.

Papadias, D., Karacapilidis, N., and Arkoumanis, D. (1999). Processing fuzzy spatial queries: A configuration similarity. *International Journal of GIS*, 13(2):93–128.

Patel, J. and Dewitt, D. (1996). Partition based spatial-merge join. *Proceedings of ACM SIGMOD*, pages 259–270.

Patel, J. M. and DeWitt, D. J. (1996). Partition Based Spatial-Merge Join. In *Proceedings of the 1996 ACM SIGMOD International Conference on Management of Data*. ACM Press.

Patel, J. M. and DeWitt, D. J. (2000). Clone join and shadow join: two parallel spatial join algorithms. In *ACM-GIS 2000, Proceedings of the Eighth ACM Symposium on Advances in Geographic Information Systems, November 10–11, 2000, Washington, D.C., USA*, pages 54–61. ACM.

Petrakis, E. and Faloutsos, C. (1997). Similarity searching in medical image databases. *IEEE TKDE*, 9(3):433–447.

Price, R., Tryfona, N., and Jensen, C. S. (2000). Modeling part-whole relationships for spatial data. In *ACM-GIS 2000, Proceedings of the Eighth ACM Symposium on Advances in Geographic Information Systems, November 10–11, 2000, Washington, D.C., USA*, pages 1–8. ACM.

Ramakrishnan, R. (1998). *Database management system*. McGraw Hill.

Ritter, G., Wilson, J., and Davidson, J. (1990). Image algebra: An overview. *Computer Vision, Graphics and Image Processing*, 49:297–331.

Roussopoulos, N., Kelley, S., and Vincent, F. (1995). Nearest neighbor queries. In *Proceedings of the 1995 ACM SIGMOD International Conference on Management of Data*. ACM Press.

Samet, H. (1990). *The design and analysis of spatial data structures*. Addison-Wesley.

Sarawagi, S. and Stonebraker, M. (1994). Efficient organization of large multidimensional arrays. In *Tenth International Conference on Data Engineering*, pages 328–336. IEEE Computer Society.

Schneider, R. and Kriegel, H.-P. (1991). The tr*-tree: A new representation of polygonal objects supporting spatial queries and operations. In *Lecture Notes in Computer Science, Vol. 553*, pages 249–264. SSD '93.

Scholl, M. O., Voisard, A., and Rigaux, P. (2001). *Spatial database management systems*. Morgan Kaufmann Publishers.

Seidl, T. and Kriegel, H.-P. (1998). Optimal multi-step k-nearest neighbor search. In *SIGMOD 1998, Proceedings ACM SIGMOD International Conference on Management of Data, June 2–4, 1998, Seattle, Washington, USA*, pages 154–165. ACM Press.

Selinger, P. G., Astrahan, M. M., Chamberlin, D. D., Lorie, R. A., and Price, T. G. (1979). Access path selection in a relational database management system. In *Proceedings of the ACM SIGMOD International Conference on Management of Data*, pages 23–34. ACM Press.

Sheikholeslami, G., Chatterjee, S., and Zhang, A. (1998). Wavecluster: A multi-resolution clustering approach for very large spatial databases. In *VLDB '98, Proceedings of 24rd International Conference on Very Large Data Bases, August 24–27, 1998, New York City, New York, USA*, pages 428–439. Morgan Kaufmann.

Shekhar, S., Chawla, S., Ravada, S., Fetterer, A., Liu, X., and Lu, C. (1999a). Spatial databases—accomplishments and research needs. *IEEE TKDE*, 11(1):45–55.

Shekhar, S., Coyle, M., Liu, D.-R., Goyal, B., and Sarkar, S. (1997). Data models in geographic information systems. *Communication of the ACM*, 40(4).

Shekhar, S. and Huang, Y. (2001). Discovering spatial co-location patterns: A summary of results. In *Proceedings of the 7th International Symposium on Spatial and Temporal Databases, SSTD 2001, Redondo Beach, CA, USA, July 12–15, 2001*, volume 2121 of *Lecture Notes in Computer Science*, pages 236–256. Springer.

Shekhar, S. and Liu, D.-R. (1997). A connectivity-clustered access method for networks and network computation. *IEEE TKDE*, 9(1):102–117.

Shekhar, S., Lu, C., Chawla, S., and Ravada, S. (1999b). Efficient join index based join processing; a clustering approach. *TR99-030 (Also to appear in IEEE TKDE)*.

Shekhar, S., Schrater, P. R., Vatsavai, R. R., Wu, W., and Chawla, S. (2002). Spatial contextual classification and prediction models for mining geospatial data. *IEEE Transactions on Multimedia*, 4(2):1–15.

Shekhar, S., Vatsavai, R. R., Chawla, S., and Burk, T. E. (1999c). Spatial pictogram enhanced conceptual data models and their translation to logical data models. *Integrated Spatial Databases: Digital Images and GIS. Lecture Notes in Computer Science*, 1737:77–104.

Shin, H., Moon, B., and Lee, S. (2000). Adaptive multi-stage distance join processing. *SIGMOD Record*, 29(2):343–354.

Silberschatz, A., Korth, H., and Sudarshan, S. (1997). *Database system concepts, 3rd Ed.* McGraw-Hill.

Song, J.-W., Whang, K.-Y., Lee, Y.-K., Lee, M.-J., and Kim, S.-W. (1999). Transformation-based spatial join. In *Proceedings of the 1999 ACM CIKM International Conference on Information and Knowledge Management, Kansas City, Missouri, USA, November 2–6, 1999*, pages 15–26. ACM.

Stonebraker, M. and Moore, D. (1997). *Object relational DBMSs: The next great wave*. Morgan Kaufmann.

Takeyama, M. and Couclelis, H. (1997). Map dynamics: integrating cellular automata and gis through geo-algebra. *International Journal of GIS*, 11(1):73–91.

Theodoridis, Y. and Sellis, T. (1996). A model for the prediction of r-tree performance. In *Proceedings of the Fifteenth ACM SIGACT-SIGMOD-SIGART Symposium on Principles of Database Systems*, pages 161–171. ACM Press.

Theodoridis, Y., Stefanakis, E., and Sellis, T. (1998). Cost models for join queries in spatial databases. In *Proceedings of the Fourteenth International Conference on Data Engineering*, pages 476–483. IEEE Press.

Theodoridis, Y., Stefanakis, E., and Sellis, T. (2000a). Efficient cost models for spatial queries using r-trees. *IEEE TKDE*, 12(1).

Theodoridis, Y., Stefanakis, E., and Sellis, T. K. (2000b). Efficient cost models for spatial queries using r-trees. *IEEE Transactions on Knowledge and Data Engineering*, 12(1):19–32.

Tobler, W. (1979). Cellular geography. In *Philosophy in Geography, Eds., S. Gale and G. Olsson.* D. Reidel Publishing Company: Dordrecht, Holland.

Tomlin, C. (1990). *Geographic information systems and cartographic modeling*. Prentice-Hall.

Ullman, J. and Widom, J. (1999). *A first course in database systems*. Prentice-Hall.

van der Lans, R. F. (1992). *The SQL guide to Oracle*. Addison-Wesley.

Vatsavai, R. R., Burk, T. E., Wilson, B. T., and Shekhar, S. (2000). A web-based browsing and spatial analysis system for regional natural resource analysis and mapping. In *Proceedings of the Eighth ACM Symposium on Advances in Geographic Information Systems ACMGIS*, pages 95–101.

Wang, W., Yang, J., and Muntz, R. R. (1997). Sting: A statistical information grid approach to spatial data mining. In *VLDB '97, Proceedings of 23rd International Conference on Very Large Data Bases, August 25–29, 1997, Athens, Greece*, pages 186–195. Morgan Kaufmann.

Worboys, M. (1995). *GIS: A computing perspective*. Taylor and Francis.

Yoshitaka, A. and Ichikawa, T. (1999). A Survey on Content-Based Retrieval for Multimedia Databases. *IEEE TKDE*, 11(1):81–93.

Index